Design for
a Study of Entry
into Careers

Design for a Study of Entry into Careers

Volume I: Entry into Careers Series

Luther B. Otto
Vaughn R.A. Call
Kenneth I. Spenner
Boys Town Center

LexingtonBooks
D.C. Heath and Company
Lexington, Massachusetts
Toronto

Library of Congress Cataloging in Publication Data

Otto, Luther B.
  Design for a study of entry into careers.

  (Entry into careers series; v. 1)
  Bibliography: p.
  Includes index.
  1. United States—Occupations. 2. Occupations. 3. Work. 4. Vocational
guidance. I. Call, Vaughn R.A. II. Spenner, Kenneth I. III. Title. IV. Series:
Otto, Luther B. Entry into careers series; v. 1.
HB2595.087   331.7'02'0973   79-48034
ISBN 0-669-03643-9   AACR2

Copyright © 1981 by D.C. Heath and Company

Published simultaneously in Canada

Printed in the United States of America

International Standard Book Number: 0-669-03643-9

Library of Congress Catalog Card Number: 79-48034

2184597

To our parents

Contents

List of Figures

List of Figures

List of Tables

Preface and Acknowledgments

In 1974 the Board of Directors of Father Flanagan's Boys' Home approved major programmatic expansion into research on the causes of problems that affect the nation's youth. Central to the plan was the establishment of the Boys Town Center for the Study of Youth Development. Its mission is to generate significant research and communicate useful knowledge in service to youth and families.

Given the difficulty youth experience in choosing careers and Boys Town's historic interest in the problem, it followed that the Boys Town Center would make an early long-term commitment to research and dissemination of career information. In early 1976 Luther B. Otto was named director of the Career Development Program. Vaughn R.A. Call joined the staff in early 1977. Kenneth I. Spenner joined the research team later the same year.

Attention to the process by which careers develop required longitudinal data on a suitable sample of respondents through early career. We first explored the possibility of launching a new long-term study but later rejected that option in favor of doing a follow-up study of respondents on whom appropriate earlier data were already gathered. We examined several data sets.

One possibility was to do a follow-up of the educational- and occupational-plans study of male and female high-school students conducted in 1966-1967 by Gordon McCloskey, Walter Slocum, and William Rushing, then of Washington State University. This data set, eventually extended in a thirteen-year follow-up, had much to recommend it. The technical characteristics of the data were exemplary. The sample was approximately half male and half female. Moreover, the data set lay dormant and largely unanalyzed.

In 1976 Washington State University authorized transfer of the original data file and archives to the Boys Town Center. This enabled us to make a detailed examination of the quality of the original data in assessing the feasibility of a follow-up study. The arrangements were facilitated through the good offices of Donald Dillman, chairman of the Department of Rural Sociology, and James F. Short, Jr., director of the Social Research Center. Gordon McCloskey, director of the original study and professor emeritus, also approved the transfer.

During the spring of 1977 we conducted a thorough verification of the educational- and occupational-plans data. This satisfied us concerning the technical characteristics of the data and the integrity of the data file. In the summer we accomplished a pilot study of our proposed tracking procedures with a random sample of respondents. The pilot study demonstrated the effectiveness of the tracking procedures and, together with the verification studies, assured the feasibility of conducting the thirteen-year follow-up study of the original respondents.

The substance of the proposed follow-up was not self-evident, however. The literature of the middle and late seventies reflected various currents of thought in sociology generally and stratification studies in particular. There was increased dissatisfaction with status-attainment research, which had dominated the journals for a decade. There was a rebirth of interest in structure as evident in the shift away from achievement research to studies of labor markets. Life-course research was casting developmental issues in broader substantive contexts and setting the stage for methodological advances including dynamic modeling. Evaluation and policy research raised the visibility of social-problem studies. The Career Development Program of the Boys Town Center took shape during this period and in various ways reflects these currents of thought in its program design.

The long-term direction and timetable were set in fall of 1977. During that period, we arrived at a consensus and refined our conceptualization of the dependent variable: careers and career lines. We laid out a five-year work program—including data gathering and preparation, analysis and publication, dissemination and application—that has governed our collaborative efforts. We articulated our research agenda in an extramural funding proposal. The efforts produced a grant award from the National Institute of Education that gave added impetus to the research program.

We implemented the work plan in early 1978 with the full-scale tracking of the original study participants. We acquired the 1970 Census Public Use Samples that provided the data base for estimating and analyzing career lines. We designed and began the estimation of career lines. We prepared detailed specifications and let bids to several external contractors to gather follow-up data on the participants in the educational- and occupational-plans study. We prepared instruments for gathering life-course-event histories in the follow-up study.

Fieldwork for the data-gathering component of the Career Development Study began in early 1979. A contract was let with Audits & Surveys, Inc., of New York City to interview the original study participants whom we had tracked. We designed and administered an extensive mail questionnaire to follow and supplement the telephone-interview information. We estimated job and worker characteristics to complement the career-line information on the basis of data in the *Dictionary of Occupational Titles* (1965) and the 1970 census data.

We began data preparation in 1979. Much of that effort continued into 1980. The in-house data coding included assignment of some forty-eight thousand, 6-digit census occupation-industry codes to jobs and nearly sixty thousand codes to education measures. All data were double entered and verified for accuracy. Complex editing involved cross-checking each respondent's detailed life-course information through a series of specially developed computer-software programs. Concurrently, we designed hard-copy graphic displays of the 384 sets of destination and recruitment career lines. Finally, we completed this first volume in the Entry into Careers series at the end of 1980.

The original educational- and occupational-plans study could not have been extended were it not for the thorough and careful documentation of the wave 1 data recorded by Walter L. Slocum. His attention to detail in the collection, coding, and archiving of the data and project records is a lasting tribute to his professional standards and research practice. We acknowledge his legacy and express our gratitude to Mrs. Esther Slocum, who encouraged us to continue his work and assisted us in recovering his professional files.

An effort of this magnitude and duration could not have been accomplished without the extensive collaboration and cooperation of numerous institutions, agencies, and study participants and the assistance of skilled personnel. Many who carried out the exacting operational tasks are not acknowledged here by name, but their excellent work is recognized and greatly appreciated.

Washington State University encouraged and supported our efforts at all administrative levels. The principals and superintendents of the twenty-five high schools in the state of Washington who were part of the original study gave us excellent cooperation. We thank them for their participation and help.

Glen Elder, David Featherman, Sy Spilerman, and Ivan Charner gave collegial and professional counsel at strategic points in designing the program of studies. Robert Stump, senior associate and project officer at the National Institute of Education, was a ready source of encouragement and administrative counsel.

We were pleased with the telephone interviewing services provided by Audits & Surveys, Inc. Dexter Neadle, Nina Mathus, Rhoda Brooks, and George Sexton were patient, accommodating, resourceful, and conscientious in mounting the complex telephone-interview schedule on the CATI system and in conducting the survey. The Boys Town mailing division and print shop served us well during the tracking and mail-questionnaire efforts.

The Boys Town Center made many contributions to the program of research outlined in this book. The Center provided a sustained hard-money funding base, an institutional identification, and necessary support services including administration, computing, and library resources. In particular, we gratefully acknowledge the initial confidence expressed and enacted by Ronald A. Feldman, who, as center director, gave program status to Career Development and nurtured its early growth and development.

The Research Computing Division at the Center, Edmund D. Meyers, Jr., director, and the word-processing center staffed by Dorothy Runte, Mary Pat Roy, Marilyn Pittillo, and Donna Plaisted were extraordinarily accommodating. We thank them for their perseverance and help.

Our work would have been impossible without David Chapin's computing expertise. From the automation of tracking procedures to complex editing of completed interviews, from the estimation of career lines to the manipulation of large matrices on a minicomputer, Chapin translated our candy-store visions into software realities. Large-scale and long-term research is increasingly dependent on automation, and Chapin masterfully guided us through that dependency.

Many telephone trackers, interviewers, coders, data editors, and clerical assistants faithfully lent their labors to the project. Ruth Rabalais capably supervised the telephone-interview data through occupation coding, data cleaning, and editing. The spirit and cohesion that she generated in supervising several data-coding and editing operations made accuracy and precision relatively painless features of the lengthy ordeal. Among the clerical assistants, Martha Inman, Carolyn Seybold, Joyce Milroy, Mary Baumstark, and Patty Haug warrant special mention for their long-term service. During his time on the project, James Peterson also provided very able computing assistance.

The success of any panel study depends initially on locating the original respondents. Although many individuals contributed to the effort, Cynthia Evahn and Elisabeth Trembath assumed major supervisory responsibilities. Their persistence, patience, innovativeness, and ingenuity are reflected in relocating 98.2 percent of the original 1966 respondents. In addition, we recognize Evahn's diligence in supervising the day-to-day questionnaire mailing, coding, data entry, and file-maintenance activities. Her ability to organize and her attention to detail were great assets in completing these tasks efficiently and with care.

John Larma and Marie Rademacher exhibited skill, endless patience, and care in preparing the graphic displays of career lines—384 in all.

Finally, Sandy Wendel has served the Career Development staff since the inception of the program at the center. She has been extraordinarily efficient as a secretary, administrative assistant, and copy editor. We thank her for her continued loyalty and conscientious service over the years.

The program of research introduced by this book has been funded from various sources including the Office of Education, Washington State University, and the Boys Town Center. The material reported here was also performed pursuant to grant NIE-G-79-0046 from the National Institute of Education, Department of Health, Education and Welfare. However, the opinions expressed do not necessarily reflect the position or policy of these agencies or institutions, whether public or private, and no official endorsement should be inferred. Total responsibility for the content rests with and is accepted by the authors.

**Design for
a Study of Entry
into Careers**

1 Introduction

In his classic statement on the historical meanings of work, Tilgher (1930) traces the evolution of different ideas of work and describes how these have directed and controlled people's day-to-day lives. Tilgher reasons that people organize their lives around ideas, especially the prevailing ideas about work. What work has meant through the ages—whether, for example, curse or means of salvation, remedy for temptation or expression of inherent creativity—is the basic belief that has structured human existence since the time of the Greeks and the Romans. Speaking of the modern idea of work and life, Tilgher (1930, p. 131) argues that "consciously or unconsciously, man projects upon a cosmic plane and extends to the whole universe what he has learned in factories . . . "

Work continues to occupy a central place in people's lives. In *The American Occupational Structure*, Blau and Duncan (1967, pp. 6-7) argue that the great significance of the occupational structure is that it serves as the connecting link between different elements of social organization, including the economy, the family, and the hierarchy of political power. They argue that a person's occupational role within that structure is the most important definition of that person's position in the social structure. Thus, Kohn (1977) marshals the evidence of three studies to demonstrate that there is a relationship between positions in the stratification order and people's values; that values influence behavior; and that values originate in different conditions of life, particularly occupational life.

Social and behavioral studies have related work functions to economics, social integration, and psychological well-being. Work fulfills an economic function in the production of essential goods and services for the individual and society. Various forms of personal and social integration and disorganization are traced to such conditions of the labor market as employment, unemployment, and underemployment. And a person's psychological makeup—sense of worth, esteem, power, feelings of happiness, and general sense of well-being—is related to conditions of the work place. Whether examined from the vantage point of a society or of the individual, work shapes the life-styles that people endure, experience, or enjoy.

The accumulated literature outlines various approaches to the study of work. Economists, for example, have responded to a growing and widespread interest in the economics of education. The logic of the investment-returns model has been used to explain, among other things, the positive effect of educational achievement on occupational prestige and earnings. Psychologists and psychometricians have answered the military and industrial need to screen, train, and assess job performance. Vocational guidance and scientific management are additional applications that have developed from the occupational aspects of economics and psychology. These efforts have concentrated on inventorying interests and abilities, cataloging job characteristics, and matching the two. Among sociologists considerable attention has been focused on issues of intergenerational mobility, equality of opportunity, and the achievement process.

This volume introduces the Career Development program of research. It investigates how people enter careers. The chapters that follow are a blueprint for the inquiry. The book presents the design for a series of studies that will map the sequences of jobs people hold over time, will examine the individual factors that open and close doors to career possibilities, and will explore the ways people manage their lives as they make the transition from adolescence to adulthood. The chief components of the design are the theoretical perspectives that inform the research program and the data bases on which the analyses are based.

In chapter 1, the first section sets the study of work in the context of social roles. In the second section we sketch the major theoretical perspectives that guide the inquiry. A montage of themes and sensitizing concepts that apply to various levels of social organization emerges. The third section presents an overview of the principal data bases that will be used in scheduled analyses. The chapter concludes with reflections on the systematic study of work and an outline for the remainder of the volume.

Work as Social Role

We view the study of work as the study of the major social roles people occupy by virtue of the work they do. The research concentrates on the dynamics of work roles as these emerge over time. Careers are viewed as sequences of work roles. Our goal is to understand them.

Social role is a central concept in this program of studies. It warrants more precise definition relative to other levels of social organization that bear on explanations of careers. Conceiving of occupations as social roles is neither new nor novel. Indeed, students of occupations have typically begun their writing in a similar vein. Hall (1959, pp. 5-6), for example, provided this definition: "An occupation is the social role performed by adult members of society that directly and/or indirectly yields social and financial consequences and that constitutes a major focus in the life of an adult." However much the denotations and connotations of the concept have been debated in the literature, the underlying theme in definitions and usage is that role is an intermediary concept that links the individual with society. Roles interpret individual behavior in terms of social expectations.

Jobs and careers are work-specific examples of social roles. For example, elementary school teachers are expected to meet formal certification requirements, to work a continuous nine-month period concurrent with the academic cycle, to possess personality traits that facilitate empathizing with parents and children, and to exhibit irreproachable public behavior. A job change typically signals a change in work roles. Thus, a school teacher turned politician is thrust into a world requiring less skill at empathizing but more sixth-sense ability to read the public pulse. A career is a record of changes in the content of a person's work routines and reports changes in the social expectations that govern those routines.

Our research distinguishes between careers and career lines. *Careers* are individual-level phenomena: a person's employment biography, a particular individual's job history. *Career lines*, by comparison, are the patterns of job changes regularly made by people over the course of their work histories. Career lines record the job sequences that people follow with calculable predictability. Career lines are social-structural phenomena.

An analogy might assist the distinction. Career lines are like a detailed city map showing the intersections that join streets and avenues with highways and back alleys. Studying job changes may be likened to measuring the traffic flow. The roadways exist prior to the person's work history. They are "out there," part of the world of work. They are molds within which individual careers take shape. A career, then, is like a motorist making his way across town. The route followed is partly a matter of personal choice, but always that choice is within the road system. Similarly, individual work histories more or less conform to a prior network of age-graded career lines.

The causes and consequences of differences in work roles operate at several levels of social organization and explanation (see Baron and Bielby 1980). At the most general level, differences between societies beget differences in the division of labor. Such societal trends as industrialism and demographic changes provide the impetus for the long-term expansion or contraction of the labor force and of classes of jobs available in the economy. At the next level of social organization, institutional considerations such as regional variation in job opportunities offer explanations for the operation of inequalities. At a third tier, that of organizations and firms, there are differences in the settings within which the varieties of work experience are played out. At a fourth layer, social roles are encoded in positions that have normative expectations for the worker. This is where the interface between individual careers and structural career lines takes place. Finally, there is the individual level that allows for differences between workers in genetic makeup and human personality to enter explanations for differences in work-role performance.

Within the five levels of social organization, social roles are located between the individual and the increasingly complex levels of social structure. If another analytical dimension is added, that of developmental time, then the notion of a sequence of work roles is meaningfully embodied in the two concepts of career and career line. *Developmental time* refers to the aging of individuals over the life course. The significance of developmental time for career studies is that it is an important determinant of the patterning of social roles. The study of careers requires not only that the properties of normative career lines reflect the contingent nature of historical time but also that an individual's location in a career line be understood as a function of age.

Following Spilerman (1977), the notion of career lines, defined as sequences of jobs held over time, is a strategic link between structural features of the labor market and the socioeconomic attainments of individuals. The focus, therefore, is on careers as a life course phenomenon. The study of entry into careers centers on these three questions:

1. What are the job sequences people regularly follow during their work histories?
2. What are the individual-level determinants of access to the different job sequences?
3. How do people manage their early careers in the context of the multiple roles they assume during the transition from adolescence to adulthood?

Each question raises a class of issues that may be joined from differing but not necessarily competing theoretical perspectives. In the following section we summarize those perspectives.

Theoretical Backdrop

Three different literatures provide the theoretical backdrop for the study of careers. As a convenience we label them conservative or functional explanations, radical or conflict explanations, and life course perspectives.

The conservative and radical explanations bear the imprimatur of tradition and span the history of thought (Lenski 1966). Conservative explanations include functional perspectives, the industrialism thesis, the neoclassical paradigm in economics, human-capital theory, and meritocratic arguments. Radical explanations embrace major themes from Marxist writings, conflict theories, economic-segmentation arguments, internal-labor-market theses, and revisionist ideologies. The unavoidable cost of reviewing major historical themes in summary fashion is that the fine-grained texture of specific arguments is blurred if not lost in the panorama. The benefit, of course, is that classes of explanations can be compared more easily when reduced to their major premises. The life course approach is of more recent origin, is more embryonic in its development, and is more limited in scope. Nonetheless, it too offers an independent contribution to understanding careers.

As it informs the study of careers, each interpretation concentrates on a different level and unit of social organization. Where one might fix on societal trends in the economy as an explanation for mobility patterns, another engages the rhetoric of multiple social roles held by individuals or the actions of firms. The orientations also vary in the amount and kind of attention they give to historical and development time (age) as an explanation for careers. Further, each of the conservative, radical, and life course perspectives contains multiple strands of theories and hypotheses. For other purposes these could be unraveled and examined separately. There is variety, at times incoherent, in the explanations. Of interest to us here are the broad themes each lends to the study of careers. Differences among perspectives and in the details of their predictions will be pursued in the context of specific analyses.

Conservative Explanations

Conservative explanations view stratification and social inequality as necessary features of a social order. They rise from the efficient logic of industrial development, the economy, and the firm. The image of the worker is that of a rational, purposive maximizer of desirable outcomes. For example, the industrialism thesis views societies as subject to similar forces as they industrialize (Kerr et al. 1964). Work becomes more complex, and positions become more finely differentiated. Education becomes increasingly important. It trains and certifies potential workers. It provides for the rational placement of workers in jobs. Rationality and efficiency at a societal level are the engines that drive the organization of work and the mobility linkages between jobs.

In economics the neoclassical theory of the firm complements the industrialism thesis but centers on organizations as the level of analysis. Firms produce outputs from different combinations of factor inputs, including labor and capital. Firms use factor inputs in combinations designed to assure that revenues exceed costs and, across inputs, that profits are maximized. The structure of work is defined indirectly by this production function. From the standpoint of neoclassical theory, the existing regime of careers and mobility linkages are those that promote profit maximization in the firm.

Human-capital theory may be viewed as an extension of the conservative argument applied to individuals (Leigh 1978). Human-capital theory emphasizes that the worker tries to maximize personal returns. Note that this explanation for the evolution of careers is not necessarily inconsistent with the functionalist argument expressed in the industrialism thesis and neoclassical theories of the firm. Human-capital theory argues that workers choose among jobs on the basis of their skills and training, their preferences and tastes. Individuals maximize job rewards, particularly earnings. In accepting employment, a worker "buys" and the employer "sells" opportunities to further the worker's stock of human capital in anticipation of greater long-term yields. Firms, in turn, regard schooling as evidence of a person's actual or potential skill. Firms offer on-the-job training, promotion hierarchies, and higher wages in response to demands for skilled labor and profitable production. Workers with higher levels of human-capital stock are more productive; hence, they are able to translate their training, job performance, and work experience into rising wages and a progression of jobs that approximates the classic career.

From the conservative perspective—viewed in terms of the individual, organization, and society—the ingredients from which good careers are made include training, choice, productivity, and profit. Stable careers will flourish where organizations can profitably convert inputs to outputs and where workers have high performance capabilities. But at any level of explanation—societal, organizational, or individual—the prerequisites for stable careers may go awry. Expanding economies may stagnate. Organizational infrastructures may become disjointed. An adequate supply of human-capital stock may not be present in the available work force. Conservative perspectives best explain how individual differences are translated into differential occupational and earnings returns. To the extent that careers are the products of individual rational choice, organizational efficiencies, and societal conditions, conservative arguments provide an explanatory backdrop. But the same explanations are less successful in accounting for the variation in job histories that are tied to such ascribed individual characteristics as race and gender and to market imperfections. Conservative explanations have given little attention to the extent that work careers are established along these other dimensions of social organization. Radical perspectives have.

Radical Explanations

Radical perspectives are more cynical about human motives. Radical theorists argue that individuals maximize their own interests through the exercise of power and coercion. Institutions are established and maintained because they provide mechanisms for exploitation. They provide privilege to those in power. From a radical perspective, formation of mobility chains and the quality of work life flow from the structural arrangements that promote the interests of capitalism. Current radical perspectives on work roles are found in economic-segmentation theories.

In the extreme, segmentation perspectives suggest that larger societal forces lead to divisions within the economy. One often-cited societal trend is monopoly concentration by firms attempting to control markets. In the core or primary segment, the quality of work life is high, wages are good, and job ladders that form careers are available to workers who have secured employment in entry-level positions. Educational credentials are viewed merely as screening devices, controlled by advantaged groups, that employers use to detect good workers. In the secondary sector, workers are readily substitutable, few promotion opportunities exist, work quality is low, and job instability is high.

Some segmentation perspectives stress the insulation of one labor-market segment from another. Consider the internal-labor-market thesis. Once workers have passed through entry-level positions in internal labor markets, they are more or less guaranteed stable work histories. But only those inside the market have such protection and security. Workers in secondary markets, by comparison, are thrown into greater competition among themselves. In the secondary sector, jobs and wages are more subject to the capriciousness of market supply and demand (Doeringer and Piore 1971). Moreover, workers with certain ascribed premarket characteristics—notably blacks, females, and youth—are typically relegated to secondary segments. Rather than explaining career outcomes in terms of rational actors making decisions that maximize individual-level returns, segmentation theorists reason that a worker's career attitudes and aspirations are shaped and defined by his work location.

Whereas conservative perspectives view careers as individual achievements accomplished through efficiency and productivity, radical perspectives view careers and work life as ascribed rather than achieved. Once a worker has gained access to favored work status through the initial employment gate, his career outcomes are largely guaranteed by virtue of economic segmentation.

The radical perspective has been criticized by Cain (1976; see also Baron and Bielby 1980). Frequently, its predictions are ambiguous or no different from those of the conservative perspectives. Further, critics argue that radical perspectives tend to shift focus between different levels of social organization. Nonetheless, conflict arguments are credited with introducing new ideas and discovering empirical anomalies in the neoclassical paradigm.

Conservative theories speak to issues of individual achievement and the rational operation of firms. But conservative theories say little about how individuals are shaped by structure. Radical theories address questions concerning institutional arrangements and their consequences for individuals, but these perspectives largely ignore how individuals shape their own lives and, in turn, affect the social structure. A third orientation, the life course perspective, speaks to weaknesses in the conservative and radical theories. The life course perspective cannot claim a long-standing intellectual pedigree. It is of more recent origin, is more limited in scope, and is more of a conceptual framework than a theory. But it adds depth to the understanding of career development.

Life Course Explanations

Several ideas are central to the life course approach. First, life in industrial societies is characterized by significant social transitions (for example, adolescence to adulthood, school to work, single to married status). Second, the transitions involve movement through multiple, interlocking work and nonwork roles. Roles can be thought of as social positions that involve expectations for performance. The life course perspective views multiple roles not as separate areas of activity but as sets of complex interrelationships that must be analyzed in these larger contexts. Third, the individual is viewed as an actor, decision maker, negotiator, and adapter to multiple role demands that often compete. How the individual meets those expectations has career ramifications. Fourth, events are normatively timed. Both synchronies and asynchronies have consequences for subsequent events. The life course consequences of early marriage, for example, differ from those of late marriage, and the consequences for both early and late marriages differ from those for normative marriages. Fifth, events are normatively sequenced. There are social expectations regarding the assumption of parenting roles relative to marriage, for example. Failure to observe the normative sequences may also have consequences for subsequent events. Finally, individual needs, interests, and options change over time. Developmental time (age) is an important determinant of the social expectations that are assigned to individuals.

Life course considerations introduce additional complexity to the study of careers. But lacking is a clear statement of variables and hypotheses that relate them. Indeed, there is little consensus about the number or identification of the appropriate dimensions on which life course events may be plotted, and there is only limited agreement about the events that mark transitions. We manage the ambiguities by restricting focus to four life course dimensions—family, school, work, and military histories—over a defined period roughly corresponding to the twelve-year period from completion of high school through age 30. Further, we limit consideration to the major transitions that occur over that period, giving primary attention to the effect of familial, educational, and military transitions on work histories.

The life course perspective sensitizes research to the complexity that is ignored in explaining work roles and careers at any single level of social organization, to say nothing of the problems attending multiple-level explanations. We use the life course perspective as a unifying framework within which to examine social-structural and individual-level explanations for careers. This possibility is considered following presentation of the data sources on which the analyses are based.

Data Sources

Although past research has most often focused on either structural or individual-level explanations of careers, the Career Development Program juxtaposes the two. The program is organized around the analysis and development of two data bases. Although each involves unique issues, this program of study requires complementary use of the two.

The first task is to investigate career lines. We used the 1970 Census Public Use Samples (U.S. Bureau of the Census 1972) to generate the essential information. The 1970 census contains detailed occupation-industry information for respondent's labor force participation in 1970 and identical information for labor-force participation in 1965. Thus the data provide opportunity to assess the amount and direction of job change and job stability individuals experienced over the five-year interval. By stringing together job-history information from the five-year interval into age-graded sequences, we developed a picture of the patterns of job sequences that occur over time under a set of simplifying assumptions. Moreover, the age-specific jobs through which workers regularly enter each job sequence or career line are identified. For each career line, estimates are produced of the work-role features of the entry-level job. These include requirements for entering a line of work, characteristics of the work role, and returns or rewards that accompany occupancy and performance of the work role. The estimation strategies are based on strong assumptions, and the outcomes have specified limitations. Yet, we view the procedures as reasonable first steps in studying career lines and the results as useful first approximations.

The concepts and career-line information generated in the first phase of the analysis serve as major dependent variables for the second phase, which examines the individual-level determinants of career-line access. This phase of the analysis requires measures of several life course dimensions over time. We use a rich set of panel data on a sample of male and female respondents ($N = 6,729$). As juniors and seniors in high school in 1965-

1966, the respondents provided extensive information on their backgrounds, social-psychological concepts, post-high school plans, and life course events through age 18. Thirteen years later in 1979, when respondents were about 30 years old, we tracked and gathered detailed life course histories.

The tracking effort confirmed the whereabouts (current address and/or telephone number) of 98.2 percent of the original respondents through direct contact with the respondents or their immediate families. The procedural details of the tracking effort are the subject of a separate volume. We gathered detailed life course histories from 90.6 percent of the original respondents: 88.9 percent were successfully surveyed by telephone interview, and 1.7 percent, who were not available for telephone interview, completed and returned a reduced-form mail questionnaire.

The histories include information on job transitions, formal and informal schooling, family, and military experiences as these occurred month by month. Supplementary information was gathered on psychological and social-psychological variables. Detailed educational histories, as recorded in school transcripts and yearbooks, were also retrieved. The individual-level data (hereafter the Career Development Study) were gathered to provide information on the determinants of careers. However, the data are also appropriate for conducting triangulation studies, including partial validation of the career lines constructed from the Census Public Use Samples, and for pursuing life course analyses.

The opportunity for validating the career lines arises in the partial overlap of the data bases (figure 1-1). The 1970 Census Public Use Samples are drawn from a population of individuals age 23 to 62 in 1970 who were age 18 to 57 in 1965. The Career Development Study consists of panel data on respondents through age 18 and very detailed life course information on the same respondents up to about age 30. The two data bases overlap—one provides structural-level information, the other provides detailed individual-level information—for the twelve-year period after high school. The detailed life-history information from the Career Development Study also provides the data source for testing hypotheses drawn from the life course literature.

Discussion

A survey of the social- and behavioral-sciences literature indicates various approaches to the study of work. Temme (1975*b*, p. 6), for example, concluded that there exist "disparate bodies of knowledge, all seeking to account for

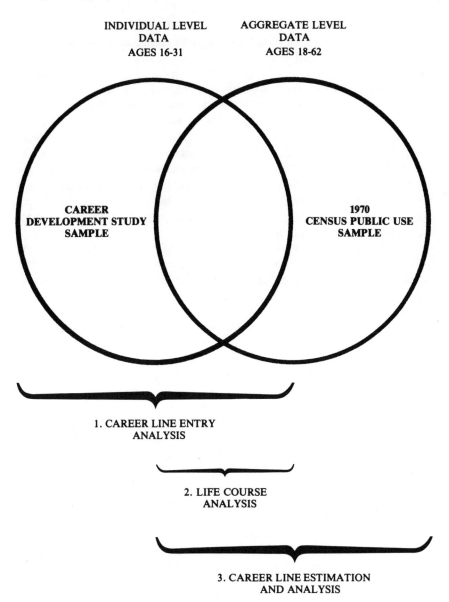

Figure 1-1. Age Coverage of the Career Development Study Data and the 1970 U.S. Census Public Use Samples Data by Components of the Research Design

the same phenomenon, man and his work, but each developing with little concern for the other." Several facets of work have been examined, but no comprehensive theory of work exists within which to anchor further inquiry into understanding how people enter careers in contemporary U.S. society.

We are heirs to the fragmentation that characterizes past approaches to the study of work. We have not inherited a treasure chest whose theoretical contents can be critically examined and carefully arranged. There are no estate assets from which to deduce an orderly and exhaustive set of propositions. Indeed, were that theoretical heirloom to exist, we would still suffer the limitations of data that lack full correspondence to the requirements for testing a carefully specified theory. However, ours is not an empty legacy either. There are sensitizing concepts and important ideas that bring theoretical considerations to bear on data and suggest substantively meaningful interpretations for findings.

Although work has been a central feature of human existence since the proverbial curse in the Garden, the systematic study of work continues to be in infancy. It is useful, then, to remind ourselves that the process of scientific inquiry has multiple goals and that they are sequential goals. Before intervention and control can be exercised, there must be explanation; and before explanation there must be description based on analysis of the relationships between basic variables. The study of work is still searching for the basic variables.

This is not to say that we will be content to count noses or that we naively believe that the facts will speak for themselves. Rather, we observe an interdependence of theory and research, and we nurture the symbiosis wherever possible. We proceed deductively where luxury allows and inductively where necessity dictates. We admit to a preference to progress empirically and to build incrementally. We view our efforts as a modest attempt to extend past theory and research so that future efforts might yield an even more cumulative understanding of entry into careers.

The remainder of this book is organized in three major sections. The first section provides our prospectus for studying the dependent variable, the nature and structure of career lines in the U.S. economy. Chapter 2 presents a conceptual and measurement framework for studying careers. Chapter 3 discusses estimation procedures and analysis of career lines. The second section outlines the study of individual entry into careers. Chapter 4 reviews individual-level determinants of access to career lines as these are informed by the literature. Chapter 5 presents the Career Development Study data base. Chapter 6 casts this set of studies in the context of complementary research and anticipates the potential significance and impact of the program of research. The third section consists of several appendixes that record the Career Development Study instrumentation and related primary materials.

2 A Conceptual and Measurement Framework for Studying Careers

A good job means more than present-tense work conditions and rewards. A good job also connotes future possibilities and, sometimes, assurances. The future implications of a person's current work were dramatically revealed in the Work in America survey (U.S. Department of Health, Education and Welfare 1973), which indicated that good chances for promotion are an important job consideration to more than three-fourths of the workers who were studied. Strong job dissatisfaction was voiced by workers who believed they were trapped in dead-end positions. But whatever workers may believe about the importance of future job prospects for their present work, the historical study of work has given relatively little attention to intragenerational mobility patterns.

Given that some jobs lead to other jobs and that sequences of jobs form careers, several questions surface. The first are descriptive: what sequences of jobs or career lines exist in the world of work? How may these be typed? The second set is analytical: why do certain jobs lead to other jobs and not to others? What are the salient dimensions that differentiate career lines?

This chapter offers an initial framework for examining the nature and structure of careers. The chapter is divided into three sections. First, we review old concepts and develop and illustrate new concepts for studying careers. Second, we consider measurement issues and present a measurement strategy for the empirical study of this conception of career lines. Third, we consider the dimensions and social organization of jobs and careers.

Career Concepts

Historical Origins

The historical roots of contemporary notions about careers can be traced back half a century to Sorokin (1927), who believed that regularities in job sequences occur over the work histories of individuals. Davidson and Anderson (1937) initiated research on career patterns a decade later. About the same time, Buehler (1933) identified five psychological life stages: the growth stage, exploratory stage, establishment stage, maintenance stage, and a stage of decline. Form and Miller's (1949; Miller and Form 1951)

13

sociological classification of work stages largely corresponded to the age limits of Buehler's life stages in distinguishing the preparatory work period, initial work period, trial work period, stable work period, and the retirement period (Super 1957, p. 71).

Miller and Form examined whether the sequences in work periods were patterned in different ways for various occupational and socioeconomic groups. Four types of career patterns were noted: stable career patterns in which individuals went directly from school to a type of work they consistently followed; conventional career patterns in which individuals progressed through initial and trial periods en route to stable employment; unstable career patterns in which stable work periods were interrupted by trial work periods; and multiple-trial career patterns that featured frequent changes of employment without a dominant work period. In their career patterns, Miller and Form also displayed the relationship between father's education and father's occupation, between father's occupation and son's education, and between son's education and son's occupation. Miller and Form's research was noteworthy for three reasons. First, it defined careers in terms of work histories rather than jobs held at some point in time. Second, their definition of careers did not denote upward mobility to the exclusion of other types of career patterns. Third, their study examined the determinants of careers. There have been subsequent empirical descriptions of careers.[1] Nonetheless, excepting Spilerman (1977), there have been few attempts to systematically describe and type the variety of career lines that occurs in the labor market on the basis of empirical data.

Not only are there few empirical studies of career patterns that appear in the economy, there is also little agreement on the meaning of the concept that for the past quarter-century has regularly appeared in the economic, psychological, sociological, and vocational guidance literatures. Temme (1975b), for example, provided reasonably specific definitions for work, jobs, and occupations, but he left the precise meaning of careers unattended. Typically, career neither denotes nor connotes a work history or succession of jobs over time. Usually the term is used synonymously with job or occupation.

Those who incorporate the notion of job succession in definitions differ on other requirements of the definition. Slocum (1975, p. 5), for example, asserted that an occupational career may be defined as "an orderly sequence of developments extending over a period of years and involving progressively more responsible roles within an occupation." Hall (1975, pp. 267-268) stated that "a 'normal' career . . . is generally a normal progression that carries with it not only a higher income over a period of time but also some prestige, which accrues with the status of having seniority or tenure, being experienced, being an old-timer, and so on." Sørensen's work (1974, 1975, 1977; see also, Hudis and Kalleberg 1977 and Rosenfeld 1980) on occupational careers used the job shift as the basic datum for analysis of earnings and socioeconomic differences across individuals. More recently these analyses were extended to incorporate individuals who stay in the same job over time (Kalleberg and Hudis, 1979). In summary, the concept of career is used equivocally. It lacks precise definition.

Spilerman (1977) observed that the key themes around which past studies were organized focused on preparation for work, securing entrance into occupations, remuneration and rewards, mobility, occupational associations, and phasing into retirement. Spilerman criticized the literature for selectively studying careers—for example, orderly careers—and for its reliance on case histories of single occupations, firms, or industries to the near neglect of careers that cross institutional boundaries. He noted that although the empirical description of careers has not been entirely neglected, over the past quarter-century career studies have largely deferred to the study of status and earnings change as these have been formulated in socioeconomic attainment models. Moreover, to anticipate the discussion that follows, there has been little effort to describe the multidimensional characteristics of careers or to predict and explain their differential accessibility within and between populations.

New Perspectives and Concepts

The limits of past research expose several necessary features of a definition and concept of career that informs research. A conceptual and operational definition must meet these requirements:

1. The concept should embrace consideration of the entire labor force, not just a single occupation, firm, industry, or class of workers.

2. The concept must incorporate the dimension of developmental time (individual's age) that allows statements about work histories as experienced by individuals, not merely job occupancy at a single point.[2]

3. The concept ought to be sensitive to a variety of institutional structures around which work roles vary (for example, occupation, industry, firms, labor markets) rather than grant exclusive priority to a single institutional axis.

4. The concept should provide for an examination of various features of work roles, not just their job status or economic remuneration.

5. The concept must avoid the evaluative trappings of past definitions of careers that often assume that careers denote upward social mobility to the exclusion of other types of career lines.

6. Finally, the definition, conceptualization, and analytical treatment of careers ought to be based on detailed and empirically verified work histories of men and women.

Our conceptualization draws on Spilerman's (1977) seminal discussion of careers. Jobs are considered to be a set of work roles or positions that have requirements for entry, imply a set of routines that characterize the content of the work role, and provide rewards for work-role occupancy and performance (Temme 1975b; Wise, Charner, and Randour 1976; Spenner 1977). *Career*, then, is defined as an individual's sequence of jobs over time. Careers are always and only individual-level phenomena. They are person-specific job histories.

The concept career line is informed by the observation that labor markets are patterned. *Career lines* are the determinable regularities in job sequences that exist in populations over time. They are structural features of the labor market, subject to the formative influences of industries, firms, and occupations. Career lines are normative patterns of job changes that set expectations for significant numbers of workers over their work histories. Moreover, career lines have identifiable work-related consequences for their incumbents, and there are empirical regularities that govern access to career lines through a limited number of jobs. Following Kerr (1954; see also, Doeringer and Piore 1971; Althauser and Kalleberg forthcoming), Spilerman (1977) refers to these jobs as entry portals.

Career-line sets consist of all career lines originating from an entry-portal job or leading to a destination job.[3] Treating career lines as empirically linked sequences of jobs formed by institutional and labor-market structures goes beyond theoretical traditions in economics (human capital), sociology (status attainment), and the trait-factor assumption in psychology that give only selective attention to job linkages (for example, occupation- or industry-based lifetime-earnings profiles).[4]

It is necessary to distinguish between an entry portal and any other particular job that a person may hold, be that the first job, current job, job at a specific age, job at mandatory retirement, or the like. Entry portals, like career lines, are not individual-level but are structural phenomena. They are properties not of careers but of career lines. An *entry portal* is a job through which a significant portion of the labor force gains access to a career line.

Entry portals are variable with respect to their age-width, that is they are jobs that may open the door for entry to a particular career line for only a few years or for many years. Some career lines have entry portals that are narrow age-width openings. For example, unless one is a physician at age 25 to 33, lengthy training requirements and medical school policies largely preclude that person from becoming a specialized surgeon. The age-door that is open for entrance to surgical specialties is comparatively narrow. Other career lines may have very broad age-width entry portals. For example, one may become a truck driver over a considerable number of years during the life course. The particular jobs that individuals hold—be they first, second, or last—vary in the timing and the extent to which they grant access to one or more career lines.

Inasmuch as entry portals control access to career lines, they portend the expected job sequences and consequences or rewards for workers located in that position at a given time in their work histories. Focusing on entry portals provides for examining a number of questions central to the proposed research. For example, in their aspirations and eventual labor-force entry, to what extent do young adults choose not only a job but also one or more career lines implicated in that job choice? Which entry portals offer the greatest flexibility at a later date, that is, skill generalizability or access to other career lines? Which aspects of family background and educational and military histories have significant bearing on access to certain types of entry portals and movement through career lines?

The strategy of focusing on entry portals assumes that individuals selecting jobs in the early years of their labor-force participation are at the same time, whether consciously or not, choosing jobs that have later career consequences. Limited information from status-attainment research suggests that this is not an unreasonable assumption (Blau and Duncan 1967; Kelley 1973; Featherman 1973; Featherman and Hauser 1978). First job is the best predictor of occupational status more than a decade later. Nonetheless, the mechanisms involved in the process are not well understood and have not been examined exhaustively.

Several recent conceptual and empirical studies draw on notions of careers and career lines in a way that is consistent with this use. The general model for intragenerational mobility proposed by Sørensen and colleagues defines career as a sequence of jobs held by the individual (1974, 1975, 1977; see also Hudis and Kalleberg 1977 and Rosenfeld 1980). In these studies, careers are measured by a person's succession of job shifts. Moreover, their structural model incorporates a system-level parameter for measuring growth in opportunities along with reporting variation in individual-resource variables. Further, the theoretical typology of labor markets proposed by Althauser and Kalleberg (forthcoming) incorporates ports of entry and job ladders as central components of certain types of labor markets. Finally, recent research by Rosenbaum (1979a, 1979b) examines panel data from a single organization to form career trees (sets of career lines) from workers' job histories. These developments are compatible with our conceptualization and design for the study of careers.

Issues in Measuring Career Lines

Suppose one had the ideal data for measuring career lines. What would be the properties of such a data set? The requirements are nontrivial. Suppose, also, that the ideal data requirements could not be met. What are the alternatives? A consideration of these issues follows.

Data Requirements

The measurement of career lines refers to the empirical identification of the age-graded sequences of jobs that regularly occur in the labor force. Since the concept of career line embodies a statistical notion of relatively frequent, age-specific job transitions, the ideal data set would include complete work histories covering the life course of a large sample of individuals. Note that this requirement alone far exceeds the properties of any existing data set. Inasmuch as career lines are sensitive to different institutional arenas, the work histories should also contain occupation, industry, and firm information and the dates of job transitions. The classification of jobs, hence the detail of career lines, should be at as homogeneous and disaggregated a level as possible. Finally, to assess historical changes—period and cohort effects—in the structure of career lines, the data set would ideally include multiple panels five or ten years apart, with each panel followed over its work life.

But even if such a data base existed, the conclusions generated from it would likely refer to a labor market of ten, twenty, or more years earlier. They may not accurately characterize the experiences of current cohorts due to the effects of inflation, migration, growth and decline in opportunities, and the like. These disjunctions between the real and the ideal, the attainable and the impossible, give pause to reflect on two issues. First, measures and operations for the career-line conceptualization are problematic. Spilerman (1977) suggests a synthetic-cohort strategy that has inherent limiting assumptions. These will be discussed. Second, the career-line concept does not give explicit attention to the dimensions or the social organization of the dimensions of jobs and careers. The nature and structure of jobs and careers are considered next.

Analysis Strategies

Two procedures are available for measuring career lines: a longitudinal analysis of job histories based on one or more birth cohorts of individuals and a synthetic-cohort strategy that employs cross-sectional data. In reality, neither approach meets the requirements of the ideal data set sketched. Consider the limitations.

The longitudinal job-history approach has the obvious advantage of incorporating the complete job record of individuals (see Blum et al. 1969;

Karweit 1973; Rogoff Ramsøy and Clausen 1977; Rosenbaum 1979a; Gitelman 1966). Unfortunately, few bodies of data contain the necessary detail. Of those that do, the data are usually restricted to a single firm or set of industries restricting the estimation to a few career lines. Rosenbaum (1979a, 1979b), for example, generated a career tree (career-line set) that originates from the same job for new employees entering a single firm in the same year. Five job categories and five time points over a thirteen-year history were used. The full sample of some thirteen thousand employees produced a subsample of 671 individuals for the career-line set in question, which contained about twenty-five distinct career lines. Even at this extreme level of aggregation, many of the career lines are based on the job histories of only one, two, or three people—hardly a basis for generalizing to known populations. In addition, longitudinal data may be dated when applied to subsequent cohorts whose experiences reflect different historical effects.

Consider also the synthetic-cohort strategy. Synthetic-cohort analysis takes age-graded "snapshots" of labor force transitions at one point. By stringing together consecutive snapshots—treating the destination of one group as the origin for the next oldest group, and so on for all age-graded groups—a moving picture or synthetic version of the true career line can be estimated under simplifying assumptions.

There are two major disadvantages and one practical consideration that bear on the synthetic-cohort strategy. The first disadvantage is that synthetic-cohort analysis is predicated on Markov-like assumptions about the irrelevance of the earlier history of a worker's jobs. No history other than what flows through the previously measured point-in-time job enters the estimation of transition probabilities (Mayer 1972; Rosenbaum 1979a; Spilerman 1977). The second disadvantage is that there is a possible confounding of marginal changes in the occupational structure reflecting growth and decline in job opportunities with age variations in transition probabilities. In addition, there is a practical consideration to estimating career lines under synthetic-cohort assumptions. Career lines are patterns of movement common to a portion of the labor force. Rules of statistical inference require substantial case numbers to constitute each transition probability. Only the largest of census samples permits such estimates. Spilerman (1977) notes that although the feasibility of this strategy is not in doubt, the analysis does require considerable computer time. These and related issues are discussed in chapter 3.

The primary measurement strategies for estimating career lines, then, involve analysis of longitudinal job histories and cross-sectional synthetic cohorts. Both have inherent limitations, and the shortcomings of each require the complementary use of the other. We use synthetic-cohort analysis in the Career Development research because it has a singular advantage. The synthetic-cohort strategy based on large cross-sectional samples represents the only reasonable and available option for estimating a large variety of career lines for the U.S. labor force. The challenge lies in learning the limits of the strategy, improving on it, and complementing it with longitudinal data where possible.

Career-Line Analysis

This section extends the discussion prospectively in search of the types, structure, and salient dimensions that describe career lines in anticipation of establishing the determinants of individual access to career lines.[5]

Description of Career Lines

Spilerman (1977) defined the principal task of career-line analysis as elucidating the properties of the job sequences. Within that agenda, Career Development assigns first priority to the goal of describing and typing the career lines that are generated by the synthetic-cohort analyses. The task is substantial. It assumes, of course, that career lines have been estimated for a manageable and substantively meaningful number of job sequences. To anticipate the results of the career-line estimates that are illustrated in chapter 3 and are the subject of a later volume in the Entry into Careers series, some ten thousand career lines that appear in nearly four hundred sets of career lines are constructed. Each career line or set of career lines originates in a job category. Each traces the job sequences of successive cohorts as these occur over hypothetical work histories in the labor force.

Several questions may be posed to guide the description of career lines. How do career lines differ with respect to their holding power on people in entry-level positions? Is there systematic change in career-line holding power over time? How do career lines differ with respect to the number, narrowness, or breadth of entry portals? How are career lines patterned with respect to early or late mobility options? What are the patterns of mobility that occur among some jobs to the exclusion of others? What are the dimensions over which career lines vary? Can the career lines be reduced to a manageable typology?

There are several ways that the study of career lines per se can inform the study of individual access to careers. One way is to construct a career-line typology and then predict access to particular kinds of career lines on the basis of individual-level variables. The individual-level data (see the review of theories of individual-level determinants in chapter 4 and the overview of the Career Development Study data in chapter 5) are designed to address issues of access as these involve variations among people. If the variation in career lines can be summarized in the form of several types that emerge from the census-data analyses, then the question of access reduces to the distributive question of who gets what type, why, and how? Further, who remains in or exits a given type and why? The substantive types could also be used to generate individual-level scores that measure the kind of career lines a person has held. These variables, then, could be used in equations that predict variance in occupancy of career-line types. In summary, the findings from the first part of the research provide the operational definitions of the dependent variable in the second part of the research.

Another strategy for linking the data sets involves the estimation of expected career-line characteristics for each age-specific entry portal. Examples include expected earnings and complexity of work. In this case the dependent variable would index the expected career-line outcome for those whose careers follow a particular career line or, alternatively, for those whose careers appear within a particular set of career lines. The specific variables could be estimated from the census data as weighted averages for workers following a particular career line. The expected career-line characteristic variables for jobs that individuals have held in their careers could then be merged to individual data records in the Career Development Study. The variables could be modeled with other independent variables as measured for individuals.

Dimensions and Organization of Work

Gross, Mason, and McEachern (1958, p. 17) noted that uses of the concept of role engender three basic ideas, namely, that individuals "(1) in social locations (2) behave (3) with reference to expectations." Work roles have requisites for entry, include expectations for behavior with respect to role routines or content, and offer rewards for occupancy and performance. The dimensions of jobs refer to the distinct features of work roles by which jobs are differentiated. The central issues can be framed by several questions. What dimensions of jobs are important over the careers of individuals? What are the relationships between dimensions, and how do societal structures generate these relationships? More generally, how is work organized into jobs, occupations, industries, and career lines (Davis and Taylor 1976; Braverman 1974; Baron and Bielby 1980)?

In certain respects these are classic questions raised earlier by Marx, Durkheim, and Weber, and different answers have been given. For example, in Marxist studies of the class structure (Parkin 1971; Giddens 1975; Wright and Perrone 1977), unit relationships of control over production prevail as paramount dimensions of the social organization of work. Neoclassical economics explains internal job structures in terms of the production function: considerations of productivity and scarcity determine the nature of jobs and internal promotion ladders. In studies of status attainment and mobility, socioeconomic status or prestige, as concept and as measurement metric, is the major stratification dimension (Klatzky and Hodge 1971; Featherman and Hauser 1977; Treiman 1977). Finally, the effects of occupational role on psychological orientation show the prominence of occupational self-direction as an organizing dimension for work (Kohn 1969; Kohn and Schooler 1978; Miller et al. 1979).

Identification of the appropriate dimensions of jobs and careers is an issue that has not been resolved. The more general concepts and measures, such as socioeconomic status and prestige, inform the study of stratification and intergenerational status transmission but do not provide the necessary detail for analyzing the dynamics of intragenerational job choices and shifts. Dimensionality and social organization of jobs are important because the understanding, definition, and mixture of individual definitions of costs and rewards likely vary as a function of age, family, and other role responsibilities and career-line position. Moreover, undoubtedly the dimensions and the mix of job dimensions specific to certain classes of career lines are in some measure organized by their location in labor markets (Doeringer and Piore 1971; Althauser and Kalleberg forthcoming; Kalleberg and Sørensen 1979).

Several recent studies provide a beginning, however tentative, to defining the nature and structure of careers. Baron and Bielby (1980), for example, identify unresolved issues in structural explanations of work organization. They argue that the "new structural" stratification research—by which they mean explanations for individual achievement in terms of such structural factors as class, authority, organizational size, and labor-market sector—proceeds without a clear notion of the social structure that underlies and organizes attainment and without consensus on which structures to study. Moreover, the literature fails to give adequate consideration to alternate explanations for economic segmentation. Current research fails to generate competing testable hypotheses driven by the two major perspectives, namely, the neoclassical theory of the firm (conservative theories) and segmented labor-market theories (radical theories). Baron and Bielby (1980) urge refocusing research on firms as the strategic unit of organization, suggesting that firms yield a more meaningful picture of the structure of work than that provided by occupational or industrial data. They reason that the following are key questions that will guide research during the 1980s. To what extent is there economic segmentation of labor markets? Given economic segmentation, what are its underlying components and dimensions? What is the effect of segmentation on work organization within firms? And, what is the trend in economic segmentation over time?

We append two additional questions to the Baron and Bielby formulation. First, assuming its existence, does economic segmentation determine the shape and salient dimensions of career lines? Second, does classic economic theory of the firm offer better-fitting predictions about the dimensions of jobs and careers? These issues will be addressed in subsequent work.

Other Perspectives to Career-Line Dimensions

Economic-segmentation arguments offer one explanation for the dimensions and social organization of jobs and careers, but other literatures also address the topic. The program of research by Kohn and colleagues (Kohn 1969; Kohn and Schooler 1973, 1978; Miller et al. 1979) provided the most sustained and systematic sociological program of research that examined a large array of detailed job characteristics. Regressing psychological functioning on occupational conditions and controlling for job status, Kohn and colleagues reported that the largest net effects are associated with occupational self-direction variables: substantive complexity of work, routinization, and closeness of supervision. This and related research (Temme 1975b; Spenner 1977) indicated that the colinearity between indicators for these constructs and socioeconomic status is quite high, in many cases above $r = .75$.

The question must be asked: what does it mean, how does it affect understanding of the dimensionality and structure of jobs, if the effects of occupational conditions on psychological functioning are estimated controlling on job status, following Kohn's analytical strategy (Kohn and Schooler 1973)? Lacking a theory of the dimensionality and structure of jobs, the relationship of the part to the whole remains undefined. Indeed, even the definition of what is part and what is whole is problematic.

We ask whether controlling for status when estimating the effects of job conditions is to remove some of the covariation that is of interest. To grant equal conceptual status to the overall indicator of resources and to the subcomponents of roles that constitute that overall resource level results in serious colinearity problems when, for example, one attempts to separate the effects of socioeconomic status from those of substantive complexity of work. A major unresolved issue, then, concerning the dimensionality and social organization of jobs and careers is clarification of the conceptual status of such overall constructs and measures as prestige and socioeconomic status in relation to the more disaggregated job characteristics, however specified.

Other recent studies employ both inductive and deductive strategies to generate job dimensions from a large array of job characteristics. Temme

(1975*b*), in a conceptual and empirical treatment of occupation, and Spenner (1977), in a study of the intergenerational transmission of the components of jobs, used a tripartite conception of labor-force positions: requirements (requisites), routines (job content) and rewards. Bielby and Kalleberg (1975) inductively arrived at related dimensions: requirements, resources, and rewards. Similarly, Mortimer (1974) reports work autonomy, functional foci, and characteristic rewards. Yet other studies, using inductive and deductive strategies, arrive at still other dimensions for jobs. Spaeth (1979), for example, produced three highly correlated vertical dimensions: prestige, authority, and complexity. Kalleberg's (1977) theory provided for six dimensions of work values and job satisfaction: intrinsic, convenience, financial, relations with co-workers, career opportunities, and resource adequacy. Vanneman and McNamee (1978) presented three dimensions—rewards, working conditions, and organizational size—in their study of labor-force characteristics and job rewards.

These studies pose several additional issues. First, consensus is clearly lacking on what constitutes the appropriate domain of job characteristics that generate or reflect the dimensions of jobs and careers. The literatures identify more than one hundred features of jobs, perhaps fifteen to thirty major ones. Problems of conceptualization and data reduction must not be underestimated. Second, the studies uniformly show that jobs are constellations of modestly to highly correlated characteristics, creating the estimation problems that accompany the separation of colinear effects. The presence of constellations of job features emphasizes the need for stronger theoretical and measurement models that speak to the question of what it is about jobs that is important and why.

The accumulated literature discourages the notion of a single dimension, a single theoretical statement, or a single measurement model for jobs and for the social organization of jobs that will fit all substantive problems at a disaggregated level of analysis. At least in the near term, theories and measurement models for career and job dimensions will probably be most effective if they are tailored to more narrowly defined classes of substantive problems. Examples include those dealing with structural and labor-market forces operating on jobs and those dealing with such individual perceptions of jobs as job satisfaction and aspirations. This, we submit, is a reasonable strategy until there is a better understanding of the dimensions and social organization of jobs and careers for sociologically similar questions. Then researchers may have achieved the leverage needed to address larger issues of synthesis.

Summary

There exists little theoretical and empirical research that cumulatively informs understanding of career phenomena. Moreover, there is little agreement on the meaning of the concept. Following Spilerman (1977), career lines are defined as structural regularities in job sequences that affect significant numbers of workers over their work histories. Consideration is given to the merits and limitations of two analytical strategies for measuring career lines: longitudinal job-history analysis and cross-sectional synthetic-cohort analysis. The literature reports numerous characteristics of jobs but lacks an integrating conceptual statement on the nature and dimensions of jobs and careers. Our research will describe and type career lines in anticipation of establishing the individual-level determinants of access to careers.

Notes

1. See, for example, Lipset and Bendix 1952a, 1952b; Palmer 1954; Spilerman and Miller 1973; Sørensen 1974, 1975, and 1977; Parnes and Nestel 1975; Wilensky 1961; Thompson, Avery, and Carlson 1968; Rosenbaum 1979a; 1979b; and Dauffenbach 1980.

2. The variation that occurs in careers and career lines over time may not be solely a function of age. For example, Tuma (1976, p. 357) suggested that the (negative) correlation between rate of mobility and age results from the association of age with duration in jobs and from decreasing mobility with jobs of increased duration. The effect is time dependent, but it is an effect of job durations, not age. Our point here is to stress the time-dependent nature of careers and career lines, whether the specific effects are those of duration, age, or both.

3. The distinction between lines originating from versus leading to a job corresponds to outflow and inflow displays, respectively, in any job transition or mobility matrix.

4. But see Featherman 1971, 1973, and Kelley 1973.

5. This section draws on a paper, "Emerging Issues in the Study of Careers," by Spenner and Otto (1979).

3 Estimation and Analysis of Career Lines

Lacking the ideal data base for producing a motion picture of evolving career lines, we produce estimates of career lines using existing cross-sectional data. A synthetic-cohort strategy takes age-graded snapshots of labor-force transitions at one time for workers of various ages and, under simplifying assumptions, strings them together into a synthetic version of the true career line. This chapter presents the methodology for estimating career lines, discusses assumptions and related issues, presents empirical examples of career lines, and illustrates job and worker characteristics for representative job categories.

Methodology for Estimating Career Lines

Data

A career line is operationally defined as a post-high school job sequence for successive five-year age cohorts experienced by a nontrivial portion of the labor force. Informed by Spilerman's (1977) procedures, we produce estimates for the empirically occurring career lines based on the cross-sectional synthetic-cohort information provided in the 1970 Census Public Use Samples (U.S. Bureau of the Census, 1972). The combined 3 percent neighborhood, county, and state public use sample numbers about 3.3 million cases. The population from which the sample was drawn is defined as individuals age 23 to 62 in 1970 and age 18 to 57 in 1965. Additionally, analysis was restricted to those individuals reporting a codable occupation and industry in 1965 and 1970 ($N \doteq 1.874$ million). This restriction imposes the additional qualification of limiting the sample to those active in the labor force, by census definition, in the 1965-1970 quinquennium. The sample was divided into 8 five-year age cohorts (ages 18-22, 23-27, . . . , 53-57). The age groupings roughly correspond to the earliest age of formal entry into the labor force and the midpoint between early and mandatory retirement. Given the job categories discussed later, we constructed a three-dimensional array of 1965 job origins by 1970 job destinations by age cohorts.

Construction of Job Categories

The elemental components of career lines are jobs, whether the jobs are positioned in primary or secondary sectors, internal or external labor markets, within or outside the context of firms. *Job* refers to the 1970 six-digit detailed census occupation-industry classifications (U.S. Bureau of the Census 1970).

To make the 1970 census classifications manageable and of sufficient numerical size to develop stable estimates of transition probabilities, we reduced the 421 three-digit census occupations and 221 industries to 384 occupation-industry categories. We constructed the categories to maintain compatibility with the 1970 census job codes and to maximize within-category homogeneity.

The 384 categories were constructed in several steps. First, univariate marginals were examined for all three-digit occupations and industries for 1965 and 1970 jobs. Second, in the case of very large or small categories ($N > 4,000$; $N < 1,000$), six-digit occupation-industry marginals were also examined. In the case of very large, heterogeneous categories, further industry breakdowns were made. If a job category were small, then we sought other jobs within the same occupation group that might serve as a basis for combination (for example, computer systems analysts and computer specialists, not elsewhere classified). Third, preliminary occupation-industry breakdowns and combinations were made and critically reviewed. Instructive precedents were provided by the 1970 industrial classifications and categories earlier constructed by Temme (1975*b*). Means and variances of *Dictionary of Occupational Titles* (DOT) characteristics for census categories were also considered (Spenner, Otto, and Call 1980). We sought as much industry detail within an occupation category as the available distribution of cases would permit. Further, in the case of occupation combinations, we sought maximum within-group homogeneity on DOT job characteristics. Finally, the job categories were adjusted, revised, and rechecked until a satisfactory final set was obtained.[1]

We report the final 384 career-line job categories with corresponding 1970 U.S. Census occupation-industry elements in appendix A.

Construction of Career Lines

Career lines consist of job sequences originating in a single age-specific entry portal that occur with sufficient frequency in the sample to qualify for inclusion on the basis of decision criteria that will be discussed.

We constructed career lines by linking consecutive five-year-interval job transitions reported by successive age cohorts. For example, beginning with the cohort age 18 to 22 in 1965, we calculated the probabilities of moving from each job category in 1965 to each job category in 1970. We used the 1970 destination job category for the 18-to-22 age cohort in 1965 as the 1965 origin job category for those in the cohort age 23 to 27, and we again calculated job transition probabilities. We repeated this process for each of the eight age cohorts. The procedure yielded a career line or set of career lines for every origin job category. Figure 3-1 graphically illustrates the construction of a set of synthetic career lines.

Figure 3-1A displays hypothetical information for 1965 to 1970 job transitions for one origin job, A^1, for the cohort age 18 to 22, and for three jobs—A^2, B^2, and J^2—for the cohort age 23 to 27.

In figure 3-1B the rearranged display presents the beginnings of a set of synthetic career lines. The transitions for the cohort age 23 to 27 are repositioned to appear horizontally and in temporal sequence. The resulting career lines are synthetic, inasmuch as the transition probabilities are estimated from two different age cohorts based on job reports for 1965 and 1970 rather than probabilities at two 5-year intervals for the same cohort.

In figure 3-1C we simplify the graphic presentation and present the form used in subsequent examples. We followed the same procedures for joining the transition probabilities of the cohorts age 23 to 27 with those for the cohort age 18 to 23 and with the remaining cohorts. This produced a complete set of career lines originating with job A in the age 18-to-22 cohort and extending through the age 53-to-57 cohort.

It is technically possible to compute probabilities for all transitions over the eight successive five-year periods. However, such detail may not be meaningful or necessary for most analyses. In the extreme case, if all probabilities were included, it would mean that if only 2 of 1.8 million people changed from job X to job Y from 1965 to 1970, that transition would be defined as an element in a career line. Our software permits alternate decision rules.

As the decision rules are relaxed, the number of transitions increase, and career-lines sets become more complex. As stricter decision rules are employed, the number of transitions decreases, and the career-line sets become less complex. In examples that illustrate career-line sets, the decision criteria are transition probabilities $P_{ijk} \geq .04$, and the transition frequencies are $f_{ijk} \geq 10$ individuals.

Methodological Issues and Assumptions

The data and analysis strategy used to construct career lines raise several methodological issues:

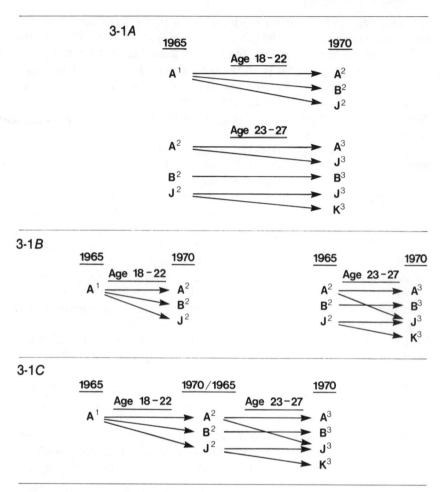

Figure 3-1. Construction Steps for Career Lines under a Synthetic-Cohort
          Assumption

1. the validity of Markov assumptions
2. the validity of steady-state assumptions concerning the nature of work
   and the structure of career lines over time
3. the confounding effects of marginal changes in the occupational structure
4. the measurement error in retrospective job reports
5. other institutional axes that structure career lines (for example, firms
   and regional labor markets)

These assumptions and issues are considered in the following section.

Markov Assumptions

Synthetic-cohort analysis requires an assumption about the nonrelevance of a worker's earlier job history to his or her present opportunities and future job prospects. This is true because only the previous point-in-time job enters the estimation of transition probabilities to other jobs in Markov models (Mayer 1972; Rosenbaum 1979a; Spilerman 1977). For example, in the case of a worker age 45 in 1970, the assumption of synthetic-cohort analysis is that the entire effect of his or her prior employment history—including seniority, tenure, and skill acquisition—is captured in the measurement of the 1965 job at age 40. Equivalently, individuals in the same detailed jobs in 1970 and 1965 are assumed to have equivalent job histories.

Undoubtedly, this assumption introduces some level of distortion in the estimation of transition probabilities for career lines. Markov models are recognized as offering a poor fit for intergenerational mobility and at best provide an improved but loose fit to intragenerational mobility (Mayer 1972). Hodge (1966), for example, using a sample of men age 35 to 64 with longitudinal data on occupation in 1940 and 1949 from the Six Cities Labor Mobility Study, reported that the Markov assumption introduces 4 to 7 percent distortion in transition probabilities for highly aggregated occupation groups over the nine-year period. Whether this level of distortion is large or small depends on the alternatives. Further, there is a literature of extensions and elaborations to the basic Markov model aimed at achieving better empirical predictions (for example, see Ginsberg 1971; McFarland 1970; Spilerman 1972; Singer and Spilerman 1974; Stewman 1975; Tuma 1976). Generally, the advances assume data requirements or levels of aggregation that are more tractable with our individual-level data on careers, but this does not hold for the estimation of career lines with census data. Largely for reasons of simplicity and tractability, we chose to pursue a first set of estimates for career lines under a synthetic-cohort assumption in the census data. In the present case, lacking an estimation alternative, we proceed recognizing the limitation and trying to assess its effects.

Steady-State Assumptions

Synthetic-cohort analysis requires a steady-state assumption with respect to the nature of work and jobs and in the stability of the transition probabilities through recent history. This assumption, too, is not completely true and introduces some distortion in the estimated career lines. Although the empirical evidence is far from definitive, theoretical arguments about temporal changes in work content have ranged from "no change" through "the degradation of work in the twentieth century" thesis to "the upgrading of the content of work as a function of technological change and automation" arguments (Hall 1975, p. 314-322; Braverman 1974; Edwards 1979; U.S. Department of Health, Education and Welfare 1973; Eckaus 1973). However, the little systematic empirical evidence that is available suggests that apart from changing distributions of workers to jobs, true change in the skill content of jobs in the last thirty years has probably been very small. Spenner (1979), for example, found little change in the skill requirements of a sample of jobs from the *Dictionary of Occupational Titles* for the period 1965 to 1977.

Other research with the same data base shows little change between 1947 and 1965 (Horowitz and Herrnstadt, 1966). If the data are reliable and valid, then there appears to have been little change in average skill requirements of jobs since World War II. Perhaps even less answerable is the extent to which jobs—their content, structure, and place in career lines—have changed relative to one another, as distinct from simple mean upgradings or downgradings of jobs, career-line requirements, or changes in the number of individuals moving through jobs and career lines.

Marginal Changes in the Occupational Structure

A question might also be raised concerning temporal changes in transition probabilities. Featherman and Hauser (1978, p. 214) conclude that there is substantial temporal constancy in the mobility regime for American men between 1962 and 1973 given adjustments for the varying marginal distributions of workers to aggregate occupation categories over the years. Nonetheless, they report very small but statistically significant changes in the transition probabilities that link first jobs to current jobs between 1962 and 1973. The size of the net change is 1.5 percent of the total association in a full (10 x 10) mobility table. Comparable data for longer periods of time are not available. Lacking a better option, we proceed with caution acknowledging the small changes that have been reported over an eleven-year period.

A further confounding effect that may distort transition probabilities concerns compositional changes in the occupational structure and changes in the age and industry structure. The assumption of synthetic-cohort analysis is that the economy and social structure are relatively constant over time and that young workers undergo the same set of experiences and move according to the same transition processes as did older members of the labor force. There is some indication that this may not be the case. There have been changes in the composition of the occupational structure over time such as a decline in the proportion of the labor force employed in agriculture accompanied by growth in clerical, professional, and service occupations. It may be argued that as some areas expand, the probabilities of taking jobs in these areas increases; and as other areas contract, the probabilities of taking jobs in these decreases. So, also, there has been growth in the nation's economy, in the total number of workers in the labor force. The absolute supply of workers has increased.

But the demand side of the equation is not always balanced by the supply side. Demographic changes, as influenced by birth rates, on the one hand, and mortality rates, on the other hand, are not always in synchrony such that labor supply matches labor demand. Moreover, economic conditions have sometimes imposed dramatic changes in demand with the result that the probabilities of having a job, any job, change over time.

In theory, these problems may be remedied in part by equiproportionally adjusting the three-way marginals of the input job-structure matrix while leaving intact the odds ratios inherent in the transition regime (Hauser, Dickinson, Travis, and Koffel 1975; Hauser, Koffel, Travis, and Dickinson 1975; Deming 1943; Goodman 1970). For example, adjustment might remove the artificial component of mobility or lack of mobility to agricultural career lines resulting from the substantial decrease in workers employed in agriculture. Other potentially important adjustments to the synthetic-cohort data might allow for differential death rates and for biased age-sex distributions in estimates from the 1970 census data (Sommers and Eck, 1977). Such adjustments may provide plausible relief for problems associated with labor-force expansion and marginal changes.[2]

But, there is also some evidence that the steady-state assumption may be appropriate. Hauser and colleagues (1975a, 1975b) have demonstrated the stability of certain basic mobility processes even though jobs undoubtedly have been upgraded in their entry requirements (Thurow 1975). The extent to which adjustments will alter career lines is an empirical question. The conditions under which use of unadjusted versus adjusted career lines is advised require careful consideration.

Measurement Error in Retrospective Reports

One potentially important measurement issue that arises with use of census data is whether retrospective reports of jobs are accurate. Several papers (U.S. Bureau of the Census 1970a; Miller 1977) have questioned the accuracy of retrospective job reports. Walsh and Bukholdt (U.S. Bureau of the Census 1970a), for example, drew on a 1968 survey in which respondents who were members of a 1968 population survey reported retrospectively about the occupations they held five years earlier. Unfortunately, the sample included males in their mid-teens, where the error was disproportionately located. Further, the reports assumed that the 1963 respondent reports were completely accurate and that whatever discrepancy in reports occurred over the five-year period was error attributed to the 1968 retrospective report.

The Career Development Study does not sample respondents in their mid-teens. Moreover, in important recent work Featherman and Hauser (1977, p. 57) reanalyzed some of the same data for males age 19 and over and concluded that "memory of occupation is not subject to much more decay in the long run [five years] than it is in the short run [several months], as witnessed by the similarity of reliability (.8726) and stability (.8020) correlation coefficients." More important, the error structure in retrospective reports of jobs, particularly for nonblacks, is random with respect to background variables, education, and current occupation (Bielby 1976; Bielby, Hauser, and Featherman 1977a, 1977b). In sum, recent analyses indicate that measurement error in retrospective reports of jobs is not a serious problem for the estimation of career lines.

Other Institutional Axes

The initial estimates of career lines leave unspecified the effects of certain institutional axes, such as regional labor markets and career patterns within firms, insofar as these are not captured by occupation-industry categories. Spilerman (1977) estimated career lines from census data for six metropolitan areas in the Northeastern states. A cost of such regional restrictions on estimates is a severe reduction in sample size that reduces the reliability of transition probabilities. This is not to say that regional variation is unimportant. Rather, we opted for increased reliability and number of cases over regional variations in career lines. That career lines are structured and operate within firms even though the individual may be in the same occupation and industry over his or her entire work life is a more serious bias in the proposed estimates (for reviews on intrafirm career structures see Doeringer and Piore 1971; Baron and Bielby 1980; Collins 1979). Although the current round of estimation does not deal with intrafirm variations, the individual-level data in the Career Development Study allow for some attention to the ways in which individual careers are embedded in firms.

Implications of Working Assumptions

We have assumed a position on a very complicated problem. The assumptions have implications that pose a potential threat to the validity and reliability of inferences, as is always the case. However, information with which to assess the magnitude of the problems associated with nonrandom historical trends is not readily available. Neither are there simple solutions for dealing with them.

Our approach is pragmatic. Lacking workers' detailed lifelong job histories, the synthetic-cohort strategy is one of the limited options for bringing empirical information to bear on the study of careers. There is a problem of correspondence between the theoretical and measurement models. However valid the concept, there are operational limitations to the synthetic-cohort approach. Under the limitations of data, we submit that careful application of the approach is required, not disregard for an empirical approximation.

Eckaus advised that there are equally burdensome methodological problems with the only other analytical option (1973, pp. 71-79). Using longitudinal retrospective data, one would have an equal reluctance to employ the life histories of those who are currently 60 to 70 years old in predicting the career lines of 18-to-25 year olds entering the labor force in 1980. Thus, the most viable alternative assumption is also problematic.

That the steady-state assumption is an oversimplification of reality is not to be denied. We acknowledge the limitations of our inferences. We proceed on the conviction that, given our bias for dealing with empirical data, the steady-state assumption is a rational decision, and the analytical strategy will yield a plausible interpretation of important aspects of work careers.

Empirical Examples of Career Lines

The Case of Elementary School Teachers

Figure 3-2 graphically displays an empirical example of the career lines that originate with employment as an elementary school teacher at age 18 to 22 in 1965. The figure labels the jobs that occur in the career lines of elementary school teachers, extends the construction of career lines through all eight synthetic-cohort stages, and graphically portrays the significant job changes ($P_{ijk} \geq .04$, $f_{ijk} \geq 10$) that occur for successive cohorts.

Two numbers for each job transition quantify the amount of movement between the job categories in 1965 and 1970. The percentages indicate the proportion of the total number of people in the 1965 job-age group that made the transition to a particular 1970 job category. For example, 67 percent of the elementary school teachers age 18 to 22 in 1965 continued as elementary school teachers in 1970; and 12 percent of the elementary school teachers age 18 to 22 in 1965 changed to secondary school teachers over the same five-year period. The number in parentheses indicates the number of cases represented by the percentage. Thus, 1,818 elementary school teachers in the age group 18 to 22 in 1965 were also classified as elementary school teachers in 1970. Similarly, 319 changed to secondary school teachers over the same period. Both the percentage and the number of cases in a given transition are based on the actual number of cases in the 3 percent 1970 U.S.

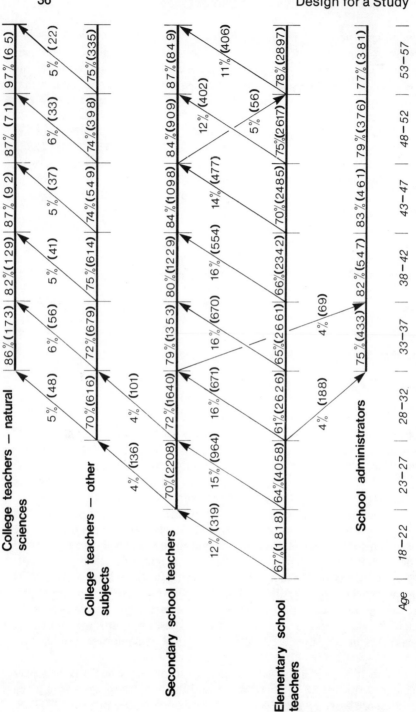

Figure 3-2. Career-Line Set for Elementary School Teachers

Census Public Use Samples of an age group that was in a job category in 1965 and made the transition to a 1970 job category.

Career lines for elementary school teachers illustrate several concepts. First, the figure graphically portrays a set of career lines. Figure 3-2 embodies forty-four different combinations and permutations of job changes, each presenting a career-line possibility. Career-line sets from other job-origin positions show quite different patterns. Some sets contain many more lines. Others contain just one line. The transition probabilities vary from one set of lines to another. Finally, the age-width of entry portals and the age or life course location of entry portals vary systematically between sets of lines.

The career lines for elementary school teachers illustrate the variability in the age-width of entry portals. At every age elementary school teachers change to secondary school teacher positions. The percent of elementary school teachers making the transition is relatively constant, 11 percent to 16 percent over the career span. Thus, elementary school teaching provides a wide entry portal to secondary school teaching. By comparison a significant number and proportion of elementary school teachers become school administrators but only in the age 28 to 32 cohort, at which time 4 percent make the transition. From a probability point of view, elementary school teaching offers a very narrow entry portal to school administration. The change occurs in only one 5-year period and then in a very small amount.

One is tempted to also observe that secondary school teaching is a very narrow entry portal to both school administration and elementary school teaching and that college teaching of other subjects is a wide entry portal to college teaching of natural sciences, whereas the latter is not an entry portal to the former. Although probable, these conclusions would be premature, since they are not based on job-change information for job categories in the early cohorts. Such information is available only by referencing the complete career-line information for the appropriate origin job categories.

Career lines for elementary school teachers are patterned. Elementary school teachers tend to remain elementary school teachers across age cohorts, as is also the case for the other job categories represented in figure 3-2. Typically, from two-thirds to three-fourths of the elementary school teachers stay in elementary school teaching positions over successive five-year periods. The percentage who remain elementary school teachers systematically increases from about 60 percent to nearly 80 percent after age 32. Indeed, after age 32 the options open to elementary school teachers are limited to secondary school teaching. Prior to age 32, elementary school teaching provides a wide entry portal for secondary school teaching and narrow but significant entry portals to college teaching—both of other subjects and of natural sciences—and school administration.

Study of the career-line set for elementary school teachers reveals other patterns. First, the display is highly successful in capturing most of the job changes affecting elementary school teachers. Typically, the transition probabilities account for 80 to 90 percent of the job transitions for elementary school teachers in a given age group. Thus, 67 percent remain elementary school teachers, and an additional 12 percent change to secondary teaching, which accounts for 79 percent of the job changes experienced by elementary school teachers age 18 to 22 in 1965. In the later cohorts nearly 90 percent of the job changes are captured. This means that 21 percent of the first cohort or as little as 12 percent and 13 percent of the later cohorts change to other positions (not graphed) or left the labor force. What those unspecified jobs are could be determined by relaxing the decision rules to allow tracing all changes to other categories. Indeed, the number of job categories included in this residual is itself interesting and would inform other analyses.

Second, this analysis is based on the entry-portal strategy applied to the case of elementary school teachers. It traces the career implications of being an elementary school teacher in every age cohort, spanning ages 18 to 57. It is not a complete statement for other job categories that appear in the figure. For example, figure 3-2 says nothing about the career lines for school administrators prior to age 33. Were one interested in the career lines of school administrators, it would be necessary to follow the same entry-portal analysis as is illustrated for elementary school teachers.

Third, the percentage and numerical indicators associated with each job change in this illustration provide three kinds of information. They quantify the amount of change; they provide a basis for reconstructing the total number of persons in the 1965 sample by job categories; and they provide the basis for looking at the relative contraction, expansion, or stability of job categories across age cohorts. Embedded in the numbers indicating the amount of job change for specific cohorts is information on the relative size of the work forces drawn from age cohorts in a particular job category. Thus, if 1,818 cases equal 67 percent of the work force in the age 18-to-22 category, by extrapolation one can establish that the total size of the age group in the sample is 2,714. Similarly, for elementary school teachers the total size of the age group 53 to 57 is 3,714. The youngest cohort is about one-fourth smaller in size than is the oldest cohort. Thus, the percentage remaining elementary school teachers declines slightly across the first three age cohorts and then increases for each successive age cohort. The number of persons who remain elementary school teachers for successive cohorts increases, then decreases only to increase for the last cohort. The total number of elementary teachers follows the same pattern across cohorts.

The entry-portal strategy displays the implications of being in a particular job at a given time and how position and age bear on subsequent job-transition probabilities. The entry-portal strategy is not designed to trace the job origins of persons who, for example, are elementary school teachers in the age 53-to-57 cohort. Such information requires an alternate display strategy.

Examples of Variations in Career Lines

The career-line set for elementary school teachers is moderately complex, as is evident from a comparatively cursory inspection of the career lines for other job categories. Figures 3-3 and 3-4 present examples of simpler career lines, but they are simpler only in the graphic sense that fewer predictable options open to electric-power linemen and cablemen (figure 3-3), on the one hand, and to sheetmetal workers and tinsmiths (figure 3-4), on the other.

The case of electric-power linemen and cablemen presents an example of a job that provides an entry portal to only one other job category (foremen, not elsewhere classified in transportation, communications, and utilities industries). The entry portal is relatively narrow. It occurs in mid-career. The case of sheetmetal workers and tinsmiths presents an example of a job category that does not serve as an entry portal to a related line of work. Note that in both examples, 60 to 70 percent stay in the line of work during the early years where no career options surface. Thus, about one-third of the workers scatters to numerous other jobs—such that, given the decision rule, less than 4 percent takes work in another single identifiable occupational grouping—or leave the labor force entirely.

But there are also much more complicated job-change scenarios than the case presented by elementary school teachers. Note the job-change patterns for accountants in accounting firms (figure 3-5). No more job-category groups are involved in the career-line set for accountants than were involved in the case of elementary school teachers. Both feature five different job categories. Yet the pattern of movement is considerably different. Accountants in accounting firms experience substantial movement to other industries during the first fifteen years of the career; but note also that past mid-career this career-line flexibility quickly disappears.

In approximately half of the 384 career-line sets, workers do not predictably change to another line of work once they enter a particular job category, given the $P_{ijk} \geq .04$, $f_{ijk} \geq 10$ decision rules. Either workers stay in the same job classification or they change to such a large number of jobs that regularities and patterns do not appear. The other half of the career-line sets features at least one and often several other job categories. No two sets of career lines are alike.

The career-line sets for electric-power linemen and cablemen, sheetmetal workers and tinsmiths, and accountants in accounting firms are

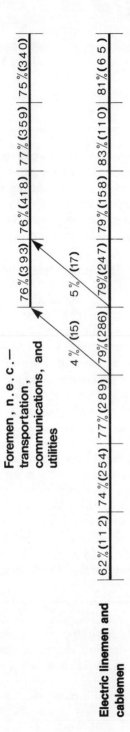

Figure 3-3. Career-Line Set for Electric Linemen and Cablemen

Sheetmetal workers and tinsmiths

56%(204)	61%(265)	66%(276)	73%(321)	75%(387)	77%(394)	79%(304)	81%(230)
18–22	*23–27*	*28–32*	*33–37*	*38–42*	*43–47*	*48–52*	*53–57*

Age

Figure 3-4. Career-Line Set for Sheetmetal Workers and Tinsmiths

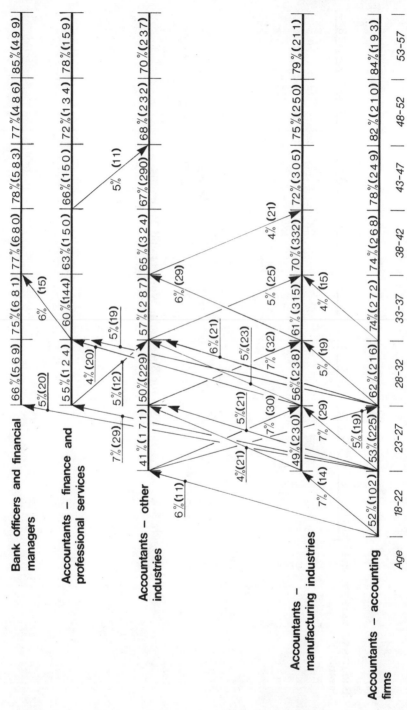

Figure 3-5. Career-Line Set for Accountants in Accounting Firms

presented merely to illustrate some of the variation in career line. The reader is invited to analyze and compare the patterns in greater detail.

Job and Worker Characteristics

To further illustrate the variation in career lines several characteristics of jobs and workers are tabulated and presented for each of the 384 occupation-industry categories. For illustration, table 3-1 reports mean estimates for the worker characteristics, job characteristics, and median earnings for elementary school teachers. Table 3-2 presents comparable information for the U.S. civilian labor force, age 23 to 62 in 1970.

The estimates are taken from two sources. Scores for work-role content variables are weighted estimates for the U.S. labor force based on information from the *Dictionary of Occupational Titles* (U.S. Department of Labor 1965). Estimation and measurement details are reported in Spenner (1980). The remaining variables that index the requirement, reward, and compositional variation in jobs were estimated from the Census Public Use Samples described earlier.

Tables 3-1 and 3-2 provide the basis for comparing job- and worker-characteristics information for elementary school teachers with average scores for the entire U.S. labor force. Compared to the average job, elementary school teaching involves more complex work with data and people, less complex work with things, greater use of cognitive and perceptual aptitudes, more vocational training, much more variety in work, generally sedentary work in terms of physical demands, and, overall, much more complex work than that entailed in the average job. Further, with respect to worker characteristics, elementary school teachers are 87 percent female, 91 percent white, generally hold college degrees, work 36 hours a week, and work less than a full year at their jobs.

Summary

Using the 1970 Census Public Use Samples as data for synthetic-cohort analysis, we construct career lines for 384 job categories. We consider the basic assumptions on which the analysis strategy is based and related issues that bear on the reliability and validity of inferences. We present empirical examples of the variations in career lines. We present the case of elementary school teachers in detail and illustrate the new concepts for studying careers. We extend the example to include consideration of representative job and worker characteristics, and illustrate comparisons with average scores for the entire U.S. labor force.

Table 3-1
Worker Characteristics, Job Characteristics, and Median Earnings for Elementary School Teachers

Worker Characteristics

Sex composition	Percent male	13
Race composition	Percent white	91
Median years of education		
Female	Years	15.36
Male	Years	16.69
Total	Years	15.31
Percent with vocational training	Percent of workers	13
Average hours worked	Hours per week	36.23
Weeks worked per year		
Working 40-47 Weeks	Percent of workers	27
Working 48-49 Weeks	Percent of workers	4
Working 50-52 Weeks	Percent of workers	22

Job Characteristics

General educational development	Above average	(4.98)
Specific vocational preparation	Average	(6.15)
Complexity of work with:		
Data	Above average	(1.97)
People	Above average	(2.01)
Things	Below average	(8.00)
Variety in work	Above average	(0.90)
Repetitiveness in work	Below average	(0.00)
Closeness of supervision	Below average	(0.00)
Responsibility	Average	(0.09)
Overall complexity of work	Above average	(21.42)

Median Earnings (1969 Dollars) by Age

	18-22	23-27	28-32	33-37	38-42	43-47	48-52	53-57
Female	4,916	1,544	2,394	4,941	6,057	6,738	7,062	6,926
Male	6,177	7,913	9,291	9,900	9,930	9,420	9,833	8,340
Total	5,236	2,846	3,972	5,982	6,650	6,943	7,281	7,035

Table 3-2
Worker Characteristics, Job Characteristics, and Median Earnings for the 1970 U.S. Civilian Labor Force

Characteristics of the U.S. Labor Force			U.S. Job Characteristics	Range	Average
Sex composition	64	Percent male	General educational development	1-6	3.61
Race composition	90	Percent white	Specific vocational preparation	1-9	5.35
Median years of education	11.46	Years	Complexity of work with:		
Percent with vocational training	27	Percent of workers	Data	0-8	3.97
Average hours worked	40.48	Hours per week	People	0-8	6.67
			Things	0-8	5.42
Weeks worked per year			Variety in work	0-1	.41
Working 40-47 Weeks	8	Percent of workers	Repetitiveness in work	0-1	.30
Working 48-49 Weeks	6	Percent of workers	Closeness of supervision	0-1	.22
Working 50-52 Weeks	69	Percent of workers	Responsibility	0-1	.22
			Overall complexity of work	-3 to 27	10.11

	Median Earnings (1969 Dollars) by Age							
	18-22	23-27	28-32	33-37	38-42	43-47	48-52	53-57
Female	3,194	2,921	3,579	3,875	4,308	4,358	4,612	4,353
Male	6,015	7,613	8,524	8,845	8,843	8,801	8,305	7,678
Total	4,916	5,843	6,734	6,992	7,134	7,115	6,880	6,419

Notes

1. Transforming the 1970 three-digit census occupations into job categories resulted in 165 job categories remaining identical to the 1970 three-digit census occupation codes. For these categories, 70 industry breakdowns are made. One hundred and sixty-six 1970 three-digit occupation categories are collapsed into 53 occupation categories with no industry designations. Finally, ninety 1970 three-digit occupation categories are collapsed into 34, which, in turn, are broken down by industry to form 160 categories.

Most of the resulting categories (95 percent) have one- to five-thousand 1965 respondents with at least fifty cases per age cohort. A small number have many more cases (for example, elementary school teachers) where further industry breaks are not possible. A few categories have fewer than fifty respondents in some age cohorts (for example, airline stewardesses and railroad conductors) where the job category is highly age-skewed.

2. There is no question about the theoretical feasibility of classic proportional-scaling adjustments of the odds ratios in the tables (Deming 1943; Bishop, Feinberg, and Holland 1975). However, there are questions concerning the practicality and substantive advisability of making such adjustments. Software considerations require that adjustments must be iterative. Moreover, large tables cannot be partitioned into smaller, manageable pieces. Most computer programs have upper limits of about fifteen thousand cells for tables, which is typically far too restrictive for the manipulations required. The Social Security Administration has managed tables in excess of thirty thousand cells however. Due to innovative design features, their software has no upper limit on cell size. In summary, the only limit to performing the adjustments on the table, which contains about 250,000 nonzero cells, is budgetary.

Beyond the feasibility of making adjustments, there is a question whether one should remove association underlying transition probabilities that occurs due to growth or decline in job opportunities. It may be argued that this variation causes meaningful differences in career lines that are themselves the subject of study. As long as the investigator is interested in studying career-line variation that might be caused by underlying mobility regimes and changes in the opportunity structure, then unadjusted probabilities are informative. Interpretation requires caution not to attribute to the mobility regime that which rightfully belongs to growth or decline in job opportunities and vice versa. This argument holds that one should simply bear in mind that marginal change in the job structure and "true" job linkages underlie the unadjusted observed transition probabilities.

4 Individual-Level Determinants of Access to Career Lines

Conceptually, the meaning of access to career lines is reasonably straightforward. It means taking a job in a position that is located in a career line or set of career lines. In probability terms, individuals have more or less access to all career lines, usually less opportunity to enter most career lines and more opportunity to enter a few. Individual-level determinants of access refer to variations among people that affect the probability of entering a career line, set, or type of career line.

Access refers not only to the probability of taking a position located in a career line but also to the consequences of taking a position. Consequences include the content of the work role and the rewards that are associated with occupancy and performance in a position. In addition, work routine and reward consequences may be projected for a career line or career-line set. In summary, studying access to career lines involves the analysis of who gets what by way of career lines, associated work-role consequences and rewards, and why those outcomes occur.

Four strategies are available to make the notion of access operational as a set of dependent variables:

1. Access to career lines can be studied with the census data by comparing the probability of entering one career line as opposed to entering another. Given entry into a career line, the probability of continuation or exit can be measured for each age group. These conditional and unconditional access probabilities could then be modelled.

2. Access can be measured by career-line types. If a valid and reliable typology of career lines can be demonstrated, then it is possible to make between-type comparisons of individuals who occupy career lines. Further, a typology generated from the structural study of career lines in the census data can be used conceptually to inform the coding of job histories in the more wealthy Career Development Study data that record detailed job histories.

3. Access can be measured also through a more explicit linkage of career-line characteristics from the census data and individual-level job histories. For each age-specific entry portal in a career line, the average earnings of all workers in the career line can be taken as the expected projected earnings associated with entering a career line at a particular age. Such predicted characteristics can be merged as variables in the data records for individuals based on their job histories. Variation in expected career-line

characteristics would be the subject of explanation. This approach requires strong synthetic-cohort assumptions that may be unnecessary if the work-role characteristic is measured for individuals for each job over their careers.

4. Finally, the Career Development Study data provide for the study of access as measured by the job histories of individuals. Person-to-person variations in work histories may also be the subject of explanation. There is neither implicit nor explicit linkage between the career lines constructed from the Census Public Use Samples and the individual job histories reported in the Career Development Study. In this case, access refers to differences in job histories reported by individuals.

We give primary attention to the second and fourth strategies in analyzing individual-level determinants of access to career lines. The examples in the remainder of this chapter are based on these strategies.

Dependent Variables

Although the definition of actual dependent variables awaits the results of systematic career-line analysis, some speculation on the outcome is possible. Assume that career lines are typed on various dimensions. Consider, for example, a type suggested by the economic segmentation perspectives outlined in chapter 1. The internal-labor-market thesis suggests that there are entry-level positions that evolve into job sequences assuring more or less stable work histories. In the sections that follow we refer to these hypothetical career-line types in the internal labor market as primary types. This kind of question can then be posed: What characteristics of individuals, their life situations and histories, are the best predictors of access to primary-type career lines? How do life course contingencies—for example, early marriage or military service—affect the probabilities of entering or maintaining a primary career line?

The study design for examining the determinants of careers—whether "determinants" are defined as pre- or postentry into the labor force—draws on an array of personal, social-psychological, and social-structural factors as these occur and are sequenced over the ages 18 to 30. Because of their theoretical and policy relevance, two major classes of explanation will be given primary (although not exclusive) attention: individual differences and the interplay of life course dimensions. The basic questions are:

1. How and to what extent do individual investments in different forms of human capital and differences in social-psychological orientations determine access to careers?

2. How does the interplay of major life course dimensions (family, education, and military) structure individuals' access to career lines?

Before proceeding it is useful to reconsider the framework for organizing the theoretical literature on careers that was presented in chapter 2. At the risk of oversimplifying, the literature may be arranged as if organized in terms of a two-by-two table. The columns represent substantive foci—namely, studies of the structure of the labor market, on the one hand, and studies of the determinants of careers, on the other—and the rows label major classes of explanations, that is, radical and conservative theories. We noted that the literature is not evenly distributed across the four cells. For example, with respect to explanations for the structure of career lines, most of the literature is identified with radical explanations. Conservative contributions are comparatively lacking. As attention now turns to explanations for determinants of career-line access, the weight of the literature also shifts. Here the preponderance of material appears in the conservative literatures, giving particular emphasis to human-capital explanations. Nonetheless, the radical explanation cell is not totally empty, and appropriate references will be made to these perspectives.

Our consideration of variables, like our discussion of analytic strategies, gives prominence to individual differences and exhibits sensitivity to the timing and sequencing of determinants in the life course context. Human-capital and life course perspectives are not necessarily competing explanations. Theoretically, they may be complementary, and temporally they may overlap. However, for presentation purposes it is useful to emphasize the main themes in each and to discuss them in sequence.

This chapter continues with individual-level explanations for access to career lines followed by discussion of life course considerations. Migration and gender effects are also considered in these contexts.

Person-Level Explanations

Whether one reviews the literature on occupations and careers from the perspective of a single discipline or from several disciplines (Crites 1969; Temme 1975b; Pietrofesa and Splete 1975), the conclusion is inescapable that there does not yet exist a comprehensive theory of careers and work roles, let alone an explanation of career entry. This study of career determinants is most accurately described as exploratory, therefore, a circumstance underscored by the new conceptualization of the dependent variable, career lines.

There are, however, suggestive hypotheses gleaned from the literature. Two considerations must be emphasized in discussing these. First, in context these hypotheses are advanced as explanations for single-time measures of occupational choice or attainment (for example, first job). Implicit tests of the null hypothesis will reveal whether the explanations also apply to access to career lines. Second, rather than embrace a monocausal explanation of career-line determinants, our strategy is to examine classes of effects within the context of more broadly specified models.

An important set of predictors reflects a human-capital perspective. By human capital, reference is made to capacities that can improve the quality of human effort and enhance its productivity (Schultz 1961, p.1). Although economists (for example, Becker 1975) tend to use the concept with reference to improved skills and knowledge, the term was earlier applied more generally to "attributes that affect particular human capabilities to do productive work" (Schultz 1961, p. 8). Schultz isolated five major categories of human capital:

1. health facilities and services, including all expenditures that affect people's life expectancy and vitality
2. on-the-job training, including apprenticeships in firms
3. formal education at elementary, secondary, and higher levels
4. other study programs, including extension programs
5. migration of individuals and families in response to changing job opportunities (1961, pp. 8-9)

Becker (1975) extended the list to include emotional health, better diet, avoidance of activities with high accident and death rates, motivation, and the like. The review that follows employs both a narrow and a broad definition of human-capital stock. An alternative explanation for individual access to careers as proposed by conflict theorists is also presented. We examine two literatures that consider education and schooling variables. The first suggests that knowledge and skill acquisition maximize career-line access possibilities. The second literature suggests that educational benefits are differentially received because school resources are differentially allocated on the basis of social status. The definition of human capital is then broadened to accommodate two additional literatures. The third literature asks: Do ambitions differentiate those who enter certain types of career lines? The fourth questions whether differences in local opportunity structures and in individual migration behavior predict differences in access to types of career lines.

Knowledge and Skill

Of the many possible forms of human capital none has received more attention over the past two decades than has the economics of education (Becker 1975, p. 1). Calculations of the rates of return on investments in education generally indicate that a four-year college education yields a 10 to 15 percent economic return (Eckaus 1973, p. vii; also see Jencks et al. 1979; Freeman 1976; and Featherman and Hauser 1978, pp. 265-269), and the status-attainment literature documents the positive effect of education on occupational prestige. Confirmation that education "pays off" has provided support for the notion that the educational system may be employed as an instrument of change and as a solution to social problems. Coleman et al.'s *Equality of Educational Opportunity* (1966) and Jencks's *Inequality* (1972) typify the debate over equalizing the opportunity for and the results from human-capital investments in education. The implicit hypothesis with respect to time-point estimates of occupational prestige and earnings is that returns are a function of educational investments. How the investment-return formula applies to careers has not been examined in detail. Typically, schooling resource levels are assumed to be fixed after entry into the labor force (but see Rosenfeld 1980, and Tuma 1976). There is, then, a need to examine the career-line implications of kinds of educational investments including curriculum, level of formal education, vocational and apprenticeship programs, on-the-job training, and the like.

Analysis is not restricted to studying the influence of precareer inputs but also elaborates the continuing effect of human-capital-investment updates on career development through the adolescent-to-adulthood transition and into early career. The initial analysis will consist of developing regression-based models for forms of training and skill acquisition. The independent variables, continuous and dichotomous, will measure length of training, high school and college curriculum, vocational education, apprenticeships, and on-the-job training. Controls will be introduced for social background. The dependent variables will include the probabilities of entering certain types of career lines. Do human capital investments return higher probabilities of entering primary-type career lines? Alternatively, are human-capital investments prior to career-line entry associated with higher career-line earnings? Does acquisition of knowledge and skill after entering a career line enhance career-line options and outcomes? The detailed life-history information in the Career Development Study provides for including explanatory variables that reflect individual skill acquisitions and training as people age.

School Resource Allocation

An alternative to human-capital explanations is voiced by Bowles and Gintis (1976) who argued that schools fail to function as the great equalizer among individuals and that the educational system is an instrument of class interests. Bowles and Gintis insisted that educational systems reflect efforts to legitimate the social hierarchy and contribute to the exploitative division of labor that characterizes the larger society. Schools socialize youth into uncritical acceptance of prevailing inequalities. Schools "are part of the web of capitalistic society," Bowles argued (1972, p. 37). Whereas the human-capital perspective emphasizes the direct effect of investments—for example, education—on outcomes, the Bowles-Gintis argument emphasized the role of formal education as an intervening variable in the intergenerational transmission of socioeconomic advantage. The Bowles-Gintis position raises two questions for the present analysis. What aspects of background, including ascribed statuses and socioeconomic origins, affect access to career lines? And what are the mechanisms by which the effects are transmitted? The design provides for elaboration of regression models for these sources of career variation.

A related literature contains elements of both the human capital and the social selection to educational investment-opportunities theses. Heyns (1974) acknowledges that resources do not determine achievement differentials between schools (Coleman et al. 1966; Jencks et al. 1972). However, she argues that school achievement differences may result from curriculum tracking and assignment policies that establish an academic hierarchy through which rewards may be distributed within the schools. Rather than assume homogeneity of educational experiences within schools (Bowles and Levin 1968; Jencks et al. 1972), Heyns's thesis is that differences in schooling outcomes are due to differential access to and use of resources within schools. The within-school explanation incorporates elements of the human-capital argument—that school investments maximize returns—and features of the Bowles-Gintis argument—that school resources are differentially allocated by social status. Alexander and McDill (1976) provided qualified support for the thesis that sorting and selecting processes are implicated in both the educational and societal stratification systems. Alexander, Cook, and McDill (1977) reported additional support but, from the same analysis, provided evidence that the major determinants of curriculum are meritocratic.

There is, then, considerable ambiguity, theoretical and empirical, concerning the effect of school-related human-capital investments—including resources measured by curricular, extracurricular, and significant-other influences—on such school outputs as achievement aspirations and attainments measured at a single time. The ambiguity of returns to investments in individually acquired capacities or credentials is further confounded in the case of explaining access to career lines, which has not been examined in the literature. The fundamental question is whether investments in school-related human capital affect access to career lines in ways different from their effect on occupation and earnings attainments measured at a single point in time. The aggregate returns of years of schooling to occupational status are well documented (for example, Mincer 1974; Blau and Duncan 1967; Duncan, Featherman, and Duncan 1972; Sewell and Hauser 1972; Featherman and Hauser 1978) and the earnings returns have been extensively studied (see reviews by Eckaus 1973; Mincer 1974; Becker 1975; Haller and Spenner 1977). The ways that individual-level resources change with age and how the returns to changing resources vary over work histories are only beginning to receive attention for outcomes other than earnings (Sørensen 1977; Tuma 1976; Rosenfeld 1980).

Schooling and related forms of human capital may affect career-line entry in unexpected ways. Does the acquisition of monopsonistic skills, knowledge, and credentials that are specific to a narrow range of work-role applications enhance the probability of following a specific career line, on the one hand, or the range of career options, on the other hand? Specialized training and credentialing in surgery, for example, may be viewed as a kind of human capital that has narrow work-role applications and also restricts career options and transferability. Other kinds of training and skill acquisition may be more generalizable to a variety of potential career lines—for example, interpersonal as opposed to surgical skills. Thus, a liberal-arts education may provide career-line flexibility, although its effect on single point-in-time measures of occupations and earnings may be modest. Are certain types of high-school curricula—for example, vocational education programs—although promoted as relevant job training and intended to relieve problems of youth unemployment, counterproductive by restricting career-line options? What enhances the prospect of immediate employment in a single career line may be detrimental if that line of employment or sector of the labor market is characterized by high turnover rates or is phasing out.

Although informed by the literature on human capital, the study design is not limited to a restrictive definition of the human-capital perspective. The individual-level data offer the opportunity to assess selected within-school process effects such as vocational-educational, college preparatory, and mixed-track effects for their interactive influences on career-line access (see Rosenbaum 1976) net of individual-level effects (Alwin 1976; Hauser, Sewell, and Alwin 1976; Alwin and Otto 1977; compare Sørensen and Hallinan 1977). Similarly, measures are also present for examining the career-line implications of knowledge of the world of work, participation in apprenticeship training programs and extracurricular activities including part-time work experience. Does early experience in jobs in primary sectors of the labor market increase the probability of later employment in primary-type career lines? Does early experience in secondary labor-market jobs depress the probabilities of early or later access to primary-type career lines? Are there institutional barriers that surround the secondary sector (Doeringer and Piore 1971; Reich, Gordon, and Edwards 1973)? If the segmentation theorists are correct that work careers are established not on the basis of individual differences but on the basis of larger structural arrangements, then human-capital concepts may have little explanatory power in these contexts. Although labor-market theories tend to address ways that career lines are structured as opposed to explaining access to them, we will also apply these conflict perspectives where they inform the study of career-line entry.

Ambition

The human-capital perspective, narrowly defined as investment in education and training, provides one class of explanations for how individual characteristics differentiate access to career lines. But the broader definition of human capital—namely, "attributes that affect particular human capabilities to do productive work"—admits to other explanations (Schultz 1961, p. 8). Another prominent line of person-level explanations originates in the psychological and social-psychological literatures. It suggests that individual interests, aspirations, and motivations—ambitions, generically speaking—differentiate those who enter certain types of career lines (for a review and citations see Holland 1973; Temme 1975b, pp. 21-37; and Spenner and Featherman 1978.)

These explanations have provided only modest predictive power for single-point estimates of occupational achievements, and it is doubtful that they will prove to be dramatically more powerful determinants of access to career lines. It is, nonetheless, appropriate to examine the matrix of achievement orientations or ambitions as they might explain access to career lines of a given type and quality under alternative assumptions and specifications regarding implicit measurement error. The correlates include aspirations and expectations for careers, locus of control, self-esteem, future orientation, delay of gratification, competence, intelligence, and intrinsic-extrinsic motivations. The Career Development Study data (described in chapter 5) include multiple indicators of these affective, behavioral, and cognitive components of ambitions. Further, in the case of most affective measures and many of the behavioral measures, the data provide measures of intensity as well as direction. Thus, the refined measures of school-related human-capital stock are complemented by a broad range of psychological and social-psychological indicators that, together, tap an array of person-level explanations for differential access to career lines.

Community Structures and Migration

Schultz also identified "migration of individuals and families to adjust to changing job opportunities" as a major category of human capital (1961, p. 9). The research agenda for analyzing data on career-line access will also take into account individuals' structural location and migration behavior.

In a number of ways the structures of local communities define the availability of career lines. In some measure all career lines depend on a reasonably healthy economy to sustain them. Indeed, one would expect that long-term growth in the economy might accommodate increased numbers of workers and, when coupled with increased complexity in the division of labor, would generate new career lines while allowing others to phase out. Changes in the economy and job structure—whether induced by the logic of capitalism (Braverman 1974), the imperatives of technology (Solow 1971), knowledge (Bell 1973), or industrialization (Kerr et al. 1964)—are a major source of change in types of available career lines and in differentiating access to them. Farming, for example, has experienced a steady decline as a career-line option whereas a number of computer-related jobs and career lines have experienced steady growth. Both were mandated by larger changes in the economy and society (U.S. Department of Labor 1976).

The study design does not permit systematic inferences about historical sources of change. However, in some respects the cross-sectional census data minimize historical variations, since all measurements of jobs are for workers in 1965 and 1970, subject to then-existing labor markets, economic conditions, and the like. In other respects the synthetic-cohort continues these variations inasmuch as each age cohort of workers has endured a segment of history that only partially overlaps that of other cohorts and may or may not differ in crucial respects from the experiences of other cohorts. Further, as noted (see chapter 3, note 2), in a limited way it is technically possible to adjust for some of the larger historical variations, that is, changes in the marginal distribution or composition of jobs across age cohorts. However, these procedures, if implemented, would be designed to control the quality of inferences so as not to attribute to individuals that which is due to structural change. The design does not provide for the explicit study of structural change.

There is a second feature of community organization to which the Career Development Study design gives greater attention: intercommunity variations in career accessibility at a single point in time. In entering the labor force, individuals encounter a community and regional occupation-industry-firm mix that defines the opportunity structure to which they have access. Thus, Sewell and Orenstein (1965) reported that low occupational aspirations of male seniors in Wisconsin were associated not only with intelligence and socioeconomic background, but also with place of residence, whether farm or small community, medium or large city. Spilerman and Habib (1976) provided an insightful study of how community of residence in conjunction with ethnicity structures job opportunities. Although status-attainment processes may be remarkably similar across large metropolitan areas (Mueller 1974), variations in career line outcomes and content are likely among large urban areas, small towns with one industry, and rural areas. Such variations may also be important among regions (Blau and Duncan 1967; Hogan and Featherman 1977).

Several features of local opportunity structures might influence access to types of career lines and career-line content. First, community of origin, particularly residence during late adolescence, will be examined as an independent variable. The hypothesis is that a person's notions of work, careers, and of the labor-force opportunity structure vary by community of origin and, in turn, affect movement into entry portals and along career lines. Individual-level data in the Career Development Study are well suited to these analyses. Youth respondents in communities ranging from metropolitan to small town were surveyed concerning their perceptions of local and regional educational and occupational opportunities and their willingness to move from community-of-origin to further their education and work careers. If early analyses indicate that intercommunity differences exist in the probabilities of entering types of career lines, then the design permits later analyses modeling dimensions of community differences that may underlie those differences. These include community size, dominance of a single industry in small communities, the occupation-industry mix in communities (where that information is recoverable for the communities from which study participants were drawn), and social-psychological orientations that might facilitate or mitigate the community effects. Examples include perceived closeness to family of origin and willingness to relocate to improve job opportunities.

Also, the follow-up design will extend the analysis to community-of-residence effects at the time of entry into the labor force and during the early career years. Although respondents will have dispersed to different parts of the country, thereby precluding the simultaneous assessment of inter-and intracommunity variations possible with community of origin, the data include measures of a number of variables relevant to the analysis of early career development. Do those who migrate from communities of origin for reasons of education or work gain access to different or better types of career lines than those who remain? Are there rural-urban origin differences? Does access occur earlier for those who migrate? Does community-of-residence location and size during early years of employment predict the type of career line that individuals enter and such career-line content characteristics as expected levels of earnings? Does an individual's willingness and ability to migrate for career-related reasons have measurable career-related outcomes?

The person-level explanations for access to career lines embrace different forms of human capital. The narrow definitions focus on schooling and education variables. The broader definitions admit to the potential effects of individual differences in ambition, of differences in local opportunity structures, and of migration behavior. In addition, there is the conflict perspective that explains differences in career-line outcomes not in individualistic terms, but in social-structural terms. In the section that follows we consider how individual differences in the way people manage multiple and sometimes competing roles affect their access to career lines.

Life Course Determinants of Access to Career Lines

The literature on careers has been presented as if drawn from a two-by-two conceptual table in which the columns differentiate studies of the structure of the labor market from studies of the determinants of individual access to careers, and the rows differentiate radical from conservative explanations of access to career lines. Given the four-cell structure relating substantive focuses and theoretical explanations, where does the life course or developmental perspective fit? Is the life course perspective another substantive focus or an additional set of explanations? Is it both? Does it add a third axis along which to order the literature?

Career Development uses the life course perspective as neither a separate substantive focus nor an independent set of explanations. Rather, we employ the life course perspective as a theoretical overlay that adds a sense of depth to career issues and explanations (see figure 4–1). Our use of the life course perspective deepens understanding of career phenomena in three ways: (1) It takes into account variations that occur within life course dimensions. (2) It offers a perspective to the interpretation of effects that occur between life course dimensions. (3) It allows for the influence of significant others on ego's plans, decisions, and activities.

Each life course dimension hosts a variety of identifiable events. For example, the family dimension includes marriage and parenthood. A major assumption undergirding most models of social processes is that events are normatively timed and sequenced (Glaser and Strauss 1971; Winsborough 1975; Hogan 1978, 1980; but see Sweet 1977, for a compelling argument against the assumption of a single, life course model). But, if there is uniformity across life course sequences, many individuals do not follow the normative pattern. Does nonconformity have consequences for subsequent events and outcomes in the same life course dimension? For example, there is a literature that emphasizes the detrimental effects of asynchronies in marital timing on marital stability (Bartz and Nye 1970) and on several dimensions of fertility including the probability of parenthood, timing of first birth, child spacing and parity (Otto 1979). Are there any salutary effects?

The life course literature also offers a perspective for examining effects that occur between life course dimensions. Again, there is a literature emphasizing the consequences of asynchronies and disrupted sequences across

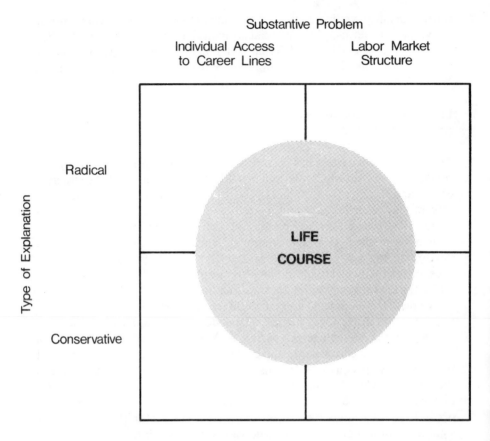

Figure 4-1. Relationship between Theoretical Explanations, Substantive Problems, and the Life Course Perspective

life course dimensions (Bartz and Nye 1970; Bumpass and Sweet 1972; Hogan 1976; Marini 1978; Call and Otto 1977, 1979; Kerckhoff and Parrow 1979a, 1979b). However, this literature is not always in agreement on the relationship between marital timing and outcomes on such other life course dimensions as levels of educational attainment, occupational prestige, and earnings. Does early marriage have a negative impact on the educational attainment of males, as Kerckhoff and Parrow (1979a, 1979b) suggest? Or is there no significant effect, as Call and Otto's (1977, 1979) analyses indicate? The life course perspective sensitizes the investigator to issues of normative influence.

Finally, the life course perspective takes into account the influence of significant others on a person's career development. The assumption of additional roles, as occurs in such major transitions as those marked by marriage and parenthood, typically complicates life by introducing added considerations to the basis for decisions and behavior. Most notable are spouse effects, whether these be behavioral, as exemplified in dual-career families, or attitudinal, as illustrated by sex-role ideologies. Are job changes for husbands and wives associated with the event of childbirth and family expansion? Are job changes for either husbands or wives associated with marital instability? Are husbands' and wives' educational attainments affected by spouses' work history? The life course perspective adds such interactive considerations to the explanations of individual-level determinants of access to careers.

The intricacies of life course analysis are potentially disabling because of the number of possible variables and permutations in the ordering of events within and between life course dimensions. Rapoport and Rapoport (1965, p. 387) propose a reasonable strategy for managing the complexity without sacrificing the details of life course transitions. They suggest that it may be useful to concentrate on "critical" major role transitions, which occur when the structural elements of both personality and social system are somewhat "fluid," and new structures are being formed.

Like the Rapoports, we focus on selected life course dimensions occurring over a specified period. Attention is limited to educational, familial, military, and job histories with primary emphasis given to the effect of education, family, and military transitions on career development. The separate dimensions are conceptualized not as separate analytical spheres but as complex interrelationships with calculable career consequences (see reviews by Elder 1975 and Sweet 1977). This is not to deny the influence of work roles on the other life course dimensions, which are also of interest, but it is to maintain a central focus on the individual-level determinants of access to career lines.

As families are formed, as individuals move between family, school, military, and work, their career interests, needs, and options likely change. The transitions are especially numerous and complex during the years from completion of high school through establishment of early careers, about age 30. During this twelve- to thirteen-year period, educational, familial, military, and work roles are assumed, perhaps terminated, and sometimes resumed. In the pages that follow, we attend to issues of timing and sequencing that occur with respect to the four life course dimensions. The chapter concludes with consideration to significant-other influences and gender-specific determinants of access to career lines.

Educational Histories

We considered the probable effect of level and kind of education on careers from the human-capital perspective. The life course perspective considers issues of schooling duration, interruptions, and reentry as these also affect access to career lines.

Featherman and Carter (1976) report for a limited sample that discontinuities in educational attainments are largely independent of background characteristics. Further, the consequences of educational discontinuities, when compared to members of the cohort with continuous education histories, appear to be negative for levels of eventual schooling, status of first job, and job status and earnings fifteen years after high school. More comprehensive assessments of the nature and extent of the effects of educational discontinuities are not available. The increasing numbers of people returning to school for "retooling" or basic adult education (Grant and Lind 1976) underscore the lifelong nature of the education-to-work and work-to-education transitions (Featherman and Carter 1976, pp. 136-137). The conditions for and the consequences of these transitions are not understood. We include consideration of the transitions into and out of formal education as well as transitions from college to vocational-technical schools, vocational-technical training, and other two-year training programs to college four-year programs, and transitions into and out of other forms of nonformal education. In addition, we examine the career-line consequences of leaving school without certification.

Family Histories

The principal elements of family histories that bear on access to and maintenance of career lines are marital timing, transitions to parenthood, child spacing, marital dissolution, and remarriage. Bartz and Nye (1970) report that past research reveals negative effects of early marriage on future attainments, and conventional wisdom suggests that the financial demands of establishing a household encourage schooling interruptions if not terminations.

More recent research suggests a more differentiated pattern of effects, however. Voss (1975) and Marini (1978) demonstrate a negative effect of early marriage on female attainments, but the same authors and Call and Otto (1977, 1979) fail to find the hypothesized negative effects for males. One interpretation is that marriage is more important to females than males, and, therefore, females are willing to put more of their resources into marriage or to make greater sacrifices in other areas (Otto 1979). But these hypotheses have not been tested directly. On balance, the research relating early marriage to single-time estimates of attainments is equivocal. The effect of marital timing on career-line access and maintenance has not been studied for either males or females. Further, given that later marriages and earlier entry into career sequences also occur, the effects of attainments on marital timing—and, also, the possibilities of marital-timing effects on attainments—have not been studied and are not understood.

Otto (1979) reviews other reported associations with marital timing. These include several within-family dimensions and between-family and other life course dimension relationships. Within-family dimensions associated with marital timing include the probability of achieving motherhood, length of time required to conceive, length of time required to bear children, child spacing, and parity. Otto (1979) notes, however, that the effects of marital timing on fertility patterns may not be direct and suggests that marital role enactment, spouse employment considerations, and whether wife works may operate as intervening variables. Between-dimension effects include the observation that the later females marry, the more likely it is that they will be gainfully employed. Otto also argues that given that the wife works, her fertility patterns are likely to be directly affected by her employment. However, such fertility considerations—whether or not the wife bears children, her age, and her fertility expectations—will also affect the probability of her working (Waite 1980; see also Stolzenberg and Waite 1977). Cogswell and Sussman (1979) argued that female fertility is inversely related to labor-force participation and that life course transitions are typically associated with lower fertility. The individual-level data in the Career Development Study were designed in part to unravel these intricacies.

LeMasters (1957) suggested that parenthood, not marriage, is the independent variable that produces crisis. Extending the argument to careers, the hypothesis is that the birth of a child may invoke decisions favoring or changing labor-force participation and the curtailment or interruption of education. The study design examines the effects of marital timing, timing of birth of first child, child spacing, and marital instability on the types of career lines available to individuals.

Military Service

Although it has been asserted that military service provides opportunities for continuing education and for learning a trade, the literature generally suggests that military service has negligible or negative effects on young men's futures (Cutright 1974). Nonetheless, the consequences of military service for career-line access and maintenance are not well understood. This is especially true of the Vietnam cohort, which the Career Development Study sample includes. Featherman (1978) raised five questions that inform the design and analysis:

1. Do people consider the military as an option instead of going back to school or looking for a job?
2. Why do people volunteer for military service and what do they hope to get out of it?
3. What determines how long people remain in the military?

4. What happens to a person's civilian skills and aspirations/plans during the period of military service?
5. How is social maturity or "competence" advanced by military service?

In addition, we will examine whether military service has effects net of those due to schooling interruption or curtailment. Military service provides specialized training opportunities. Are there forms of military training programs that improve a person's career prospects? The military draft as opposed to enlistment may represent an unanticipated and involuntary transition in the life course and for that reason imposes detrimental career-line consequences. Is this hypothesis confirmed? We will focus on forms of induction (particularly enlistment), duration of military experience, and perception of military service (for example, whether viewed as a source of benefits in training and skill acquisition, a career opportunity, or a life course interruption) as independent variables. The dependent variables include access to career-line types and career-line content characteristics before and after military service.

Job Histories

Our research design uses the life course perspective primarily to identify determinants of access to career lines. However, as a separate life course dimension, job histories might also be the subject of conceptualization and analysis of empirical regularities. Three possibilities illustrate the proposed analysis:

1. Empirical regularities can be examined regarding issues of timing in job histories, for example, date of entry into the labor force, dates of job transitions, and durations of time spent in successive jobs.

2. Interruptions in job histories can be analyzed. Are there normative periods of short- or long-term unemployment; of voluntary and involuntary job exits?

3. Empirical regularities, synchronies and asynchronies can be examined. These include analysis of the comparative duration of successive jobs. Do developmental age and number of jobs interact and affect career outcomes apart from the effect of duration of jobs?

In past research, sociologists have given simple and superficial attention to change in studies of job histories. Time and change seldom enter analyses as dimensions of job histories and when they do, then only crudely in data collection and analytic designs (Hannan and Tuma, 1979). Typically, panel or cross-sectional designs relate mean levels of a characteristic of one job to the same characteristic in another job.

But two jobs measured at or for arbitrary time periods may incompletely capture the full event history of jobs for an individual. The event-history approach, by contrast, records the time, duration, and state (whether currently employed or unemployed), and the kind of job for all moves in a job sequence (Hannan and Tuma 1979, p. 305). Most analyses from panel and cross-sectional designs are static. They assume a system in equilibrium. Without event histories one is forced to make strong assumptions about the nature of the processes underlying state changes in the dependent measures. Further, incomplete event histories severely limit the researcher's ability to examine the veracity of assumptions about stochastic processes underlying job changes and, hence, to analyze life course effects appropriately.

Several developments in the use of continuous-time, discrete-state stochastic models hold promise for a new generation of research on careers in the life course context (Tuma, Hannan, and Groeneveld 1979). Continuous time refers to the modeling of instantaneous rates of transition between discrete states, that is, jobs, career lines, and career-line types. The probabilistic process that describes change in rates of transition can explicitly depend on the passage of time or time-dependent changes in independent variables. Such models are most powerfully estimated with complete event-history data. In a sense, the core of the life course perspective—namely, the passage of time—can be modeled in mathematical form more explicitly as a result of these developments.

Tuma's (1976) study of the rate of job leaving illustrates the strategy. The Tuma research models the instantaneous rate of job leaving. The rate of mobility from jobs is a function of: rewards of the job; stationary resources of the worker, such as education and origins; changing worker resources, including the number, duration, experience, and skill levels of previous jobs; age and other life course features; system features, including the state in which the job is held; and the elapsed time or duration in the job. Tuma (1976) partitions the rate of mobility from a job into the rate of quitting, the rate of firing, and a residual rate that reflects other reasons for leaving. As duration of a job-person match continues, both the rates of mobility and involuntary terminations should decline, since termination of the match becomes more costly for both employer and employee because of the changing ratio of resources and rewards. In short, as duration increases there is an increasing adaptation of employer and employee to the job-person match. Empirical results from a limited sample generally support the predictions.

From this perspective, initial career-line location might be conceptualized as a stationary resource, and present career-line location might be considered to be a changing resource. The time spent in successive jobs over the early life course can be specified as an explicit function of initial and current career-line locations. These kinds of models and methods are new to sociology. We anticipate their use in specifying life course variation, particularly as it shapes the time-dependent rates of movement in and out of jobs.

Significant-Other (Spouse) and Gender Effects

To this point the discussion has emphasized individual movement through the life course. It is also useful to consider how significant others in general and spouses in particular affect each others' careers. Thereafter, we consider gender differences in career-line access and content.

The timing of educational investments and employment for one spouse may dramatically affect the timing and sequencing of education and employment for the other. For husbands, wife's employment or inherited wealth may facilitate continuation in post–secondary education (Otto 1979) thereby affecting his career-line options. Waite (1976), for example, reported that a wife's wage potential has its greatest effect on her labor-force participation in the period between marriage and birth of the first child. Therefore, when the wife is employed, husbands enrolled in post-secondary education should experience fewer schooling interruptions or terminations prior to the birth of the first child. The wife's reentry into the labor force after the birth of the first child may structure the timing and sequencing of the husband's education and work transitions by permitting him to reenter school, hence restructure his access to career lines. For females, the timing of husband's entry into the labor force and his anticipated earnings may substantially define her career behaviors and options. Conventional wisdom suggests that married women are much more likely to find their careers to be secondary to their husbands' (Otto 1979), but under what conditions? Relatively little is known about the differentiating and integrating processes that affect husband's and wife's career-line options under more and less traditional structures and definitions of the family division of labor.

Spouse's sex-role ideology—as expressed in attitudes toward education, labor-force participation, and psychological support—may influence career-line outcomes beyond the effects of timing and sequencing. With respect to wife's reentry to college, Tittle and Denker (1977) suggest that a major barrier is husband's and relatives' attitudes. This argument has also been applied to wife's labor-force participation. Certainly, a wife's orientations may also affect the husband's education and job behavior, but these are empirical questions. Are a wife's attitudes toward the disruption of a stable household and family life a major barrier to husband's returning to school? The study design provides for examining the extent to which spouse attitudes affect the education and career-line decisions of husbands and wives, but especially those of wives.

Whether gender differences exist for the individual-level determinants of access to career lines and anticipated career content characteristics is another empirical question. In their recent monograph on how women contend with career contingencies, Angrist and Almquist (1975; see also Ginzberg, 1966) argued that women choose a life-style rather than an occupation or career. Only after assigning priorities to education, work, fertility expectations, family, and so on might the question of pursuing a particular career line become a relevant issue for women.

Our research design focuses on how gender structures access to career lines in two ways. First, due to the newness of the dependent variable, it is appropriate to investigate how the individual-level determinants of access to career lines and associated content characteristics differ for male and female respondents. Therefore, the examination of the determinants of access to careers—forms of human capital and individual differences, family, education, and military contingencies—will proceed with explicit consideration to gender variations.

The second line of investigation pertains to models of labor-force orientation and participation. Where earlier research typically focused on work plans, we extend consideration to career-line dependent variables including career-line types and career-line content. The major question in this portion of the analysis concerns how women combine and coordinate their education, prior work experience, work plans, fertility experience and aspirations, and related family considerations with their location in career lines.

Recent contributions to this research have been offered by Waite and Stolzenberg (Waite 1976; Waite and Stolzenberg 1976; Stolzenberg and Waite 1977) who developed a basic reduced-form structural model of labor-force participation plans and fertility expectations for women. Adjusting for background, they reported that work plans determine fertility expectations to a much greater extent than fertility expectations determine work plans. Moreover, in support of their learning hypothesis, Waite and Stolzenberg noted an increasingly negative effect of work plans on fertility expectations across successive cohorts of older women. They reason that as women age, their knowledge about the labor force increases as does their knowledge about the detrimental consequences of interruptions on labor-force participation. The hypothesis is tested indirectly but points to the larger issue: the need for better specification of the ways work experience defines forms of female labor-force participation and vice versa.

The content of one's prospective career lines may operate as the crucial factor in linking work experience with familial behavior. Analysis is required that examines how the accessibility and content of male and female career-line options are restricted, given particular familial circumstances. Such analysis will extend considerably beyond earlier research that typically focused on gender differences in work plans and in labor-market experiences.

Summary

The Career Development research design for examining the individual-level determinants of career-line access draws on personal, social-psychological, and social-structural classes of explanation. We consider how and to what extent individual differences—including investments in different forms of human capital, ambition, local opportunity structures, and migration behavior—determine access to career lines. We also consider structural explanations posed by conflict theorists. Thereafter, we shift attention to the interplay of life course dimensions—educational, family, military, and job histories—and to how variation within and between dimensions affects access to career lines. We conclude with a discussion of significant-other influences, mainly spouse effects and gender considerations, as these affect career development. The selection of variables, and of the analytical strategies, gives prominence to their life course occurrence and sequencing.

5 The Career Development Study: Sample Design and Data

The Career Development program of analysis requires multidimensional life-history measures of individual-level determinants of access to career lines. Chapter 4 outlined the important variable sets in reviewing explanations for career-line entry. This chapter presents the sample design, data-gathering procedures, instrumentation, and results of preliminary comparisons with established data bases for the data that provide the basis for the analysis of careers and access to career lines. Here and elsewhere the data are referred to as the Career Development Study.

The chapter has four major sections. The first presents the data requirements and a sample design statement for the data gathered to meet those requirements. The second section summarizes the time 1 survey procedures and instrumentation. The third provides comparable details for the time 2 data-gathering effort. Because the follow-up achieved a noteworthy response rate, we make generous use of footnotes to document the procedures. Section four compares the survey data with state and national populations and with samples of similar studies on key demographic variables.

Data Requirements and Sample Design

Individual-Level Data Requirements

The individual-level data requirements are summarized as follows:
1. The sample must reference a heterogeneous population.
2. The sample should include males and females.
3. Testing the explanations for entry into careers minimally requires a longitudinal design with extensive social-psychological and background information during late adolescence together with detailed personal histories on work, family, and education through age 30.
4. Given the focus on careers and career lines, the data requirements include accurate measurement of event histories for all jobs. Given interest in the life course context within which careers develop, event histories are required of educational, familial, and military experiences. The required content of the event histories includes accurate reporting of dates and type of activity. For example, beginning and ending dates of each job are required.

Formal education as opposed to military training programs is an example of educational experiences that are distinguished.

5. The data must be comparable to other established samples on key demographic measures.

The respondent data, although not without limitations, meet these design requirements.

Sample Design

The source for the individual-level measures is an extensive panel data base (N = 6,729) of male and female respondents who were first studied as juniors and seniors in high school in 1965-1966. A research team from Washington State University designed and conducted the time 1 study. The principal investigator was Gordon McCloskey, and his associates were Walter Slocum and William Rushing.[1] We restudied the same respondents thirteen years later in 1979, when they were 28 to 31 years old and were established in their early careers.

The study population consisted of juniors and seniors enrolled in public high schools in the state of Washington during the 1965-1966 academic year, except for those enrolled in thirty rural high schools, who participated in a complementary study of farm youth in 1964-1965. The original research team divided schools into six strata based on the number of enrolled juniors and seniors as follows:

1. 750 and more students
2. 500 to 749 students
3. 250 to 499 students
4. 100 to 249 students
5. 50 to 99 students
6.   0 to 49 students

The researchers divided the four strata with fewer than five hundred students into two equal substrata, according to the proportion of students enrolled in vocational courses. They sampled schools randomly from each stratum until the proportion of students drawn from that stratum equaled the population total.

The researchers randomly divided the sample schools in each stratum into two groups. This was done to accommodate the administration of two coordinated but somewhat different survey instruments that reflected the different substantive interests of the research team. The two instruments share a common core of basic demographic and stratification questions. They differ in the level of detailed information gathered. One form gathered more detailed information on stratification variables. The second gathered more detail on social-psychological variables. Following the original investigators, we refer to the former subsample as sample A and the latter as sample B. We refer to the instruments as Form A and Form B (appendixes B and C).

Time 1 Survey Procedures and Instrumentation

Student Questionnaire

McCloskey, Slocum, and Rushing sent an individually typed and personalized form letter to the superintendents of the selected schools. The letter explained the objectives of the study, requested school cooperation, assured the confidentiality of information, and outlined procedures for administering the questionnaire. All but three sample schools agreed to participate in the study. The researchers replaced the three that declined with alternates that were selected in the original random selection of schools.

Administration of the Classroom Questionnaire

Local school staff handled all administrative arrangements. This included scheduling questionnaire and interview sessions, explaining the purpose of the study, assuring the voluntary nature of participation, and the confidentiality of information. Classroom teachers administered questionnaires in the schools. A letter explaining the study to the student accompanied each questionnaire. Written instructions requested teachers to refrain from interpreting any question for the students to minimize possible intervention effects. The Final Report states that "the administration of questionnaires went smoothly" (Slocum and Bowles 1966 p. 3).

School staff administered questionnaires to all juniors and seniors in each school who were willing to participate, 86 percent of the target sample.[2] The nonrespondents included refusals and students absent on the day the questionnaire was administered.

Interview Subsample

The research team drew a subsample of respondents from the completed questionnaires for more detailed information regarding the respondents' educational and occupational plans. In sample A schools, the researchers sorted questionnaires by sex and educational plans into four categories:

1. males who planned to attend a junior college or receive less education
2. males who planned to attend a college or university or receive more education

3. females who planned to attend a junior college or receive less education
4. females who planned to attend a college or university or receive more education

Within each category the original investigators drew a systematic random subsample. The final subsample was 23 percent of the original sample.

In sample B schools, the criteria for including males and females differed. The investigators first sorted females into three categories according to responses on question 45 of the Form B student questionnaire (see appendix C):

1. those who said that they did not want to spend much effort in homemaking
2. those who said that they did not want to work at all or wanted to work only part-time after marriage
3. those who said that they would want to work most of the time or that work would be their major interest although they still wanted to have a family

The researchers included all females who responded in category 1 in the interview subsample. They included an equal number of females from each school that answered in category 2. They included no females from category 3.

They sorted males into four categories according to their highest level of educational aspirations:

1. quit high school or graduate from high school
2. take business or vocational training either in business or vocational school or in a junior college
3. attend a junior college, take a regular college course, or attend a four-year college or university
4. graduate from a college or do graduate work

They varied the sampling pattern slightly from school to school to maximize the number of males with low educational aspirations in the sample. In general, they included either 45 or 50 percent of the males in each school in the subsample. Of these, they included all males who indicated high school graduation or less as their highest level of aspiration in the subsample. The researchers distributed equally the remainder of the sampling quota for each school between the other three categories of educational aspirations.

Student, Counselor, and Parent
Interviews and Questionnaires

Trained graduate and undergraduate students enrolled in the social sciences at Washington State University conducted interviews with students in the schools (for Form A see appendix D, for Form B see appendix E). They recorded data for 93.4 percent of the students in the interview subsample.

In addition, the counselor or, where counselors did not exist, an administrator in each school completed a brief questionnaire about each student in the interview subsample (for Form A see appendix F, for Form B see appendix G). The counselors evaluated the respondent's educational and occupational potential. In the Final Report the principal investigator reported that counselors were generally cooperative and that all schools returned the questionnaires (Slocum and Bowles 1966, p. 5).

The research team mailed a questionnaire to a randomly selected parent of the subsample respondents. The parent questionnaire elicited information on the parent's assessments, attitudes, and expectations for the respondent's educational and occupational future (for Form A see appendix H, for Form B see appendix I). An accompanying letter explained the purpose of the study and asked for the parent's participation. If the parents did not reply within two weeks, project staff mailed a follow-up letter. If a reply was not received in the next two weeks, a second follow-up letter and another copy of the questionnaire were forwarded. The rate of return was 77.5 percent for the parent questionnaire.

Finally, school personnel arranged to forward respondents' grades and IQ scores from school records. This completed the inventory of information gathered at time 1.

The research staff coded and edited all instruments. A second coder independently verified the records. The final response rate for respondent questionnaires was 86 percent ($N = 6,795$). Table 5-1 summarizes the time 1 data available.

Time 2 Follow-up Study

Tracking Respondents

The possibility of reconstructing the life course histories of 1965-1966 juniors and seniors since leaving high school was contingent on successfully tracking the original study participants. To determine the feasibility of the follow-up survey, we carried out a pilot study of the proposed tracking procedures on a random sample of respondents ($N = 100$).

Table 5-1
Summary of the 1966 Data Collection

	Form A Number	Form B Number	Total Number
Number of schools participating	12	13[a]	25[a]
Student questionnaires	3117	3678	6795
Student interviews	631	938	1569
Parent questionnaires	441	701	1142
Counselor questionnaires	631	938	1569
Grade and IQ records	631	938	1569

[a]One extremely small rural school (n = 14) was included with the Form B schools in 1966. However, the data for these fourteen individuals were removed from the sample by the original investigators. No explanation was provided for this omission. The fourteen individuals were used as part of the 1979 pretest sample.

We designed tracking procedures based on the most advanced follow-up techniques reported in the literature (Willits, Crider, and Bealer 1969; Crider, Willits, and Bealer 1972, 1973; Temme 1975*a*; and Clarridge, Sheehy, and Hauser 1977). We employed Dillman (1972, 1978) and colleagues' (Dillman and Frey 1974; Dillman, Christenson, Carpenter, and Brooks 1974) techniques for increasing response rates through personalization and a four-wave mail sequence to parents. We personalized all mailings using automated word-processing techniques. We affixed stamps on envelopes by hand and personally signed all letters. Postage-paid, business reply envelopes accompanied the letters. After locating 75 percent of the original respondents by mail, we introduced telephone procedures. We contacted the respondents' parents, the respondents, and, where necessary, school and community personnel, who assisted the effort.

The tracking procedures in the pilot study proved successful in relocating 100 percent of the original study participants in the feasibility subsample. We established direct contact with 98 percent of the subsample. Twenty-seven percent of the respondent subsample continued to live in their original communities of residence; 44 percent had moved to other localities within the state; 26 percent had moved out of state; and 3 percent had moved out of the United States.

The feasibility study demonstrated that approximately 85 percent of the respondents' current addresses would be supplied by parents who were still living in the same communities or from class reunion lists containing addresses no more than eighteen months old.

Having established the effectiveness of the tracking procedures, we initiated the full-scale tracking effort on 10 January 1978. We conducted the mail procedures in cooperation with the Social Research Center at

Washington State University. Telephone tracking procedures followed the mail sequence. We conducted these from the project offices at the Boys Town Center for the Study of Youth Development, Omaha, Nebraska. The tracking effort yielded a 98.2 percent successful relocation rate. Details of the tracking procedures are reported in a subsequent volume in this series.

Time 2 Information and Instrumentation

We designed the thirteen-year follow-up to gather three kinds of information on each respondent: (1) detailed life course histories; (2) various demographic and social-psychological measures; and (3) official high-school records. Each type of information focused on a different period in the respondent's life. The life course histories covered the period from leaving high school through the date of the follow-up study, when respondents were about 30 years old. The demographic and social-psychological measures tapped time-of-interview characteristics and attitudes. The school transcript records supplemented and corroborated the 1966 high school information available for each respondent.

The life course histories concentrated on four major life course dimensions: education, family, military, and work. We gathered educational information including a record of every formal and nonformal educational experience since the respondents left high school. The information included material for each enrollment, whether full- or part-time, in every school at which the respondent enrolled in three or more courses. If the respondent took two or fewer courses, we recorded the type of educational experience on a modest checklist. Military experiences elaborated on active service in the U.S. armed forces, reserves, and national guard. We gathered detailed family information on first and last or current marriages. In cases where an individual married three or more times, we limited the details for intervening marriages to the date of marriage, date of dissolution, and reason for the termination. We recorded work experiences for both full- and part-time jobs. We gathered detailed data for each full-time job and more limited information for part-time jobs.

The study design required extensive information regarding respondent's current attitudes. This included attitudes about work in general, the individual's current job, sex-role orientations, and several social-psychological concepts. We required descriptive information on the characteristics of firms for which the respondent worked, the level of the individual's authority in the firm, marriage and family relations, and respondent's leisure-time activities. We measured many of these variables with extensive scales and checklists. We decided to complement the time 1 self-report data with more detailed official school records. Privacy laws enacted restricted access to school records after the time 1 data were collected. This required authorizations from the respondents to release copies of school transcripts.

The kind and quantity of the individual-level information we sought necessitated a multistage survey design. There were several considerations. First, although the literature suggested that questionnaire and interview length may not greatly affect response and completion rates (Dillman 1978), the study requirements risked exceeding the reasonable length and limit of information that we could ask. Second, there was some question about the feasibility of using the best survey procedure for gathering detailed life course data, namely, personal interviews. Blum, Karweit, and Sørensen (1969) had suggested that gathering reliable life histories required extensive interaction between a respondent and an interviewer. But face-to-face interviews were prohibitively expensive, given the geographic dispersion of respondents across the United States and to many foreign countries. Third, we believed that a well-designed telephone interview was a possibility, but the telephone format was not well suited for the large number of social-psychological and demographic questions. In working through these considerations, we decided to gather the life course histories in a telephone interview and to ask all remaining questions in a mail questionnaire following the telephone interview.

Assuring Cooperation in the Follow-up

The telephone interview, mail questionnaire strategy required special techniques to gain and assure the respondent's continuing cooperation over the protracted study period. We followed five principles:

1. We made an effort to minimize the number of direct contacts with respondents prior to actual data collection. In the tracking phase we initiated the search by always trying to obtain the respondent's address from parents or relatives, then verifying the address with telephone directory-assistance operators. This procedure reduced the probability of respondents developing negative attitudes about the study based on limited information. The effort was successful in maintaining a very low preinterview attrition rate. When direct contacts were made with respondents to verify addresses, only six people refused to continue participation.

2. Washington State University sponsored the original study, and the University assisted the follow-up in two important ways. First, it authorized identifying the follow-up study with the University as a collaborating institution. This gave the study important continuity, legitimacy, and credibility. Second, through the Social Research Center the University took an active role in receiving and processing the mail questionnaires.[3]

3. We informed high school principals and superintendents of the participating schools about the study in advance, and we regularly updated them as the survey progressed. This further legitimized the study and anticipated questions that might arise in local areas. In addition to informing key opinion leaders in the communities, the information effort established good-will and useful contacts with school officials who later helped in the tracking effort and in processing the requests for transcripts.

4. We adopted Dillman's (1978) total design method in principle. We modified Dillman's techniques by using state-of-the-art letter-generation procedures, additional mailing waves, monetary incentives, and by giving attention to postage and envelope forms.[4] Dillman (1978) suggested that the major costs incurred by survey respondents are time, effort, self-disclosure, and monetary expenses. We tried to counter these respondent costs in the mail questionnaire by designing our communications to regard the respondent as an important individual rather than as a subject in a study.

5. We made a considered effort to get essential advanced information to study participants. The goal was to identify the questions that they might have, address them succinctly, and present the information in a factual and interesting manner. We designed a small, trifold, question-and-answer brochure that accompanied a brief cover letter (appendix J). The brochure idea is not new. For example, the National Longitudinal Study of the class of 1972 used a four-page, question-and-answer document to introduce its study. Telephone interviews later verified that the Career Development Study brochure was widely read and achieved the desired result by preparing potential respondents for cooperating in the telephone interview and mail-questionnaire surveys.

The Computer-Assisted Telephone
Interviewing System

We employed an external contractor to conduct the telephone interviews. This offered economy and efficiency in gathering and storing the complex life history information. The contractor was Audits & Surveys, Inc., in New York City. Audits & Surveys is an established market research firm with experience in conducting social science surveys. Their resources included the Computer Assisted Telephone Interviewing (CATI) system.

The CATI system provided numerous telephone-interviewing efficiencies. On the basis of key information input at the outset of each interview, the program automatically branched to appropriate sections of the interview schedule. For example, if a female respondent reported that she had never entered the military but had married twice, the computer-generated program skipped all military questions but included appropriate questions for each marriage. By automatically bypassing inappropriate sections of the interview schedule, we reduced the magnitude of the interviewing effort and cost considerably. The interview schedule in typing-page form prior to entry on the CATI software was 175 pages long. A simplified and edited copy, which deletes substantive redundancies, program language, and other software requirements, is produced in abbreviated form in appendix K.

The survey organization employed a sufficient number of experienced personnel to conduct interviews from midafternoon to very late in the evening, Eastern Standard Time. The estimated six thousand hours of interviewing time was scheduled across all hours of the interview day so that respondents, who regularly were not home at one time, could be reached at other hours.

Interviewers recorded all information at CRT consoles (terminals with video screens). This was efficient. It preserved the information in readable form. It also substantially reduced the task, associated error rates, and financial costs of data coding. Interviewers keyed-in responses to open-ended questions as open-ended responses. Our subsequent coding procedures used automation wherever possible in processing the open-ended codes.

One advantage of the CATI system was the absence of a lengthy physical interview schedule within which an interviewer could "get lost" searching for the next set of questions. With the CATI system, the appropriate question automatically appeared on the screen before the telephone interviewer; the interviewer read the question to the respondent; the respondent answered; and the interviewer keyed the response directly into the computer file. One disadvantage in using the CATI program in detailed life-history telephone-interview situations is that the respondent does not have a physical record to reference in recalling the progression of events. Such a chart, as used in the Johns Hopkins Social Accounts project, provides useful memory markers to ease respondent recall of critical information and to signal inconsistencies and overlaps in reconstructing the individual's life history. To compensate for this limitation, we provided the telephone interviewer with a timetable on which to graph the progress of educational, military, family, and job histories as the interview proceeded. This enabled the interviewer to ask questions and the respondent to answer relative to such markers as the time of college graduation, job termination, marriage, or birth of a child.

We provided written instructions and personally trained all telephone interviewers. Interviewers practiced supervised interviews before actual interviews were conducted. We pretested the software on fifty-six individuals who attended high school with the study respondents but for whom time 1 information was not available.

The CATI-equipped survey facility provided for audio monitoring of surveys in progress. This assured various forms of quality control. Problem situations were immediately discussed and resolved as they occurred with floor supervisors. The CATI system automatically recorded such details as the interviewer's name, the length of the interview, and the time the interview was conducted. This information provided the supervisors and project director with a quality-control mechanism for monitoring the operations of the telephone survey.

Telephone-Interview Procedures

Preliminary telephone fieldwork began on 27 February 1979. The project director sent a letter to high school principals informing them that the telephone-interview survey had begun. At the same time, an advanced-notice letter with the accompanying information brochure was sent to the fifty-six pretest individuals (appendix J). Project staff coordinated the work flow to the survey organization with the mailing of the advance-information letter from the project offices at the Boys Town Center.

We randomly divided respondents into ten units of approximately 588 cases each. This grouping served a twofold purpose. First, it divided the total sample into manageable numbers for processing as units. Second, it randomly subdivided the sample so that in the event of budget limitations, interviewing could be terminated without biasing sample estimates. The project office referred the information on respondents to the survey organization in the form of computer-generated, self-adhesive labels.[5]

Results of the Telephone Interview

Telephone interviewing began on 28 March 1979 and extended through 19 July 1979. During that period the survey organization conducted 5,446 interviews. We scheduled an interruption in interviewing during the months of August and September. This enabled us to obtain current telephone numbers for the reported "telephone disconnected" records, for pursuing new leads on yet unlocated individuals, and for ascertaining more likely contact times for individuals who were difficult to reach during the previous interviews. We resumed full-scale telephone interviewing during October and November. We conducted a few interviews during December 1979 through February 1980 with people who were very difficult to locate or extremely hard to contact.

Project staff made a special effort to contact 369 people who reported unlisted telephone numbers or were without telephones. We mailed a special advanced letter requesting that these individuals telephone the survey organization collect. We included a $5 incentive check as a token reimbursement for their extra efforts.[6] Fifty-two percent (N = 192) telephoned and were interviewed. The special effort netted a 2.9 percent increase in the total response rate. A few months later 38 more of the 369 hard-to-locate individuals responded to a mail questionnaire bringing the total number of respondents to 230. This was 62 percent of the respondents who reported unlisted telephone numbers or no phone.[7]

Once reached, some of the hard-to-locate respondents demonstrated remarkable cooperation. For example, one female respondent lived in the isolated regions of Alaska. Every three months she traveled 120 miles to a small town for supplies. In return correspondence she promised to call and be interviewed when she next came to town. And she did. But when she telephoned, she was apprehensive about the length of the interview because she had placed the call from an outside telephone booth in freezing weather. When the interviewer asked whether she could get to an inside telephone, she indicated that there were only two other telephones in town, but that she would try to gain access to one of them. A short while later she telephoned again, this time from the local welfare office that allowed her to use its telephone, provided the interview did not take too long. The interview was completed.

On balance, the cooperation of respondents was very good. The survey organization interviewed 96.5 percent (N = 5,880) of the names that we forwarded (N = 6,095). Only 3.1 percent (N = 191) of the individuals contacted refused to participate. When interviewing terminated, only 0.4 percent (N = 24) of the names remained. These were the very hard to reach.

The average interview lasted 40.4 minutes. The interviews ranged from less than five minutes to just under four hours. The number of jobs reported ranged from none held since leaving high school to twenty-two jobs for one female and twenty-one for one male.

One of the shortest interviews involved an individual who responded "no" to every major branching question in the interview schedule. The respondent reported no further education, no military experience, no marriages, and no job since leaving high school. Looking at the blank life course record, the puzzled interviewer queried, "But what have you been doing for the last thirteen years?" The respondent answered that he entered a monastery after leaving high school and had remained there ever since.

The life-history data are detailed and complete. Inspection of the completed interviews reveals that only thirty interviews are not usable. Ironically, most of the unusable interviews were due to automation, that is, to computer system failures over the course of months of interviewing. If interviews were lost the survey organization reinterviewed most of the affected participants, but a few refused to spend the time to go through the interview again, even when offered monetary incentives.

In summary, the telephone procedures produced 5,850 usable interviews, 86.9 percent of the total sample ($N = 6,729$). Removing individuals from the original sample who were not eligible for interviews at time 2—115 who were deceased, 23 who were institutionalized, and 7 foreign-exchange students—yielded a final response rate of 88.9 percent of the original eligible respondents ($N = 6,584$) for the telephone-interview phase.

Mail-Questionnaire Procedures

Two mail questionnaires were used in the Career Development Study, a postinterview questionnaire and a special life-history questionnaire. At three-day intervals the survey organization forwarded photocopied records of interviews completed and the accompanying computer data tapes to the Omaha project offices. There, project staff checked the records for address corrections and constructed a master name-address file. We established a software track file to maintain record of the initial mail dates and the current response status for the postinterview mail questionnaire. The two files informed the timely generation of mailing lists and the production of personalized letters.

Each initial mailing included a personalized cover letter (appendix L), a sixteen-page postinterview questionnaire (appendix M), an information request form (appendix N), a stamped, return envelope, and an incentive check in the amount of $1. We assigned a handwritten case identification number to each postinterview questionnaire, information request form, and return envelope to maintain a record of the response status for each case. We used identical questionnaires for males and females except for two changes. We made the pronouns and spouse designations sex-specific, and we included questions 17A and 17B, which refer to sexual harassment, in the female questionnaire but not in the male version.

We sent all outgoing mail with first-class postage and with address correction requested.[8] The address correction request assured that the letter would be forwarded if the respondent had moved and that the new address would be returned to project offices. We individually typed respondent's name and address on the mail envelope and accompanying correspondence in all mailings. We accomplished this task by creating special software. Up to five mail contacts were made for each nonrespondent.

The final response rate to the mail questionnaire was 83.9 percent ($N = 4,936$) of the 5,880 individuals interviewed and 84 percent ($N = 4,916$) of the 5,850 usable interviews. This represents 74.7 percent of the 6,584 eligible time 2 respondents.

Additional-Information Request Form

We included a short information-request form with the postinterview mail
questionnaire (appendix N). The brochure requested authorization to obtain a copy of the respondent's high school transcript and standardized test
scores. Of the 4,936 people who returned the mail questionnaires after the
telephone interview, 95.7 percent ($N = 4,725$) returned the information-
request form. We made a special mailing to obtain more transcript request
forms from the telephone-interview respondents. Sixty-two additional
respondents returned information request forms in response to the second
mail request. As a result of these procedures we received transcripts for 81.5
percent of those interviewed. At the conclusion of data gathering we received transcripts for 74.3 percent ($N = 4,894$) of the eligible time 2
respondents.

We made arrangements with each high school to obtain copies of the
respondents' transcripts. High school personnel located and forwarded all
but ten transcripts. Project staff entered all courses, grades, attendance
records, and class rankings into the respondent's computer file on a
semester-by-semester basis. Two clerks entered the transcript data independently. We made computer checks for inconsistencies. We reconciled
all inconsistencies with the school transcripts.

The information form also appealed for assistance in contacting former
classmates who had not yet been located. This effort contributed to locating
an additional 307 respondents who were very hard to locate.

The Life-History Questionnaire

On completion of the telephone interviews, 373 eligible participants from
the original study had not been contacted. In addition, the survey organization had not been able to interview twenty-four respondents although it
made numerous attempts at all times of the day. Fifty-eight individuals had
established residencies overseas, and 291 had unlisted numbers or were
without telephones. Of the latter group, about half (151) had not called the
survey organization in response to a letter and $5 incentive requesting them
to do so. The other half were hard-to-locate individuals who were found
during the last months of interviewing but did not have telephones.

We developed a reduced-form questionnaire that covered the essential
content of the telephone interview. Since the number of conditions in the
telephone interview was too numerous to include in a questionnaire, we used the preliminary frequencies in the interview data as limiting parameters
for the content of the questionnaire.[9] We constructed an instrument that
closely replicated the content, structure, and wording of the four major sec-

tions in the telephone interview. To cover those whose histories were more complex, we instructed the respondents to add pages to the booklet for each school or job beyond those allowed in the questionnaire. In the family section, we gathered extensive information on only the current (or last) marriage. We asked limited questions on first marriages and only the major dates and reason for terminations for all other marriages.

We divided the questionnaire into four color-coded sections: schooling, military, family, and jobs. Inspection of the returned instruments verifies that the respondents recognized the transitions where necessary. Most who added pages continued the numbering sequence of questions.

We enclosed a special cover letter for participants living overseas and for all other participants who were not interviewed by telephone. We mailed the life-history questionnaire in a packet together with the postinterview information form, cover letter, and a business reply or postage-paid, return envelope. Two mailings produced a total of 113 returned life-history questionnaires, 30.3 percent of the eligible participants who were not available for interview. Sixty-nine percent ($N = 40$) were returned by 58 overseas respondents and 23 percent ($N = 73$) were returned by the 315 remaining nonrespondents.

When the life-history questionnaires were returned, we mailed the postinterview questionnaire to the respondent. A three-wave mailing sequence of packet, postcard, and packet produced seventy-five completed postinterview questionnaires, 66.4 percent of the respondents who returned the life-history questionnaire. The overseas group returned a higher percentage of the questionnaires than did the remaining nonoverseas group, 84.6 percent compared to 58.5 percent.

Response Rates

The effort to maximize time 2 tracking and data-collection efforts yielded 5,880 telephone interviews of which 5,850 were usable. The usable interviews represent 86.9 percent of the total time 1 sample respondents ($N = 6,729$) and 88.9 percent of the eligible time 2 sample respondents ($N = 6,584$). Mail questionnaires were completed by 4,916 eligible telephone respondents, which is a 73 percent reply based on the total time 1 sample and a 74.7 percent reply based on the eligible time 2 sample respondents.

Including data gathered by the life-history questionnaires increases the response rate to $N = 5,963$, which is 88.6 percent of the total time 1 sample and 90.6 percent of the eligible time 2 sample. Similarly, the response rates for the telephone interview or life-history questionnaire and the postinterview questionnaire increase to $N = 4,991$, which is 74.2 percent of the total time 1 sample and 75.8 percent of the eligible time 2 sample. Comparative analyses are scheduled to establish whether there is a methods bias in the life-history questionnaire data.

Demographic Comparisons

Use of the Career Development Study data raises a critical question: How comparable are the data to the population and to other sample data? The final data requirement is that the data are comparable to the population and to established samples on key demographic measures.

In this concluding section we compare the Career Development Study sample, to state and national figures and to several other large samples in similar studies.

State and National Comparisons

Several comparisons inform the comparability of the Career Development Study data to the state of Washington and to comparable subgroups in the United States. Table 5-2 displays the distributions of follow-up respondents' fathers' occupations compared to employed males in the state of Washington and the United States in 1970. We compare respondents' fathers to males age 35 to 44, since more fathers of sample members would be in that age cohort than any other. Nonetheless, the match of categories is only approximate. The major differences show more professional fathers for the comparison cohort than for the nation, but a comparable proportion (20 percent compared to 21 percent) for the state of Washington. Further, the sample includes about 4 percent more manager-administrator fathers than does the state. The sample also reports about 4 percent fewer operatives. We suspect that these differences are due to the fact that the comparison is based on two different sample populations. The Career Development Study sample is based on fathers with offspring enrolled in high school whereas the state information is based on all males of comparable age. Finally, the sample data for fathers reveal 4 percent more laborers than the state and nation data. We are uncertain about the reasons for this difference. Nonetheless, the comparison is reassuring. Fathers of Career Development Study respondents are very comparable to males of approximately the same age for the state of Washington and the nation. If anything, the fathers hold slightly more advantaged occupations in socioeconomic terms, but the difference is small.

Table 5-3 reports the level of educational attainment for the same group of fathers and provides comparisons with U.S. males, age 35 to 44 in 1970. The distributions are very comparable. The only noteworthy difference is

Table 5-2

Distributions by Major Occupation Group: Fathers of Respondents, Employed Males (Age 35-44) in the State of Washington and the United States, 1960 and 1970

(percent)

Major Occupation Categories	1966 Data	Washington State		United States	
		1960	*1970*	*1960*	*1970*
Professional, technical, and kindred workers	20	14	21	12	17
Managers and administrators, except farm	18	14	14	13	14
Sales workers	6	7	7	7	7
Clerical and kindred workers	2	6	6	6	7
Craftsmen and kindred workers	24	24	23	22	23
Operatives, including transport	11	17	15	20	19
Laborers, except farm	9	6	5	6	5
Farmers and farm managers	4	4	2	5	2
Farm laborers and farm foremen	—[a]	2	1	2	1
Service workers, except private household	5	4	5	5	6
Private household workers	0	—[a]	—[a]	—[a]	—[a]
	100	100	100	100	100

Source: U.S. Bureau of the Census, *Census of Population: Characteristics of the Population, Part I: United States Summary*, vol. 1, Washington, D.C.: U.S. Government Printing Office, 1960, table 204. U.S. Bureau of the Census, *Census of Population: Characteristics of the Population, Part 49: Washington*, vol. 1, Washington, D.C.: U.S. Government Printing Office, 1970, table 226; U.S. Bureau of the Census, Census of Population: *Characteristics of the Population, Part 49: Washington*, vol. 1, Washington, D.C.: U.S. Government Printing Office, 1960, table 123; U.S. Bureau of the Census, "Accuracy of Retrospectively Reporting Work Status and Occupation Five Years Ago," Bulletin PA-(75), Economic Statistics Branch, Population Division, Washington, D.C., 1970, table 174.

Note: The 1966 and 1960 columns are based on the 1960 census classification. The 1970 columns use the 1970 census classification. Also, due to rounding error, the percentage distribution may not total exactly 100%.

[a]less than 1%.

that the sample includes 5 percent fewer fathers with some high school than does the national population, and the sample includes 5 percent more fathers with some college education. As was the case for occupation, Career Development Study respondents are of slightly more advantaged socioeconomic origins, since their fathers as a group have attained a level of education that is a fraction of one year more than the national comparison group.

Table 5-3
Level of Educational Attainment: Fathers in Career Development Study and U.S. Males (Age 35-44)
(percent)

Level of Education	1966 Data	1970 United States
8th grade or less	16	19
Some high school	15	20
High-school graduate	33	32
Some college	16	11
College graduate	10	9
5 years or more of college	10	9
	100	100

Source: U.S. Bureau of the Census, *Census of Population: Characteristics of the Population, Part 49: Washington*, vol. 1, Washington, D.C.: U.S. Government Printing Office, 1970, table 199.

Table 5-4 reports the race of Career Development Study respondents compared to the state of Washington and the nation in 1970. The percent of nonwhite is very small for the sample (2 percent) and the state (4 percent) compared to the nation (12 percent). With respect to race, perhaps more than any other variable, the sample from the state of Washington is not comparable to the nation.

Comparisons with Other Samples and Studies

In table 5-5 we make more detailed comparisons of the socioeconomic origins and achievements of telephone-interview respondents in the Career Development Study. The comparison groups are males in four studies of socioeconomic achievement. The studies include: the Occupational Changes in a Generation, II (hereafter OCG-II; see Featherman and Hauser 1978); data on 1957 Wisconsin high school graduates (hereafter WISC; see Sewell and Hauser 1975); data on 17-year-old males enrolled in high school in Lenawee County, Michigan, in 1957 (hereafter LC; see Otto and Haller 1979); and data on male high school sophomores enrolled in a national sample of schools in 1955, Explorations in Equality of Opportunity (hereafter EEO; see Alexander, Eckland, and Griffin 1975).

The samples contain significant similarities and differences when compared to the Career Development Study data. The OCG-II data represent a national probability sample of male members of the civilian labor force between the ages of 20 and 65 in March 1973 ($N \doteq 37,500$). Where possible,

Table 5-4
Race Composition: Career Development Sample, State of Washington
(Total 1970) and the United States (Total 1970)
(percent)

Race	1966 Data	1970 Washington State	1970 United States
White	98	96	88
Nonwhite	2	4	12
	100	100	100

Source: U.S. Bureau of the Census, *Census of Population: Characteristics of the Population, Part 49: Washington*, vol. 1. Washington, D.C.: U.S. Government Printing Office, 1970, table 199; U.S. Bureau of the Census, *Census of Population: Characteristics of the Population, Part I: United States Summary*, vol. 1. Washington, D.C.: U.S. Government Printing Office, 1970.

we use subsamples of nonblack males age 20 to 24 and 25 to 34 in 1973, which afford maximum comparability to Career Development respondents. The major differences include the national scope of the OCG-II sample, the temporal difference between the 1973 OCG-II and the 1979 Career Development follow-up, and the life course differences between the age groups in the OCG-II sample and ages 17 to 30 in the Career Development data.

The WISC data refer to a sample of 1957 Wisconsin high school graduates ($N = 2,069$ males with nonfarm background). Respondents were followed up in 1964 to measure their levels of educational and occupational attainment, about seven years into their post–high school careers. Where possible, we use WISC data on males with a nonfarm background for comparison purposes. Since the Career Development data contain only 8 percent of respondents from a farm background while WISC and LC data sets contain higher proportions from farm origins, subsamples with nonfarm background afford greater comparability. The WISC respondents are about ten years younger than Career Development respondents, include only high school graduates, and were resurveyed at a point in their life cycle about seven years earlier than the Washington respondents.

The LC data reference the entire age cohort of the 17-year-olds enrolled in high school in 1957 in Lenawee County, Michigan ($N = 442$). Compared to Career Development male respondents, LC respondents are about ten years older and are much more likely to have farm origins. Significantly though, both data sets measure early career achievements at about the same point in the life course.

The EEO data consist of a national sample of high school males who were sophomores in 1955. Respondents were resurveyed fifteen years later in 1970. These individuals were resurveyed at the point in the life course most comparable to the resurvey of Career Development Study youth, about

Table 5-5
Means and Standard Deviations of Select Variables in Five Studies of Socioeconomic Achievement

	Variable[a]			
Study	FOCC	OASP	EDUC	CJOB
CDS: Male Washington high-school juniors and seniors of 1966 ($N = 2863$)[b]				
Mean	44.96	59.99	14.58	47.28
Standard deviation	25.32	25.39	2.21	24.58
OCG: Nonblack males age 20-24 in 1973 ($N = 3119$)				
Mean	39.50		12.80	32.55
Standard deviation	25.40		2.19	21.86
Age 25-34 in 1973				
Mean	34.15		12.74	42.74
Standard deviation	24.05		2.83	24.96
WISC: Male Wisconsin high-school graduates of 1957 with nonfarm background ($N = 2069$)				
Mean	33.10	49.38	13.30	43.30
Standard deviation	22.40	26.51	1.72	24.41
LC: 17-year-old males enrolled in high school in Lenawee County, Michigan in 1957 ($N = 340$)				
Mean	33.64	(36.19)[c]	13.48	47.05
Standard deviation	21.78	(12.56)[c]	2.50	25.21
EEO: Male high-school sophomores enrolled in a national sample of schools in 1955 ($N = 538$)				
Mean	43.35	59.88	14.72	53.52
Standard deviation	20.23	24.98	2.66	23.53

[a]FOCC = father's occupation; OASP = occupational aspirations; EDUC = current educational attainment; CJOB = current job.

[b]CDS: Career Development Study; OCG: Occupational Changes in a Generation, II (see Featherman, David L., and Hauser, Robert M. *Opportunity and Change.* New York: Academic Press, 1978); WISC: Wisconsin Study (see Sewell, William H., and Hauser, Robert M. *Education, Occupation, and Earnings: Achievement in the Early Career.* New York: Academic Press, 1975); LC: Lenawee County Study (see Otto, Luther B., and Haller, Archibald O. "Evidence for a Social Psychological View of the Status Attainment Process: Four Studies Compared." *Social Forces* 57 (1979):887-914; EEO: Explorations in Equality of Opportunity (see Alexander, Karl L.; Eckland, Bruce K.; and Griffin, Larry J. "The Wisconsin Model of Socioeconomic Achievement: A Replication." *American Journal of Sociology* 81 (1975):324-342).

[c]Figures in parentheses are not measured in the same metric as the Washington sample. Exact N's for each variable may vary from the figure listed in left column.

twelve years after high school. The variables in the comparison are father's occupation, respondent's occupational aspirations during high school, educational attainment in 1979 in years of formal schooling, and current job in 1979. All occupations in all studies, with the exception of occupational aspirations in the LC data, are measured in the metric of the Duncan Socioeconomic Status Scale (Duncan 1961). Educational attainment is measured in years of formal schooling.

The fathers of Career Development Study male respondents hold jobs that are 5 to 10 status points higher than their counterparts in OCG-II, WISC, and LC, but they are very comparable to EEO respondents. We suspect that most of the difference is a regional effect in the occupation-industry mix rather than a sample bias. Farming and agriculture-related industries are not as prevalent in the Northwest as they are in the Midwest. Rather, forestry, fishing, aircraft, defense, energy, and related industries are more prominent in the Northwest. Further, our respondent parents are half a generation younger than WISC, LC, and EEO parents. On this basis, slightly more advantaged socioeconomic origins might be expected due to temporal trends in occupational achievement (Featherman and Hauser 1978).

The occupational aspirations of Career Development Study male respondents are somewhat higher than WISC respondents but comparable to EEO respondents. Again, we suspect that the proportion of those coming from and aspiring to farming occupations is the primary source of the difference. The mean educational attainment of 14.58 years, about two and one-half years beyond high school, is slightly less than EEO respondents, about one year more than LC and WISC respondents, and nearly two years more than OCG-II respondents. The differences reflect temporal trends in schooling, age, and sample differences. The OCG-II and WISC estimates are likely truncated, since some sample members are still enrolled in school and have not completed their education, whereas others may return later and add further to their years of formal schooling. The 1979 occupational status of Career Development Study male respondents is intermediate to that found in other samples. It is higher than OCG-II and WISC, about equal to LC, and somewhat lower than EEO. The mean occupational status for OCG-II sample members who have been in the labor force for a comparable period of time, those age 25 to 34, is 42.74 and compares much more favorably with the Career Development Study figure (47.28).

In summary, initial comparisons show that male Career Development Study sample members have slightly more advantaged socioeconomic origins and achievements at age 30 when assessed against their counterparts from several other large samples in studies of a similar type. But the differences are small. The similarities are much more prominent.[10]

It is important to note that our initial assessments of bivariate and multivariate statistics derived from the Career Development Study data for

Table 5-6

Means and Standard Deviations for Select Variables by Gender (Career Development Sample)

Variable	Total Sample			Males			Females		
	Mean	S.D.	N	Mean	S.D.	N	Mean	S.D.	N
FOCC[a]	44.92	25.33	4294	44.96	25.32	1994	44.88	25.34	2300
FED	3.22	1.49	6327	3.23	1.49	3236	3.21	1.48	3091
MED	3.18	1.14	6436	3.20	1.13	3248	3.16	1.16	3188
GPA	2.54	.66	4797	2.40	.66	2385	2.69	.63	2412
URBAN	.92	.28	6617	.92	.27	3373	.91	.28	3244
NSIBS	2.72	1.77	6359	2.69	1.76	3216	2.74	1.78	3143
EDUC	14.19	2.14	5836	14.58	2.21	2863	13.81	1.99	2973
CJOB	48.86	22.91	4023	47.28	24.58	2521	51.50	19.50	1502

[a]FOCC = father's occupation, FED = father's education, MED = mother's education, GPA = grade-point average, URBAN = nonfarm background, NSIBS = number of siblings, EDUC = current educational attainment, CJOB = current job.

models of the aspiration formation and status-attainment processes also compare very favorably with those from other regional and national samples (compare Sewell and Hauser 1975; Alwin, Otto, and Call 1976; Otto and Haller 1979; Spenner, Otto, and Call 1980).

A comparison of select variables for male and female Career Development Study sample members (table 5-6) offers further insight into the nature of the sample. Father's occupation, current job, and educational attainment are measured in the metrics reported earlier. Parent education levels are measured in a compressed metric where: 1 = eighth grade or less; 2 = some high school, but not completion; 3 = high school graduate; 4 = some college, but not graduation; 5 = college graduate; 6 = more than four years of college. Grade point average is taken directly from high school transcripts. The metric is the standard 0 (F) to 4.0 (A) scale. Urban refers to nonfarm residence during high school. Number of siblings refers to the number of living brothers and sisters in 1966.

As expected, males and females report nearly identical socioeconomic origins as measured by father's occupational status and parental education levels. Consistent with findings reported elsewhere (Hout and Morgan 1975), females score slightly higher than males in grade point average during the high school years. As a whole the sample is 92 percent urban and averages between two and three siblings. In eventual educational attainment by age 30, females are nearly a year behind their male counterparts, 13.81 years compared to 14.58 years. Finally, Career Development Study sample women hold full-time jobs that are about four points higher on the Duncan scale than the current jobs of men. The status difference is small, equivalent to the socioeconomic-status difference between bank tellers and engravers.

In a final glimpse at the data, table 5-7 reports univariate distributions for select variables from the telephone-interview follow-up in 1979. The variables, taken from the life course domains of education, military, family, and jobs, provide a sense of the life course variability in the telephone-interview data.

The distributions are based on male and female respondents to the telephone interview. For education we report the highest level of formal schooling and the number of different schools attended full-time. The latter distribution indicates the quantity of education information secured through the software loop that gathered information for each full-time school attended. The information loop included the name and location of the school, the starting and stopping dates for enrollment, dates of schooling interruptions, dates for part- to full-time changes, respondent's major course of study, degrees conferred, grade point average, whether or not respondent worked full-time during schooling, respondent's participation in extracurricular activities, and respondent's plans at time of departure from school. One-fourth of the respondents did not complete any formal

Table 5-7
Percentage Distributions for Select Variables (Telephone-Interview Respondents Only)

Variable and Category	Percent[a]	Variable and Category	Percent[a]
Highest level of formal schooling		Regular military service	
Did not finish high school	2.3	Yes	23.2
High School	22.7	No	76.6
College: < 1 year	8.1		
College: Freshman	11.9	Reserves or National Guard	
College: Sophomore	13.6	Yes	7.0
College: Junior	6.4	No	92.9
College: Senior (B.A., B.S.)	21.2		
Post-Graduate, no M.A.	6.7	Current marital status	
Masters Level	3.9	Never married	12.9
Post M.A., but no Ph.D., M.D., etc.	0.8	Married	73.4
Ph.D., M.D., J.D., etc.	1.9	Separated	1.5
		Divorced	11.6
Number of different schools attended		Widowed	0.3
(Full-time, more than 2 courses in the same enrollment)			
		Number of marriages	
0	20.8	Never married	12.9
1	36.4	1	71.8
2	26.8	2	13.9
3	11.5	3	1.2
4	3.5	4	0.1
5	0.9	5	0.0
6	0.1		
7	0.1		
		Current employment status	
Number of full-time jobs[b] since high school		Never worked	3.1
Never worked	3.1	Unemployed, looking for work	1.0
1	12.4	Unable to work	0.3
2	18.0		

3	18.3
4	15.5
5	11.3
6	7.7
7	5.3
8	3.1
9	2.2
10	1.0
11	0.7
12	0.4
13	0.2
14	0.1
15	0.2
16	0.1
17	0.1
18 or more	0.1

Working full-time	
$\geq$ 25 hours per week)	72.3
Working part-time	
(1-24 hours per week)	4.9
Other	16.8

[a] All percentages are based on $N = 5,850$. Percentages do not equal 100 percent due to rounding error and missing data. A listing of 0.0 percent means at least one response to the category, which rounds to 0.0 percent.

[b] Our definition of full-time job is based on three criteria: (1) one must work at the job for twenty-five or more hours per week, on the average; (2) the job must have been held for a period of one month (effectively, two weeks or more since interviewers and respondents were told to round to the nearest month); (3) excludes military service, jobs held during regular summer school vacation and jobs held prior to departure from high school. Subsequent editing checked all jobs for these conditions. If a job were held during summer school months only and was sandwiched between two periods of full-time schooling, then the job was edited out. Full-time jobs held during regular schooling and simultaneous full-time jobs are included. An employer switch always constitutes a different full-time job for purposes of measurement.

schooling past high school. About one-third of all interview respondents completed the equivalent of four or more years of college. Of those who went on for higher education, the vast majority attended two schools at most. Only 16.1 percent attended three or more different schools on a full-time basis.

About one-fourth of all respondents experienced active duty in the military. Seven percent served in the reserves or national guard. Of those with active duty, nearly half served in the Southeast Asian conflict in a combat or combat-related capacity. We gathered separate interview information for respondents with active- and reserve-duty experience.

In the domain of family measures, nearly 13 percent of the respondents had never been married. Nearly three-fourths were currently married. About 70 percent had one marriage since leaving high school and another 15 percent had two or more marriages.

We gathered the following information for each full-time job since high school: occupation, industry, major activities-duties, class-of-worker, start and stop date, hours worked per week, firm or employer name, promotions, different jobs with the same employer, salary at the end of the job, and main reason for leaving the job. In the case of females, we also gathered information on their career definition of the job. All jobs were coded in 1970 census occupation-industry class-of-worker categories.

Nearly 97 percent of the respondents reported one or more full-time jobs since leaving high school. The average number of jobs was 3.85 (including those who had never worked). But the distribution is skewed to the right. Nearly half of the respondents have had one, two, or three different full-time jobs. About one-third of the respondents had four to six different full-time jobs since leaving high school, and the remainder had from seven to twenty-two different full-time jobs.

Finally, the distribution of current employment status shows that nearly three-fourths of the respondents work full-time, about 5 percent work part-time, small fractions are unemployed, looking for work, or unable to work, and about 17 percent are engaged in other major activities. The other category includes those who are keeping house, are in the military, or are in school, but are not in the civilian labor force. The percentage unemployed or looking for work (1 percent) is lower than the national unemployment rate, which was from 6 to 8 percent during the interview period. However, the national unemployment rate was also much lower for the comparable age-race subgroup, from 2.5 to 4 percent for those 25 years old and over. Our definition of unemployed, looking for work differs from the Department of Labor definition in that we classify as part-time workers those who were working part-time and looking for full-time employment.

Summary

Our research design requires multidimensional life-history measures of individual-level determinants of career-line access. Chapter 5 presents the sample design and data for the measures. The time 1 and time 2 survey procedures and instrumentation are summarized and the response rates are reported for the total sample and subsample components. The Career Development Study sample data compare favorably with the state and national population characteristics and with several other large and similar samples on key demographic variables.

Notes

1. The project followed implementation of the Vocational Education Act of 1963 and was funded by the U.S. Department of Health, Education and Welfare, Project No. ERD-257-65, Contract No. OE-5-585-109, Title: The Vocational Technical Research and Development Project.

The information on the time 1 survey was abstracted from the original project proposal, from copious project records, and from the project Final Report (Slocum and Bowles 1966).

2. The time 1 Final Report and project records do not report a coverage rate for the student questionnaire. On the basis of the data documentation, we estimated conservatively that the overall coverage rate was 86 percent. Originally, there were 6,795 names on file but only 6,729 data cases. This difference was due to data-editing decisions at time 1 that declared 66 cases invalid. Fifty-six of the 66 were used to pretest the time 2 telephone interview. The telephone numbers for the remaining 10 were either not available or were unlisted numbers.

3. There is a literature that argues that the identification of a survey sponsor may affect response rates. Jones (1979), for example, reported that using a university letterhead increased the response rates by 11 percent over use of a government agency letterhead in counties around the university but reduced the response rate in counties around a rival university. Unfortunately, inferences from this study are tenuous because the overall study response rate was only 21 percent. We believed, however, that continuing in-state identification with the university that sponsored the original study was preferable to linking the study with an unfamiliar institution and an out-of-state address.

4. The use of incentives to encourage returns receives considerable support in the literature, and investigators have tried all types including

turkeys, trading stamps, and monetary awards up to $10. The findings suggest that the number and amount of monetary incentives increase response rates (Armstrong 1975; Schewe and Cournoyer 1976; Chromy and Horvitz 1978); that money in hand is better than money promised (Dohrenwend 1970-1971; Armstrong 1975); that providing money on the initial approach is more productive than waiting until subsequent contacts (Huck and Gleason 1974); that newly printed or coined money is a better incentive than old money (Erdos 1957); and that incentives improve also the completeness of responses (Wotruba 1966) and the speed of questionnaire returns (Purcel, Nelson, and Wheeler 1971). Unfortunately, the literature is of uneven quality and provides few unequivocal findings that are generalizable to all populations.

We decided to try to maximize the outcomes of the mail-questionnaire survey by including a modest first-wave incentive. The incentive was a $1 check stapled inside the cover of the questionnaire with the words, "Pay to the order of" (name of respondent) and "void if not cashed within fifteen days" clearly visible. The objective was to induce the respondent to open the questionnaire and to become interested in its contents. The cover letter mentioned the attachment of a small honorarium in appreciation of the respondent's continued help.

It is not possible to partial out the effect of including the incentive in this research design. Nonetheless, the anticipated cost was considerably less than expected. Only 43 percent of the mail respondents cashed the check. In view of the response rate, it appears that the Career Development Study gained the benefit of the incentive at a modest cost by using a check instead of cash.

5. The self-adhesive labels contained the respondent's full current name, maiden name if female, current address, current telephone number, respondent's study ID number, name of high school attended, year in school in 1966, respondent's sex, and a code indicating from whom we received the respondent's current address. The survey organization affixed the labels to a daily-record card and assigned the card to interviewers for contact. Interviewers logged each attempt to contact the respondent on the daily-record card. The information also was recorded automatically on computer file. At the end of each day the survey organization photocopied and filed all cards reporting a completed interview, a refusal, or a disconnect.

The survey organization mailed the photocopy to the Omaha project office, where staff updated files on those respondents who had been interviewed and were ready for the mail questionnaire, those who had questions and needed to be called by the project director to encourage further cooperation, and those respondents who had changed address and required further tracking. Once a respondent indicated a willingness to participate or a respondent's new address and telephone number was located, project staff produced a new label and forwarded it to the survey agency for interviewing. About every third day of interviewing, the survey agency copied the computer file on tape and mailed the tape to the project offices in Omaha. A software program searched the tape and generated a file of descriptive information including date of contact, length of interview, interviewer's name, respondent's ID number, change of address, and special comments by the interviewer. Project staff used this information to update and prepare the mailing list for the mail questionnaire that followed the telephone interview.

6. Three hundred and sixty-nine hard-to-contact individuals received a $5 incentive. Of those who responded ($N = 192$), 74 percent ($N = 143$) cashed the check. Of those who did not respond ($N = 177$), 46 percent ($N = 82$) cashed the incentive check.

Among the hard-to-contact individuals, then, 13 percent responded but did not cash the check, and 22 percent cashed the check but did not respond. Each of the hard-to-locate interviews cost an average of $5.86 in incentives.

7. With these data it is not possible to establish whether the earlier incentive payment had an effect on the individuals who cashed the check but did not respond by telephone. Although 53 percent ($N = 20$) of the thirty-eight people who responded did not cash the $5 check received earlier, we cannot say whether the eighteen people who did cash the check would have responded had they not cashed the check earlier. Still later we invited the remaining nonrespondents to telephone the project director collect when the person was available for interview. A few called and the project director immediately relayed the telephone number to the survey organization and the individual was interviewed.

8. There is limited evidence that the type of stamp used on envelopes may influence response rates (Mayer 1946; Cozan 1960; Hensley 1974). The explanation offered is that different and attractive stamps draw the recipient's attention and interest and, hence, modestly increase response rates. Consistent with these reports, we used at least one recently printed, nonpolitical commemorative stamp as first-class postage on outgoing mail. We used common flag stamps on the first wave of return envelopes. We used business reply returns on subsequent mailings.

9. For example, 99 percent of the telephone respondents attended four or fewer post-secondary schools, 85 percent married only once or had not married at all, and 92 percent held seven or fewer jobs since leaving high school.

10. At this writing the Career Development Study follow-up data are not yet in final form. We will report more detailed comparisons of respondents and nonrespondents in the 1979 follow-up data in the near future.

6 Epilogue

For centuries philosopher-scholars have written about work and its meaning for people's lives. The empirical study of work by social scientists is much more recent, however. It did not begin until the early twentieth century.

Before then there was little cumulative knowledge about work and the worker. There were no comprehensive classification systems that described the American occupational structure or federal manpower administrations to monitor it. Career guidance was the province of settlement houses, not the subject of vocational and career education movements. Palmistry, phrenology, and physiognomy—these were the methods widely used to gain insight into one's future (Rosengarten 1922).

Kimmel (1969) identified three major historical trends in work-related research that have evolved in the United States since the turn of the century. These lines of inquiry focused on worker-related industrial problems, social problems, and on the development of broader and more abstract concepts. We begin this concluding chapter by noting the trends that are the heritage from which current developments in career studies, including our own, have evolved.

The empirical study of work was given initial impetus by America's involvement in World War I. The wartime economy created new jobs and immediate manpower needs. The war effort required efficient procedures to recruit, screen, train, classify, and evaluate worker performance. Industrial psychology and psychometrics developed in response to that need. Following the war, industry hired these researchers to improve worker performance and efficiency and to reduce absenteeism and turnover. The efforts focused on worker behavior.

The second line of empirical study was initiated by occupational sociologists. In the 1920s and 1930s they examined the social problems experienced by workers rather than the labor-management problems that accompanied the war effort and subsequent applications in industry. During the Great Depression, occupational sociologists studied problems of unemployment and its manifestations in industrial, community, and family disorganization. Others turned their attention to the socioeconomically marginal occupational groups: taxi drivers, waitresses, railroaders, and the like. Later, the American soldier was studied too. The interests of the occupational sociologist were quite different from those of the industrial psychologists. Yet the two had much in common. Both responded to specific issues and events. Both were problem oriented. The problems were often local and of short-term duration. So were the solutions.

The third approach concentrated on developing concepts for the study of work. This trend also began in the 1920s and 1930s, but it was less responsive to social and economic conditions. It was not particularly concerned with changing worker behavior to accommodate industry. Neither was it a humanitarian ideology dedicated to improving the lot of the individual worker. Substantively this third approach focused on job attitudes. Methodologically it used survey techniques. It gave increased attention to sampling and measurement issues. The study of job attitudes by survey researchers differed from the interests of the industrial psychologist and the occupational sociologist, to be sure. But the distinguishing characteristic was not a shift in substance. Rather, these researchers recast the issues in terms of broader social science concepts that were situationally less specific. Therein lay their greatest contribution to subsequent research.

During the last two decades social scientists have become increasingly systematic in their methodology and theory. Economists have joined the study of manpower issues; and their analysis strategies have been adopted by related disciplines, especially sociology. More attention has been given to fundamental processes. There is greater interest in developing a cumulative body of theory and research.

We associate our work with the ongoing activities of normal science characterized by a patient, rigorous, and systematic approach to the study of larger conceptual issues. We are not alone in this endeavor. Several current areas of evolving theory and method are likely to make important contributions to the study of careers during the 1980s. We acknowledge an indebtedness to these more recent lines of inquiry, and, in the sections that follow, we outline our own anticipated contribution to understanding careers.

Current Developments in Career Studies

The information contained in this book is best viewed as background for a larger set of studies. The studies take continuity and quality of work life as the initial phenomena to be explained. The conceptual and data-analysis designs coalesce around concepts of career and career line. The general approach assumes that there is a structural component and an individual component to social inequalities in careers. The structural side looks to institutional labor markets, the logic of firms, and the division of labor as sources of patterns in career lines. The individual side inquires how people gain access to career lines and, given access, how positions are maintained or changed by individuals. The concepts provide a bridge between structural-

and individual-level analyses. No doubt there are other conceptualizations of the structural- and individual-level aspects of work life that also warrant inquiry, but the Career Development program investigates the theoretical plausibility of this conceptualization.

Prospectively, several lines of thought and research are likely to advance our shared understanding of careers. We hope to be further informed by the maturation of these ideas and the continuing labors of our colleagues. Four areas of ongoing research warrant special mention.

The Role of Structure

The role of structure in the explanation of social inequality is receiving renewed attention (Baron and Bielby 1980; Berg 1981). Many of the basic ideas originated in the radical and Marxist literatures, but the new role for structure in explanations of inequality is more pervasive. The new role includes the introduction of structural variables to status-attainment models, studies of economic and labor-market segmentation, and studies of the social organization of work in firms, bureaucracies, and larger institutional contexts. Attention to structure in stratification studies holds promise of specifying the differential operation of status attainment and human-capital processes in various institutional contexts. Moreover, the neoclassical views of labor supply and demand and the operation of the firm may be sharpened and revised by renewed research informed by structural perspectives.

We await studies that will specify the nature and extent of economic segmentation in the occupational structure. Careers and career lines may become one dimension of that specification. Further, Mayhew (1980) notwithstanding, we expect studies that will incorporate several levels of analysis in mapping the effects of higher- on lower-order social structures, including the effect of higher-order structures on individual job mobility. The program of research directed by Bielby and Baron (1979, 1980) is of this genre. It seeks to map the effects of higher-order segmentation and differentiation on the organization of work in firms, industries, and occupations. Also, we expect more and better studies of the organization, causes, and consequences of economic segmentation and labor markets. The research in progress by Kalleberg, Griffin, and colleagues (1980) follows these lines of inquiry. In summary, approaches to the study of structure in the explanation of social inequality are germinating. We expect that these separate strains of research from a structural orientation will speak to what it is about work roles that is important in the explanation of positional inequality, why this is so, and how structured inequality is maintained.

Research on careers and career lines may play a part in this larger inquiry. Spilerman's (1977) statement is important because it redirects research to the notion of career line as an intermediate-level concept bridging individual job histories with firms, labor markets, and institutional contexts. The research programs of Sørensen (1975, 1977; Sørensen and Tuma 1978) and Rosenbaum (1979*a*, 1979*b*) have already contributed other insights about the role of structure in the evaluation of careers. As these programs mature, the study of careers will further benefit from an exchange of ideas and method.

Studies of Human Biography

A second set of studies involves the study of human biography. Currently, this area shows increased activity and visibility (Hogan, forthcoming). The developments bear on the study of careers and will likely continue to influence research in the 1980s. Broadly defined, human biography includes social, emotional, and cognitive change over developmental time.

In the past, studies of human development have followed the Freudian legacy in concentrating on early years, infancy, childhood, and early adolescence. The assumption has been that change and development occur primarily during this period and that human development stabilizes by early adulthood. Gerontologists have also studied change and development. They have largely defined their task as studying the characteristics of old age, the other end of the life course continuum. In sum, studies of human development have been limited to discrete age groups, primarily the early years and secondarily the older years. They have examined the young and the old with little attention to preceding and succeeding stages in the life course. As a result the literature tends to be more descriptive of differences within and between age groups than analytical and explanatory of processes contributing to the differences (Abeles and Riley 1976-1977).

More recently there has been a partial convergence of interest among developmentalists and gerontologists. The common ground has been a shared, broad life course perspective to the study of human development. Abeles and Riley (1976-1977, p. 3) outline three central premises of the emerging perspective. First, developmental change and aging are a continual process. The process of development is not limited to the early years, and the process of aging is not limited to later years. Second, the perspective views the processes of development and change across several life course dimensions. The principal domains are social, psychological, and biological. Third, development and change have multiple causes. The perspective emphasizes the interaction of life course dimensions and gives special attention to the role of historical events in the experience of special cohorts (Elder 1975).

The study of human biographies does not offer specific hypotheses to be tested or theoretical explanations for relationships between variables. Baltes (1973, p. 457) earlier observed that the theoretical and empirical rationale is still vague. The literature continues to reveal little consensus on conceptualization, approach, and focus, and a coherent theoretical framework is lacking. Despite these limitations, however, the literature does suggest promising "lines of analysis" (Elder 1975, p. 167). The approach provides a broad framework within which to frame research questions, analyze data, and interpret findings. In the decade ahead we anticipate increased interest in the life course approach to human biographies as demonstrated by developmentalists in psychology, gerontologists in sociology, demographers, and sociohistorians. The Career Development Study will share in that interest.

Dynamic Models

A third area of development that relates to the study of careers involves the treatment of time and events in individual histories and data analysis. We sketched some of these developments in methods in chapter 4. Simply stated, most sociological research relies on cross-sectional analysis in depicting the state of the system or an individual at one or more points in time. Much of the discourse on change consists of qualitative statements about the dynamics of systems. Few areas include explicit specification of dynamic relationships, whether in theoretical or corresponding measurement models. Yet, the study of careers and career lines, where time and the passage of time are built into concepts (by way of aging, job durations, event timings, and the like) are much more powerfully treated in dynamic specifications.

In recent years research by Tuma, Sørensen, and others has made important strides in applying dynamic models to research on social stratification and inequality (Tuma 1976; Tuma, Hannan, and Groeneveld 1979; Sørensen and Tuma 1978; Hannan and Tuma 1979). Although the mathematics of continuous-time, discrete-state stochastic models is not new, applications to event histories with social science data are more recent. Use of these more powerful models requires event histories and complementary continuous types of data. For certain variables and types of problems concerning educational, family, military, and job events, the Career Development individual-level data are of the event-history type and are well suited to analysis by dynamic-modeling procedures.

In the near future we will likely see the increased diffusion and application of dynamic models to sociological research. We plan to use the procedures in modeling individual access to career lines in the first decade of labor-force experience. Similarly, we hope to model other features of work and nonwork histories. Analysis by dynamic-modeling equations holds promise for unraveling some of the complexity confounding studies of human biographies.

Social Policy Research

The fourth development applies to social research more generally and goes beyond consideration of methods and theory. It reflects more of the social-problem orientation characteristic of earlier research in this century. It involves the role of policy research.

Coleman (1972, 1979; see also Cronbach and Suppes 1969) differentiates between two broad classes of social research. The first fits the classical mode and may be labeled "discipline research." It seeks a better fundamental understanding of a substantive area by developing a cumulative body of theory and research. The second class is social policy research. The goal of policy research is to illuminate the strengths and weaknesses of competing arguments (Coleman 1979, p. 172). Policy research has much in common with discipline research, but for present purposes it is useful to emphasize features that differentiate the two. The basic difference arises in the requirements of the research. In discipline research hypotheses are derived from theory. The test is whether a null hypothesis is disconfirmed. Policy research raises a different kind of question. It asks what the consequences of a given policy are or will be. Coleman argues that this concern immediately raises two related questions. First, what kind of consequences are of interest? Second, for whom does the policy have consequences?

Differentiating between broad classes of research is useful. It sharpens the distinction among initial questions, specifies the requisite data and analytic design, and dictates the form that the outcome information will eventually take. The Career Development program of research contains elements of both discipline and policy research. Earlier chapters outlined the anticipated contributions to discipline research. The following paragraphs illustrate, but do not exhaust, anticipated contributions to policy research. We limit ourselves to two examples.

At the national level there are two congressionally mandated programs that will draw nearly $800 million from the federal treasury in 1981. The first is vocational education. The second is career education. At the state and local levels there are corresponding entities in the form of vocational schools and vocational programs within high schools. Federal funding amounts to only about 10 percent of vocational and career education support nationwide. For every program—whether at the federal, state, or local level—advocates and opponents alike raise arguments concerning the intended and unintended effects of these programs. For example, the outcomes of vocational education, which commands the lion's share of the federal dollar, have been questioned by the former secretary of Health, Education and Welfare, Joseph Califano (Lewin-Epstein 1979, p. 112), the director of the National Center for Research on Vocational Education, Robert Taylor (*Education and Work* 1980), and the project director of the National Longitudinal Studies, Herbert Parnes (Peterson 1978, p. 16). Apart from the question raised independently by Califano, Taylor, and Parnes, opponents to vocational education argue that occupation-specific training is inefficient because workers typically experience considerable job turnover, especially during their early careers. But advocates for vocational education argue that the same occupation-specific training gives the employee a competitive edge in the labor market, whether or not there is job turnover.

Whether vocational education produces salutary outcomes is informed in part by the nature of the dependent variable under consideration. Access to particular kinds of career lines—as opposed to achievement measured by point estimates of occupational prestige, earnings, job satisfaction, and the like—provides a different outcome measure that, in our judgment, is potentially an important indicator. Moreover, ascertaining the policy implications of vocational education—or, for that matter, career education, cooperative education, work study, work-release programs, and the like—requires the most careful measures of independent, intervening, and dependent variables. The Career Development Study provides improved measurement of select policy-relevant variables—for example, timing, duration, and nature of vocational-technical programs—such that the analyses hold promise of producing findings that may inform the public debate.

We present a second example in less detail. It concerns school-process effects. The central issue, which began in discipline research but has direct corollaries for policy research, concerns the effects of variations in school programs on schooling outcomes. For example, does the content of the curriculum affect individual-level outcomes? What outcomes? Is participation in the extracurriculum associated with schooling outcomes? Participation in what extracurricular activities? For males, females, or both? Other examples of school-process variables could be cited. Similarly, examples could be extended to policies and practices involving family and military issues. The design for the Career Development studies provides for data that apply to selected issues in social policy as well as discipline research.

Research Agenda

The Career Development program of studies is designed to accommodate a number of research themes. The major thrust of the concepts, data collection, and analysis focuses on work life, particularly the first decade of labor-force experience, when significant life course transitions are expected and typically occur. These include school completion; entry into the labor force and job changes; marriage, family formation and possibly marital dissolution; and military service. The study design provides for research on subjects beyond work life per se over the long term. However, our research agenda for the near term begins with work life and extends from there.

Career Lines and Careers

The initial effort will concentrate on the estimation and analysis of career lines and careers with census and Career Development Study data bases. This volume provides much of the blueprint for these studies. The major tasks include elucidating the properties of career lines and specifying the determinants of career-line features. Spilerman (1977) asks: How are career lines rooted in labor-market organization? Our response, both in terms of method and statement of results, will be based on approximations. Analysis of synthetic cohorts is an approximation. The use of career-line types, as anticipated in chapter 3, is another approximation. The approximations may prove to be quite fallible. We hope to estimate the extent of distortion in the career lines and to assess its effects.

Beyond describing the properties of career lines, there is the question of access to career lines as this is embodied in the careers of individuals. Our thinking and analysis strategy for this issue were outlined in chapter 4. This part of the research agenda is far from final, but work on the subject is underway and has high priority in our work plan.

Gender

Profound social changes are occurring in gender roles and rates of female labor-force participation. Very likely there are gender differences in the composition of career lines. These warrant investigation. To the extent that women compete with men on unequal terms for "careers" in the popular sense of the term, career lines are likely to reveal differences in the gender composition among workers as they move through ports of entry. Further, gender differences in rates of progression through career lines are of interest. In a society with a growing egalitarian ideology, sex discrimination in the work place is a matter of considerable policy relevance.

Our agenda includes investigating gender differences in the supply side of the access to careers equation. Is there an equitable conversion of human-capital investments into work routines and rewards for women compared to men? How women combine and coordinate their resources, plans, and familial obligations with labor-force participation is of further interest. We hope to improve understanding of how different life course contingencies and career-management decisions affect career outcomes for females.

Education and Training

Several items on the research agenda pertain to education and training. In chapter 4 we sketched the logic of investigating the investment-return formula as it applies to career-line access and career returns. The wealth and detail of the Career Development event-history data for schooling and training provide for investigating two additional topics. First, the greater precision in measuring type of schooling or training experiences allows a closer look at various career and noncareer outcomes for a heterogeneous sample of men and women who are well into their careers. Second, the data provide for studying the ongoing returns to schooling and training. This includes consideration of the type of schooling, the timing of schooling, interruptions and delays in schooling, curricular and extracurricular effects, and specification of the conditions under which education and training are more accurately viewed as consumption rather than investment.

Life Course

A major impediment to systematic research on the life course has been the absence of detailed event-history data sets for large heterogeneous samples of men and women. We hope that the Career Development Study data are a first step in filling part of the void. Our research agenda includes several topics.

First, we ask: What mixtures of life course events maximize career outcomes? Initially we will focus only on the presence or absence of an event and perhaps its timing in the domains of school, military, family, and jobs. The unit of analysis is the individual and the person's life course. Second, we will expand consideration of life course effects to include the influence of an individual's significant others, principally a spouse or cohabitant and children. We are interested in how spouses reciprocally affect one another in managing their separate and combined career options. Finally, can the concepts and modes of analysis developed for the investigation of career lines in the world of work be applied heuristically to the life course domains of education and family? We will examine this possibility.

Perhaps the agenda is overly ambitious. Our contributions to the study of careers are likely to be modest. Yet, a comprehensive theory of careers awaits attention to topics on this agenda.

Bibliography

Abeles, Ronald P., and Riley, Matilda White. "A Life-Course Perspective on the Later Years of Life: Some Implications for Research." Washington, D.C.: Social Science Research Council Annual Report, 1976-1977.

Alexander, Karl L.; Cook, Martha; and McDill, Edward L. "Curriculum Tracking and Educational Stratification: Some Further Evidence." Center for Social Organization of Schools, Report No. 237. Baltimore: Johns Hopkins University, 1977.

Alexander, Karl L.; Eckland, Bruce K.; and Griffin, Larry J. "The Wisconsin Model of Socioeconomic Achievement: A Replication." *American Journal of Sociology* 81(1975):324-342.

Alexander, Karl L., and McDill, Edward L. "Selection and Allocation within Schools: Some Causes and Consequences of Curriculum Placement." *American Sociological Review* 41(1976):963-980.

Althauser, Robert P., and Kalleberg, Arne L. "Firms, Occupations and the Structure of Labor Markets: A Conceptual Analysis and Research Agenda." In *Sociological Perspectives on Labor Markets*, edited by Ivar Berg. New York: Academic Press, forthcoming 1981.

Alwin, Duane F. "Assessing School Effects: Some Identities." *Sociology of Education* 49(1976):294-303.

Alwin, Duane F., and Otto, Luther B. "High School Context Effects on Aspirations." *Sociology of Education* 50(1977):259-273.

Alwin, Duane F.; Otto, Luther B.; and Call, Vaughn R.A. "The Schooling Process in the Development of Aspirations: A Replication." Mimeographed. Bloomington, Ind.: University of Indiana, 1976.

Angrist, Shirley S., and Almquist, Elizabeth M. *Careers and Contingencies: How College Women Juggle with Gender.* New York: Dunellen, 1975.

Armstrong, J. Scott. "Monetary Incentives in Mail Surveys." *Public Opinion Quarterly* 39(1975):111-116.

Baltes, Paul B. "Prototypical Paradigms and Questions in Life-Span Research on Development and Aging." *Gerontologist* 13(1973): 458-467.

Baron, James N., and Bielby, William T. "Bringing the Firms Back In: Stratification, Segmentation, and the Organization of Work." *American Sociological Review* 45(1980):737-765.

Bartz, Karen Winch, and Nye, F. Ivan. "Early Marriage: A Propositional Formulation." *Journal of Marriage and the Family* 32(1970):258-268.

Becker, Gary S. *Human Capital: A Theoretical and Empirical Analysis, with Special Reference to Education.* 2d ed. New York: Columbia University Press, 1975.

Bell, Daniel. *The Coming of Post-Industrial Society: A Venture in Social Forecasting*. New York: Basic Books, 1973.

Berg, Ivar, ed. *Sociological Perspectives on Labor Markets*. New York: Academic Press, forthcoming 1981.

Bielby, William T. "Response Errors in Models of the Intergenerational Transmission of Socioeconomic Status." Ph.D. dissertation, University of Wisconsin, 1976.

Bielby, William T., and Baron, James N. "Jobs, Firms, and Industries: Economic 'Dualism' and the Organization of Work." Proposal submitted to the National Science Foundation, University of California, Santa Barbara, 1979.

_____ . "Economic 'Dualism' and Work Organization: Case Studies from the Core." Paper presented at the Annual Meetings of the American Sociological Association, 1980, New York.

Bielby, William T.; Hauser, Robert M.; and Featherman, David L. "Response Errors of Black and Nonblack Males in Models of the Intergenerational Transmission of Socioeconomic Status." *American Journal of Sociology* 82(1977a):1242-1288.

_____ . "Response Errors of Non-black Males in Models of the Stratification Process." In *Latent Variables in Socio-economic Models*, edited by D.J. Aigner and A.S. Goldberger, pp. 227-251. Amsterdam: North Holland, 1977b.

Bielby, William T., and Kalleberg, Arne L. "The Differentiation of Occupations." Paper presented at the Annual Meetings of the American Sociological Association, 1975, San Francisco.

Bishop, Yvonne M.M.; Feinberg, Stephen; and Holland, Paul W. *Discrete Multivariate Analysis: Theory and Practice*. Cambridge, Mass.: MIT Press, 1975.

Blau, Peter M., and Duncan, Otis D. *The American Occupational Structure*. New York: Wiley, 1967.

Blum, Zahava D.; Karweit, Nancy L.; and Sørensen, Aage B. "A Method for the Collection and Analysis of Retrospective Life Histories." Center for the Study of Social Organization of Schools. Baltimore: Johns Hopkins University, 1969.

Bowles, Samuel. "Unequal Education and the Reproduction of the Social Division of Labor." In *Schooling in a Corporate Society*, edited by Martin Carnoy. New York: McKay, 1972.

Bowles, Samuel, and Gintis, Herbert. *Schooling in Capitalist America: Educational Reform and the Contradictions of Economic Life*. New York: Basic Books, 1976.

Bowles, Samuel, and Levin, H.M. "The Determinants of Scholastic Achievement: An Appraisal of Some Recent Evidence." *Journal of Human Resources* 3(1968):3-24.

Braverman, Harry. *Labor and Monopoly Capital: The Degradation of Work in the Twentieth Century.* New York: Monthly Review, 1974.

Buehler, Charlotte. *Der Menschliche Labenslauf Als Psychologisches Problem.* Leipzig: Hirzel, 1933.

Bumpass, Larry L., and Sweet, James S. "Differentials in Marital Instability: 1970." *American Sociological Review* 37(1972):754-766.

Cain, Glen G. "The Challenge of Segmented Labor Market Theories to Orthodox Theory." *Journal of Economic Literature*, Institute for Research on Poverty, Reprint no. 210, December 1976.

Call, Vaughn R.A., and Otto, Luther B. "Age at Marriage as a Mobility Contingency: Estimates for the Nye-Berardo Model." *Journal of Marriage and the Family* 39(1977):67-79.

———. "On 'The Effects of Early Marriage on the Educational Attainments of Young Men': Comment on Kerckhoff and Parrow." *Journal of Marriage and the Family* 41(1979):217-223.

Chromy, James R., and Horvitz, Daniel G. "The Use of Monetary Incentives in National Assessment Household Surveys." *Journal of the American Statistical Association* 73(1978):473-478.

Clarridge, Brian R.; Sheehy, Linda L.; and Hauser, Taissa S. "Tracing Members of a Panel: A 17-Year Follow-up." In *Sociological Methodology*, edited by Karl F. Schuessler, pp. 185-203. San Francisco: Jossey-Bass, 1977.

Cogswell, Betty E., and Sussman, Marvin B. "Family and Fertility: The Effects of Heterogeneous Experience." In *Contemporary Theories about the Family*, edited by Wesley R. Burr, Reuben Hill, F. Ivan Nye, and Ira L. Reiss, pp. 180-203. New York: Free Press, 1979.

Coleman, James. *Policy Research in the Social Sciences.* Morristown, N.J.: General Learning Press, 1972.

———. "Pluralistic Policy Research and Its Design." In *Policy Issues and Research Design*, edited by James Coleman, Virginia Bartot, Noah Lewin-Epstein, and Lorayn Olson. Chicago: National Opinion Research Center, 1979.

Coleman, James S.; Campbell, Ernest Q.; Hobson, Carol J.; McPartland, James; Mood, Alexander M.; Weinfeld, Frederick D.; and York, Robert L. *Equality of Educational Opportunity.* Two volumes. Final Report to U.S. Office of Education, Department of Health, Education and Welfare. Washington, D.C., 1966.

Collins, Randall. *The Credential Society: An Historical Sociology of Education and Stratification.* New York: Academic Press, 1979.

Cozan, Lee W. "Type of Mailing and Effectiveness of Direct-Mail Advertising." *Journal of Applied Psychology* 44(1960):175-176.

Crider, Donald M.; Willits, Fern K.; and Bealer, Robert C. "Locating People in Longitudinal Studies: A Research Report and Suggested

Guidelines." Agriculture Experiment Station Bulletin 778. University Park, Penn.: Pennsylvania State University, 1972.

_____ . "Panel Studies: Some Practical Problems." *Sociological Methods and Research* 2(1973):3-19.

Crites, John O. *Vocational Psychology.* New York: McGraw-Hill, 1969.

Cronbach, L., and Suppes, P., eds. *Research for Tomorrow's Schools.* New York: Macmillan, 1969.

Cutright, Phillips. "The Civilian Earnings of White and Black Draftees and Nonveterans." *American Sociological Review* 39(1974):317-327.

Dauffenbach, Robert C. "Careers in the Labor Market: An Empirical Assessment of the Types of Careers and Their Defining Characteristics." Office of Business and Economic Research, Oklahoma State University-Stillwater, July 1980.

Davidson, Percy E., and Anderson, H. Dewey. *Occupational Mobility in an American Community.* Stanford, Calif.: Stanford University Press, 1937.

Davis, Louis E., and Taylor, James C. "Technology, Organization and Job Structure." In *Handbook of Work, Organization and Society*, edited by Robert Dubin, pp. 379-419. Chicago: Rand McNally, 1976.

Deming, William Edwards. *Statistical Adjustment of Data.* New York: Wiley, 1943.

Dillman, Donald A. "Increasing Mail Questionnaire Response in Large Samples of the General Public." *Public Opinion Quarterly* 36(1972): 254-257.

_____ . *Mail and Telephone Surveys.* New York: Wiley, 1978.

Dillman, Donald A., and Frey, James H. "Contribution of Personalization to Mail Questionnaire Response as an Element of a Previously Tested Method." *Journal of Applied Psychology* 59(1974):297-301.

Dillman, Donald A.; Carpenter, Edwin H.; Christenson, James A.; and Brooks, Ralph M. "Increasing Mail Questionnaire Response: A Four State Comparison." *American Sociological Review* 39(1974):744-756.

Doeringer, Peter B., and Piore, Michael J. *Internal Labor Markets and Manpower Analysis.* Lexington, Mass.: Lexington Books, D.C. Heath, 1971.

Dohrenwend, Barbara Snell. "An Experimental Study of Payments to Respondents." *Public Opinion Quarterly* (1970-1971):621-624.

Duncan, Otis Dudley. "A Socioeconomic Index for All Occupations." In *Occupations and Social Status*, edited by Albert J. Reiss, Jr. New York: Free Press, 1961.

Duncan, Otis D.; Featherman, David L.; and Duncan, Beverly. *Socioeconomic Background and Achievement.* New York: Seminar Press, 1972.

Eckaus, Richard S. *Estimating the Returns to Education: A Disaggregated Approach.* Berkeley, Calif.: The Carnegie Commission on Higher Education, 1973.

Education and Work. "Researchers Disagree on Impact of Vocational Education." 6(1980):5-6.

Edwards, Richard C. *Contested Terrain: The Transformation of the Workplace in the Twentieth Century.* New York: Basic Books, 1979.

Elder, Glen H., Jr. "Age Differentiation and the Life Course." In *Annual Review of Sociology*, vol. 1, edited by Alex Inkeles, James Coleman, and Neil Smelser, pp. 165-190. Palo Alto, Calif.: Annual Reviews Inc., 1975.

Erdos, Paul L. "How to Get Higher Returns from Your Mail Surveys." *Printers' Ink* (1957):30-31.

Featherman, David L. "A Research Note: A Social Structural Model for the Socioeconomic Career." *American Journal of Sociology* 77 (1971): 293-304.

———. "Comments on Models for the Socioeconomic Career." *American Sociological Review* 38(1973):785-791.

———. "The Effects of Schooling and the Transition from School to Work." In *A Research Agenda for the National Longitudinal Surveys of Labor Market Experience,* edited by James L. Peterson. Washington, D.C.: Social Science Research Council, 1978.

Featherman, David L., and Carter, T. Michael. "Discontinuities in Schooling and the Socioeconomic Life Cycle." In *Schooling and Achievement in American Society*, edited by W.H. Sewell, R.M. Hauser, and D.L. Featherman, pp. 133-160. New York: Academic Press, 1976.

Featherman, David L., and Hauser, Robert M. "Commonalities in Social Stratification and Assumptions about Status Mobility in the United States." In *The Process of Stratification: Trends and Analyses*, edited by R.M. Hauser and D.L. Featherman, pp. 3-50. New York: Academic Press, 1977.

———. "The Measurement of Occupation in Social Surveys." In *The Process of Stratification: Trends and Analyses*, edited by R.M. Hauser and D.L. Featherman, pp. 51-80. New York: Academic Press, 1977.

———. *Opportunity and Change.* New York: Academic Press, 1978.

Form, William H., and Miller, Delbert C. "Occupational Career Pattern as a Sociological Instrument." *American Journal of Sociology* 54 (1949); 317-329.

Freeman, Richard B. *The Overeducated American.* New York: Academic Press, 1976.

Giddens, Anthony. *The Class Structure of the Advanced Societies.* New York: Harper & Row, 1975.

Ginsberg, Ralph B. "Semi-Markov Processes and Mobility." *Journal of Mathematical Sociology* 1(1971):233-262.

Ginzberg, E. *Life Styles of Educated Women.* New York: Columbia University Press, 1966.

Gitelman, H.M. "Occupational Mobility within the Firm." *Industrial Relations Review* 20(1966):50-65.

Glaser, Barney G., and Strauss, Anselm L. *Status Passage: A Formal Theory*. Chicago: Aldine, 1971.

Goodman, Leo A. "The Multivariate Analysis of Qualitative Data: Interactions among Multiple Classifications." *Journal of the American Statistical Association* 65(1970):226-256.

Grant, W. Vance, and Lind, C. George. *Digest of Education Statistics: 1975 Edition*. Washington, D.C.: U.S. Government Printing Office, 1976.

Gross, Neal; Mason, Ward S.; and McEachern, Alexander W. *Explorations in Role Analysis: Studies of the School Superintendency Role*. New York: Wiley, 1958.

Hall, Richard H. *Occupations and the Social Structure*. (1959) 2d ed. Englewood Cliffs, N.J.: Prentice-Hall, 1975.

Haller, Archibald O., and Spenner, Kenneth I. "Occupational Income Differentiation in Status Attainment." *Rural Sociology* 42(1977):517-535.

Hannan, Michael T., and Tuma, Nancy Brandon. "Methods for Temporal Analysis." In *Annual Review of Sociology*, vol. 5, edited by Alex Inkeles, James Coleman, and Ralph H. Turner, pp. 303-328. Palo Alto, Calif.: Annual Reviews Inc., 1979.

Hauser, Robert M.; Dickinson, Peter J.; Travis, Harry P.; and Koffel, John N. "Structural Changes in Occupational Mobility among Men in the United States." *American Sociological Review* 40(1975):585-598.

Hauser, Robert M.; Koffel, John N.; Travis, Harry P.; and Dickinson, Peter J. "Temporal Change in Occupational Mobility: Evidence for Men in the United States." *American Sociological Review* 40(1975): 279-297.

Hauser, Robert M.; Sewell, William H.; and Alwin, Duane F. "High School Effects on Achievement." In *Schooling and Achievement in American Society*, edited by W.H. Sewell, R.M. Hauser, and D.L. Featherman, pp. 309-341. New York: Academic Press, 1976.

Hensley, Wayne E. "Increasing Response Rate by Choice of Postage Stamps." *Public Opinion Quarterly* 38(1974):280-283.

Heyns, Barbara. "Social Selection and Stratification within Schools." *American Journal of Sociology* 79(1974):1434-1451.

Hodge, Robert W. "Occupational Mobility as a Probability Process." *Demography* 3(1966):19-34.

Hogan, Dennis P. "The Passage of American Men from Family of Orientation to Family of Procreation: Patterns, Timing, and Determinants." Ph.D dissertation, University of Wisconsin, 1976.

———. "The Variable Order of Events in the Life Course." *American Sociological Review* 43(1978):573-586.

———. "The Transition to Adulthood as a Career Contingency." *American Sociological Review* 45(1980):261-276.

———. *Transitions and Social Change*. New York: Academic Press, forthcoming.

Hogan, Dennis P., and Featherman, David L. "Racial Stratification and Socioeconomic Change in the American North and South." *American Journal of Sociology* 83(1977):100-126.

Holland, John L. *Making Vocational Choices: A Theory of Careers.* Englewood Cliffs, N.J.: Prentice-Hall, 1973.

Horowitz, Morris A., and Herrnstadt, Irwin L. "Changes in the Skill Requirements of Occupations in Selected Industries." Washington, D.C.: U.S. National Commission on Technology, Automation, and Economic Progress, 1966.

Hout, Michael, and Morgan, William R. "Race and Sex Variations in the Causes of the Expected Attainments of High School Seniors." *American Journal of Sociology* 81(1975):364-394.

Huck, Schuyler W., and Gleason, Edwin M. "Using Monetary Inducements to Increase Response Rates from Mailed Surveys." *Journal of Applied Psychology* 59(1974):222-225.

Hudis, Paula M., and Kalleberg, Arne L. "Labor Market Structure and Sex Differences in Occupational Careers." Paper presented at the Annual Meetings of the American Sociological Association, 1977, Chicago.

Jencks, Christopher. *Inequality: A Reassessment of the Effect of Family and Schooling in America.* New York: Basic Books, 1972.

_____ . *Who Gets Ahead? The Determinants of Economic Success in America.* New York: Basic Books, 1979.

Jones, Wesley H. "Generalizing Mail Survey Inducement Methods: Population Interactions with Anonymity and Sponsorship." *Public Opinion Quarterly* 43(1979):102-111.

Kalleberg, Arne L. "Work Values and Job Rewards: A Theory of Job Satisfaction." *American Sociological Review* 42(1977):124-143.

Kalleberg, Arne, and Griffin, L. "Macroeconomic Processes, Economic Segmentation, and Economic Inequality: Cross-Sectional and Time-Series Analyses of Stratification in the United States, 1947-77." Proposal submitted to the National Science Foundation, Indiana University, Bloomington, Indiana, 1980.

Kalleberg, Arne L., and Hudis, Paula M. "Wage Change in the Late Career: A Model for the Outcomes of Job Sequences." *Social Science Research* 8(1979):16-40.

Kalleberg, Arne L., and Sørensen, Aage B. "The Sociology of Labor Markets." In *Annual Review of Sociology*, vol. 5, edited by Alex Inkeles, James Coleman, and Ralph H. Turner, pp. 351-379. Palo Alto, Calif.: Annual Reviews, Inc., 1979.

Karweit, Nancy, "Storage and Retrieval of Life History Data." *Social Science Research* 2(1973):41-50.

Kelley, Jonathan. "Causal Chain Models for the Socioeconomic Career." *American Sociological Review* 38(1973):481-493.

Kerckhoff, Alan C., and Parrow, Alan A. "The Effect of Early Marriage on the Educational Attainment of Young Men." *Journal of Marriage and the Family* 41(1979a):97-107.

Kerckhoff, Alan C., and Parrow, Alan A. "Reply to Call and Otto." *Journal of Marriage and the Family* 41(1979b):225-227.

Kerr, Clark. "The Balkanization of Labor Markets." In *Labor Mobility and Economic Opportunity*, edited by E.W. Bakke, P.M. Hauser, G.L. Palmer, C.A. Meyers, D. Yoder, and C. Kerr, pp. 92-110. New York: Wiley, 1954.

Kerr, Clark; Dunlop, John T.; Harbison, Frederick H.; and Meyers, Charles A. *Industrialism and Industrial Man*. New York: Oxford University Press, 1964.

Kimmel, Paul. "Research on Work and the Worker in the United States." In *Measures of Occupational Attitudes and Occupational Characteristics*, edited by John P. Robinson, Robert Athanasiou, and Kendra B. Head. Ann Arbor, Mich.: Institute for Social Research, 1969.

Klatzky, S., and Hodge, R.H. "A Canonical Correlation Analysis of Occupational Mobility." *Journal of the American Statistical Association* 66(1971):16-22.

Kohn, Melvin L. *Class and Conformity*. Homewood, Ill.: Dorsey, 1969.

_____ . *Class and Conformity*. 2d. ed. Chicago and London: University of Chicago Press, 1977.

Kohn, Melvin L., and Schooler, Carmi. "Occupational Experience and Psychological Functioning: An Assessment of Reciprocal Effects." *American Sociological Review* 38(1973):97-118.

_____ . "The Reciprocal Effects of Substantive Complexity of Work and Intellectual Flexibility: A Longitudinal Assessment." *American Journal of Sociology* 84(1978):24-52.

Leigh, Duane E. *An Analysis of the Determinants of Occupational Upgrading*. New York: Academic Press, 1978.

LeMasters, E.E. "Parenthood as Crisis." *Marriage and Family Living* 19(1957):352-355.

Lenski, Gerhard E. *Power and Privilege: A Theory of Social Stratification*. New York: McGraw-Hill, 1966.

Lewin-Epstein, Noah. "Post Secondary Non-Educational Activity." In *Policy Issues and Research Design*, edited by James Coleman, Virginia Bartot, Lorayn Olson. Chicago: National Opinion Research Center, 1979.

Lipset, Seymour M., and Bendix, Reinhard. "Social Mobility and Occupational Career Patterns. I. Stability of Jobholding." *American Journal of Sociology* 57(1952a):366-374.

_____ . "Social Mobility and Occupational Career Patterns. II. Social Mobility." *American Journal of Sociology* 57(1952b):494-504.

McFarland, David D. "Intragenerational Social Mobility as a Markov Process: Including a Time-Stationary Markovian Model that Explains Observed Declines in Mobility Rates over Time." *American Sociological Review* 35(1970):463-476.

Marini, Margaret Mooney. "Transition to Adulthood." *American Sociological Review* 43(1978):483-507.

Mayer, Edward N., Jr. "Postage Stamps *Do* Affect Results of Your Mailing." *Printers' Ink* 17(1946):91.

Mayer, Thomas. "Models in Intragenerational Mobility." In *Sociological Theories in Progress*, vol. 2, edited by Joseph Berger, Morris Zelditch, Jr., and Bo Anderson, pp. 308-357. Boston: Houghton Mifflin, 1972.

Mayhew, B.H. "Structuralism versus Individualism: Part I, Shadowboxing in the Dark." *Social Forces* 59(1980):335-375.

Miller, A. "The Measurement of Change: A Comparison of Retrospective and Panel Studies." Population Studies Laboratory, University Park, Penn.: Pennsylvania State University, 1977.

Miller, Delbert C., and Form, William H. *Industrial Sociology: An Introduction to the Sociology of Work Relations*. New York: Harper & Row, 1951.

Miller, Joanne; Schooler, Carmi; Kohn, Melvin L.; and Miller, Karen A. "Women and Work: The Psychological Effects of Occupational Conditions." *American Journal of Sociology* 85(1979):66-94.

Mincer, Jacob. *Schooling, Experience, and Earnings*. New York: Columbia University Press, 1974.

Mortimer, Jeylan T. "Patterns of Intergenerational Occupational Movements: A Smallest-Space Analysis." *American Journal of Sociology* 79(1974):1278-1299.

Mueller, Charles W. "City Effects of Socioeconomic Achievements: The Case of Large Cities." *American Sociological Review* 39(1974): 652-667.

Otto, Luther B. "Antecedents and Consequences of Marital Timing." In *Contemporary Theories about the Family*, edited by Wesley R. Burr, pp. 101-126. New York: Free Press, 1979.

Otto, Luther B., and Haller, Archibald O. "Evidence for a Social Psychological View of the Status Attainment Process: Four Studies Compared." *Social Forces* 57(1979):887-914.

Otto, Luther B.; Spenner, Kenneth I.; and Call, Vaughn R.A. "Careers and Career Lines: Concepts, Measures and Explanations." Mimeographed. Boys Town Center for the Study of Youth Development, 1980.

Palmer, Gladys L. *Labor Mobility in Six Cities*. New York: Social Science Research Council, 1954.

Parkin, Frank. *Class Inequality and Political Order*. New York: Praeger, 1971.

Parnes, Herbert S., and Nestel, Gilbert. "Middle-Aged Job Changers." In

The Pre-Retirement Years, vol. 4, edited by Herbert Parnes, Arvil Van Adams, Paul Andrisani, Andrew I. Kohen, and Gilbert Nestel, pp. 79-114. U.S. Department of Labor, Manpower Administration, Washington, D.C.: U.S. Government Printing Office, 1975.

Peterson, James L. "Conference Proceedings: Review and Commentary." In *A Research Agenda for the National Longitudinal Surveys of Labor Market Experience,* edited by James L. Peterson. Washington, D.C.: Social Science Research Council, 1978.

Pietrofesa, John J., and Splete, Howard. *Career Development: Theory and Research.* New York: Grune, 1975.

Pucel, David, J.; Nelson, Howard F.; and Wheeler, David N. "Questionnaire Follow-Up Returns as a Function of Incentives and Responder Characteristics." *Vocational Guidance Quarterly* 19(1971):188-193.

Rapoport, Robert, and Rapoport, Rhona. "Work and Family in Contemporary Society." *American Sociological Review* 30(1965):381-393.

Reich, Michael; Gordon, David M.; and Edwards, Richard C. "Dual Labor Markets: A Theory of Labor Market Segmentation." *American Economic Review* 63(1973):359-365.

Rogoff Ramsøy, Natalie. "On Social Stratification in a Temporal Framework." Mimeographed. Oslo, Norway: Institute of Applied Social Research, 1975.

Rogoff Ramsøy, Natalie, and Clausen, S. "Events as Units of Analysis in Life History Studies." Paper presented to the Social Science Research Council Conference on the National Longitudinal Surveys, 1977, Washington, D.C.

Rosenbaum, James E. *Making Inequality: The Hidden Curriculum of High School Tracking.* New York: Wiley, 1976.

————. "Tournament Mobility: Career Patterns in a Corporation." *Administrative Science Quarterly* 24(1979a):220-241.

————. "Organizational Career Mobility: Promotion Chances in a Corporation during Periods of Growth and Contraction." *American Journal of Sociology* 85(1979b):21-48.

Rosenfeld, Rachel A. "Race and Sex Differences in Career Dynamics." *American Sociological Review* 45(1980):583-609.

Rosengarten, William. *Choosing Your Life Work.* New York: McGraw-Hill, 1922.

Schewe, Charles D., and Cournoyer, Norman G. "Prepaid Promised Monetary Incentives to Questionnaire Response: Further Evidence." *Public Opinion Quarterly* 40(1976):105-107.

Schultz, Theodore W. "Investment in Human Capital." *American Economic Review* 51(1961):2-17.

Sewell, William H., and Hauser, Robert M. "Causes and Consequences of Higher Education: Models of the Status Attainment Process." *American Journal of Agricultural Economics* 54(1972):851-861.

_____ . *Education, Occupation, and Earnings: Achievement in the Early Career.* New York: Academic Press, 1975.

Sewell, William H., and Orenstein, Alan M. "Community of Residence and Occupational Choice." *American Journal of Sociology* 70(1965): 551-563.

Singer, Burton, and Spilerman, Seymour. "Social Mobility Models for Heterogeneous Populations." In *Sociological Methodology 1973-1974,* edited by Herbert L. Costner, pp. 356-401. San Francisco: Jossey-Bass, 1974.

Slocum, Walter L. *Occupational Careers: A Sociological Perspective.* 1st, 2d ed. New York: Aldine, 1966 (1974).

_____ . *Occupational Careers.* 2d ed. Chicago: Aldine, 1975.

Slocum, Walter L., and Bowles, Roy T. *Educational and Occupational Aspirations and Expectations of High School Juniors and Seniors in the State of Washington.* Final Report to the Office of Education, U.S. Department of Health, Education and Welfare, Project no. ERD-257-65. Pullman, Wash.: Washington State University, 1966.

Solow, Robert M. "Investment and Economic Growth: Some Comments." In *Investment in Human Capital,* edited by B.F. Kiker, pp. 101-108. Columbia, S.C.: University of South Carolina Press, 1971.

Sommers, Dixie, and Eck, Alan. "Occupational Mobility in the American Labor Force." *Monthly Labor Review* January (1977):3-19.

Sørensen, Aage B. "A Model for Occupational Careers." *American Journal of Sociology* 80(1974):44-57.

_____ . "The Structure of Intragenerational Mobility." *American Sociological Review* 40(1975):456-471.

_____ . "The Structure of Inequality and the Process of Attainment." *American Sociological Review* 42(1977):965-978.

Sørensen, Aage B., and Hallinan, Maureen T. "A Reconceptualization of School Effects." *Sociology of Education* 50(1977):273-289.

Sørensen, Aage B., and Tuma, Nancy Brandon. "Labor Market Structures and Job Mobility." Paper presented at the IX World Congress of Sociology, 1978, Uppsala, Sweden.

Sorokin, Pitirim. *Social Mobility.* New York: Harper & Row, 1927.

Spaeth, Joe L. "Vertical Differentiation among Occupations." *American Sociological Review* 44(1979):746-762.

Spenner, Kenneth I. "From Generation to Generation: The Transmission of Occupation." Ph.D. dissertation, University of Wisconsin, 1977.

_____ . "Temporal Changes in Work Content." *American Sociological Review* 44(1979):968-975.

_____ . "Occupational Characteristics and Classification Systems: New Uses of the Dictionary of Occupational Titles in Social Research." *Sociological Methods & Research* 9(1980):239-264.

Spenner, Kenneth I., and Featherman, David L. "Achievement Ambitions." In *Annual Review of Sociology,* vol. 4, edited by Ralph H. Turner, James Coleman, and Renee C. Fox, pp. 373-420. Palo Alto, Calif: Annual Reviews Inc., 1978.

Spenner, Kenneth I., and Otto, Luther B. "Emerging Issues in the Study of Careers." Paper presented at the Annual Meetings of the American Sociological Association, 1979, Boston.

Spenner, Kenneth I.; Otto, Luther B.; and Call, Vaughn R.A. "Status Attainment Replication: The Washington Data." Mimeographed. Boys Town Center for the Study of Youth Development, 1980.

Spilerman, Seymour. "The Analysis of Mobility Processes by the Introduction of Independent Variables into a Markov Chain." *American Sociological Review* 37(1972):277-300.

_____. "Careers, Labor Market Structure, and Socioeconomic Achievement." *American Journal of Sociology* 83(1977):551-593.

Spilerman, Seymour, and Habib, Jack. "Development Towns in Israel: The Role of Community in Creating Ethnic Disparities in Labor Force Characteristics." *American Journal of Sociology* 81(1976):781-812.

Spilerman, Seymour, and Miller, Richard E. "The Effect of Negative Tax Payments on Job Turnover and Job Selection." In *The Final Report of the New Jersey Graduated Work Incentive Experiment,* vol. 1, edited by Harold W. Watts and Albert Rees. Madison, Wisc.: Institute for Research on Poverty, 1973.

Stewman, Shelby. "Two Markov Models of Open System Occupational Mobility: Underlying Conceptualizations and Empirical Tests." *American Sociological Review* 40(1975):298-321.

Stolzenberg, Ross M., and Waite, Linda J. "Age, Fertility Expectations and Plans for Employment." *American Sociological Review* 42(1977):769-783.

Super, Donald E. *The Psychology of Careers.* New York: Harper & Row, 1957.

Sweet, James A. "Demography and the Family." In *Annual Review of Sociology,* vol. 3, edited by Alex Inkeles, James Coleman, and Neil Smelser, pp. 363-405. Palo Alto, Calif.: Annual Reviews Inc., 1977.

Temme, Lloyd V. *The History and Methodology of "The Adolescent Society" Follow-Up Study.* Washington, D.C.: Bureau of Social Science Research, 1975*a*.

_____. *Occupation: Meanings and Measures.* Washington, D.C.: Bureau of Social Science Research, 1975*b*.

Thompson, James D.; Avery, Robert W.; and Carlson, Richard O. "Occupations, Personnel, and Careers." *Educational Administration Quarterly* 4(1968):6-31.

Thurow, Lester C. *Generating Inequality: Mechanisms of Distribution in the U.S. Economy.* New York: Basic Books 1975.

Tilgher, Adriano. *Homo Faber: Work through the Ages.* Chicago: Regnery, 1930.

Tittle, Carol Kehr, and Denker, Elenor Rubin. "Re-entry Women: A Selective Review of the Educational Process, Career Choice, and Interest Measurement." *Review of Educational Research* 47(1977):531-584.

Treiman, Donald J. *Occupational Prestige in Comparative Perspective.* New York: Academic Press, 1977.

Tuma, Nancy Brandon. "Rewards, Resources, and the Rate of Mobility: A Nonstationary Multivariate Stochastic Model." *American Sociological Review* 41(1976):338-360.

Tuma, Nancy Brandon; Hannan, Michael T.; and Groeneveld, Lyle P. "Dynamic Analysis of Event Histories." *American Journal of Sociology* 84(1979):820-854.

U.S. Bureau of the Census. *Census of Population: Characteristics of the Population, Part I: United States Summary,* vol. 1. Washington, D.C.: U.S. Government Printing Office, 1960*a.*

_____ . *Census of Population: Characteristics of the Population, Part 49: Washington,* vol. 1. Washington, D.C.: U.S. Government Printing Office, 1960*b.*

_____ . "Accuracy of Retrospectively Reporting Work Status and Occupation Five Years Ago." Bulletin PA-(75), Economic Statistics Branch, Population Division, 1970*a.*

_____ . *Census of Population: Characteristics of the Population, Part 49: Washington,* vol. 1. Washington, D.C.: U.S. Government Printing Office, 1970*b.*

_____ . *Census of Population: Characteristics of the Population, Part I: United States Summary,* vol. 1. Washington, D.C.: U.S. Government Printing Office, 1970*c.*

_____ . *Public Use Samples of Basic Records from the 1970 Census: Description and Technical Documentation.* Washington, D.C.: U.S. Government Printing Office, 1972.

U.S. Department of Health, Education and Welfare. *Work in America,* Special Task Force to the Secretary. Cambridge, MA: MIT Press, 1973.

U.S. Department of Labor. *Dictionary of Occupational Titles.* 3d ed.; 2 vols. Washington, D.C.: U.S. Government Printing Office, 1965.

_____ . *U.S. Workers and Their Jobs: The Changing Picture.* Bulletin 1919. Washington, D.C.: U.S. Government Printing Office, 1976.

Vanneman, Reeve D., and McNamee, Stephen J. "Characteristics of the Labor Force and Job Rewards: A Canonical Analysis." Paper presented at the Annual Meetings of the American Sociological Association, 1978, San Francisco.

Voss, Paul R. "Social Determinants of Age at First Marriage in the United States." Ph.D. dissertation, University of Michigan, 1975.

Waite, Linda J. "Working Wives: 1940-1960." *American Sociological Review* 41(1976):65-80.

———. "Working Wives and the Family Life Cycle." *American Journal of Sociology* 86(1980):272-294.

Waite, Linda J., and Stolzenberg, Ross M. "Intended Childbearing and Labor Force Participation of Young Women: Insights from Nonrecursive Models." *American Sociological Review* 41(1976):235-252.

Wilensky, Harold L. "Orderly Careers and Social Participation: The Impact of Work History on Social Integration in the Middle Mass." *American Sociological Review* 26(1961):521-539.

Willits, Fern K.; Crider, Donald, M; and Bealer, Robert C. "A Design and Assessment of Techniques for Locating Respondents in Longitudinal Sociological Studies." Report to National Institute of Mental Health, Contract #PH-43-68-76. University Park, Penn.: Pennsylvania State University, 1969.

Winsborough, Hallinan H. "Age, Period, Cohort, and Education Effects on Earnings by Race." In *Social Indicators Models,* edited by Kenneth C. Land and Seymour Spilerman, pp. 201-217. New York: Russell Sage Foundation, 1975.

Wise, Robert; Charner, Ivan; and Randour, Mary Lou. "A Conceptual Framework for Career Awareness in Career Decision Making." *The Counseling Psychologist* 6(1976):47-53.

Wotruba, Thomas R. "Monetary Inducements and Mail Questionnaire Response." *Journal of Marketing Research* 3(1966):398-399.

Wright, Erik Olin, and Perrone, Luca. "Marxist Class Categories and Income Inequality." *American Sociological Review* 42(1977):32-55.

List of Appendixes

**Appendix A:
Career Development
Job Categories**

CAREER LINE CATEGORY	INCLUDED 1970 CENSUS OCCUPATIONS	INCLUDED 1970 CENSUS INDUSTRIES
PROFESSIONAL, TECHNICAL, AND KINDRED WORKERS		
Accountants - accounting firms	001	889
Accountants - public administration	001	907-937
Accountants - finance and professional services	001	707-718,828-888,890-897
Accountants - manufacturing industries	001	107-398
Accountants - other industries	001	017-106,407-699,727-809, 938-999
Architects	002	all
Computer programmers	003	all
Other computer specialists (except programmers)	004,005	all
Aeronautical and astronautical engineers	006	all
Chemical engineers	010	all
Civil engineers	011	all
Electrical and electronic engineers	012	all
Industrial engineers	013	all
Mechanical engineers	014	all
Sales engineers	022	all
Other engineers	015,020,021,023	all
Foresters and conservationists	025	all
Lawyers	031	all
Librarians, archivists and curators	032,033	all
Mathematical specialists	034,035,036	all
Chemists	045	all
Other life and physical scientists	042-044,051-054	all
Operations and systems researchers and analysts	055	all
Personnel and labor relations workers	056	all
Dentists	062	all
Pharmacists	064	all
Physicians, medical and osteopathic	065	all
Other medical practitioners	061,063,071,072,073	all
Dieticians	074	all
Registered nurses - hospitals	075	838
Registered nurses - other settings than hospitals	075	017-837,839-999
Therapists	076	all
Clinical laboratory technologists and technicians	080	all
Other health technologists and technicians	081-085	all
Clergymen	086	all
Social scientists	091-096	all
Social workers	100	all
Recreation workers	101	all
College teachers - natural sciences	102-112	all
College teachers - other than natural sciences	113-140	all
Elementary school teachers	142	all
Prekindergarten and kindergarten teachers	143	all
Secondary school teachers	144	all
Other teachers - except college and university	141,145	all
Chemical technicians	151	all
Draftsmen	152	all

Electrical and electronic engineering technicians	153
Surveyors	161
Other engineering and science technicians	150,154,155,156,162
Air pilots, controllers and flight engineers	165,164,170
Other technicians (except health, engineering and science)	165,171,172,173
Vocational and educational counselors	174
Athletes and kindred workers	180
Designers	183
Editors and reporters	184
Musicians and composers	185
Painters and sculptors	190
Photographers	191
Public relations men and publicity writers	192
Other writers, artists and entertainers	175,181,182,193,194
Research workers, not specified	195
Other professionals	024,026,030,090

MANAGERS AND ADMINISTRATORS, EXCEPT FARM

Assessors, controllers and inspectors - public administration	201,213,215
Bank officers and financial managers	202
Buyers and shippers	203,205
Credit men	210
Funeral directors	211
Health administrators	212
Building managers and superintendents	216
Office managers, n.e.c.	220
Ship officers, pilots and pursers	221
Officials and administrators - public administration, n.e.c.	222
Officials of lodges, societies, and unions	223
Postmasters and mail superintendents	224
Purchasing agents and buyers, n.e.c.	225
Railroad conductors	226
Restaurant, cafeteria, and bar managers	230
Sales managers and department heads, retail trade	231
Sales managers, except retail trade	233
School administrators	235,240
Managers, n.e.c. - general building contractors, construction	245
Managers, n.e.c. - other construction industries	245
Managers, n.e.c. - manufacturing, machinery	245
Managers, n.e.c. - manufacturing, other durable goods	245
Managers, n.e.c. - manufacturing, printing and publishing	245
Managers, n.e.c. - manufacturing, chemicals, petro, rubber	245
Managers, n.e.c. - manufacturing, other nondurable goods	245
Managers, n.e.c. - transportation	245
Managers, n.e.c. - communications and utilities	245
Managers, n.e.c. - wholesale trade	245

	all
	all
	all
	all
	all
	all
	all
	all
	all
	all
	all
	all
	all
	all
	all
	all
	all
	all
	all
	all
	all
	all
	all
	all
	all
	all
	all
	all
	all
	all
	all
	all
	all
	067
	068-077
	177-209
	107-176,210-259
	338-339
	347-387
	268-337,388-398
	407-429
	447-479
	507-588

CAREER LINE CATEGORY	INCLUDED 1970 CENSUS OCCUPATIONS	INCLUDED 1970 CENSUS INDUSTRIES
MANAGERS AND ADMINISTRATORS, EXCEPT FARM--Continued		
Managers, n.e.c. - food, retail	245	628-638
Managers, n.e.c. - general merchandise, retail	245	607-627
Managers, n.e.c. - motor vehicles, retail	245	639-647,649
Managers, n.e.c. - gas stations, retail	245	648
Managers, n.e.c. - apparel and shoe stores	245	657,658
Managers, n.e.c. - other retail	245	659-698
Managers, n.e.c. - finance, insurance and real estate	245	707-718
Managers, n.e.c. - business and repair services	245	727-759
Managers, n.e.c. - personal services	245	769-798
Managers, n.e.c. - other industries	245	017-066,799-999
SALES WORKERS		
Advertising agents and salesmen	260	all
Demonstrators, auctioneers, hucksters, and peddlers	261,262,264	all
Insurance agents, brokers, and underwriters	265	all
Newsboys	266	all
Real estate agents and brokers	270	all
Stock and bond salesmen	271	all
Sales representative - manufacturing, durables	280-285	107-259
Sales representative - manufacturing, nondurables	280-285	268-398
Sales representative - wholesale: food products	280-285	527
Sales representative - wholesale: machinery equip	280-285	539
Sales representative - wholesale: other industries	280-285	017-058,507-509,528-538, 557-599
Sales clerks - retail: lumber and hardware	280-285	607-608
Sales clerks - retail: dept and mail order stores	280-285	609
Sales clerks - retail: grocery stores	280-285	628
Salesmen - retail: motor vehicles	280-285	639
Salesmen - retail: furn and appliances	280-285	667,668
Sales clerks - retail: apparel excluding shoe	280-285	657
Sales clerks - retail: drug stores	280-285	677
Salesmen and sales clerks - other retail trade	280-285	617-627,629-638,647-649,658, 669,678-699
Salesmen of services and construction	280-285	067-078,407-499,707-747
Salesmen and sales clerks in other industries	280-285	748-999
CLERICAL AND KINDRED WORKERS		
Bank tellers	301	all
Billing clerks	303	all
Bookkeepers - finance, insurance, real estate	305	707-718
Bookkeepers - manufacturing, durable goods	305	107-259

Occupation	Code	Industry
Bookkeepers - manufacturing, nondurables	305	268-398
Bookkeepers - wholesale trade	305	507-588
Bookkeepers - motor vehicles - retail	305	639-649
Bookkeepers - other retail	305	607-638,657-698
Bookkeepers - professional services	305	828-897
Bookkeepers - public administration	305	907-937
Other bookkeepers	305	017-078,407-499,727-827, 947-999
Cashiers	310	all
Clerical supervisors, n.e.c.	312	all
Collectors, bill and account	313	all
Counter clerks, except food	314	all
Dispatchers and starters, vehicle	315	all
Estimators, investigators, enumerators	320,321	all
Expediters and production controllers	323	all
File clerks	325	all
Insurance adjustors, examiners and investigators	326	all
Library attendants and assistants	330	all
Mail carriers, post office	331	all
Mail handlers, except post office	332	all
Bookkeeping and billing machine operators	341	all
Computer and peripheral equipment operators	343	all
Key punch operators	345	all
Other office machine operators	342,344,350,355	all
Payroll and timekeeping clerks	360	all
Postal clerks	361	all
Receptionists	364	all
Secretaries, legal	370	all
Secretaries, medical	371	all
Secretaries, n.e.c. - elementary and secondary schools	372	857
Secretaries, n.e.c. - colleges and universities	372	858
Secretaries, n.e.c. - health industries	372	828-848
Secretaries, n.e.c. - religious and nonprofit organizations	372	877,887
Secretaries, n.e.c. - other professional service organizations	372	849,859-869,878,879,888-897
Secretaries, n.e.c. - manufacturing industries, durables	372	107-267
Secretaries, n.e.c. - manufacturing industries, nondurables	372	268-399
Secretaries, n.e.c. - wholesale and retail trade	372	507-699
Secretaries, n.e.c. - insurance firms	372	717
Secretaries, n.e.c. - financial and real estate firms	372	707-709,718
Secretaries, n.e.c. - public administration	372	907-937
Secretaries, n.e.c. - other industries	372	017-078,407-499,727-817, 947-999
Shipping and receiving clerks - manufacturing	374	107-398
Shipping and receiving clerks - except manufacturing industries	374	017-106,407-999
Statistical clerks	375	all
Stenographers	376	all
Stock clerks and storekeepers - manufacturing	381	107-398
Stock clerks and storekeepers - except manufacturing industries	381	017-106,407-999
Telephone and telegraph operators	384,385	all
Ticket, station and express agents	390	all
Typists - banking, insurance, real estate	391	707-718
Typists - professional and related organizations	391	828-897
Typists - local, state and federal government	391	907-937

CAREER LINE CATEGORY	INCLUDED 1970 CENSUS OCCUPATIONS	INCLUDED 1970 CENSUS INDUSTRIES
CLERICAL AND KINDRED WORKERS--Continued		
Typists - other industries	391	017-706,719-827,938-999
Other clerical workers - manufacturing, durables	311,333,334,362,363,382,383,392-395	107-259
Other clerical workers - manufacturing, nondurables	311,333,334,362,363,382,383,392-395	268-398
Other clerical workers - transportation	311,333,334,362,363,382,383,392-395	407-479
Other clerical workers - wholesale and retail trade	311,333,334,362,363,382,383,392-395	507-698
Other clerical workers - finance industries	311,333,334,362,363,382,383,392-395	707-718
Other clerical workers - professional services	311,333,334,362,363,382,383,392-395	828-897
Other clerical workers - local, state and federal government	311,333,334,362,363,382,383,392-395	907-937
Other clerical workers - other industries	311,333,334,362,363,382,383,392-395	017-078,727-827,938-999
CRAFTSMEN AND KINDRED WORKERS		
Bakers	402	all
Blacksmiths, forgemen, heat treaters	403,442,446	all
Brickmasons and stonemasons	410,411	all
Bulldozer operators	412	all
Cabinetmakers and furniture finishers	413,443	all
Carpenters - general building contractors	415,416	067
Carpenters - special trade contractors	415,416	069
Carpenters - other construction industries	415,416	068,077
Carpenters - other nonconstruction industries	415,416	017-066,078-999
Carpet and floor installers	420,440	all
Cement and concrete finishers	421	all
Compositors and typesetters	422,423	all
Cranemen, derrickmen, and hoistmen	424	all
Decorators and window dressers	425	all
Electricians - special trade contractors	430,431	069
Electricians - except special trade contractors	430,431	017-068,070-999
Electric power linemen and cablemen	435	all
Excavating, grading and road machine operators; exc. bulldozer	436	all
Foremen, n.e.c. - construction	441	067-077
Foremen, n.e.c. - manufacturing, metals	441	139-169
Foremen, n.e.c. - manufacturing, machinery	441	177-209
Foremen, n.e.c. - manufacturing, transportation equipment	441	219-238
Foremen, n.e.c. - manufacturing, textiles and apparel	441	307-327
Foremen, n.e.c. - chemicals, petro and rubber	441	347-387
Foremen, n.e.c. - other manufacturing	441	107-138,239-299,328-339,388-398
Foremen, n.e.c. - transportation, communications, and utilities	441	407-479

Appendix A

Occupation	Occ. code	Industry code
(fragment — top of page)		507-698
Foremen, n.e.c. - other industries	441	017-057,707-999
Inspectors, scalers and graders; log and lumber, n.e.c. other	450,452	all
Jewelers and watchmakers	453	all
Job and die setters, metal	454	all
Locomotive firemen and engineers	455,456	177-209
Machinists - manufacturing, machinery	461,462	107-169,210-259
Machinists - manufacturing, durables (except machinery)	461,462	017-106,260-999
Machinists - other industries	461,462	all
Air conditioning, heating and refrigeration repairmen	470	all
Aircraft mechanics and repairmen	471	all
Automobile body repairmen	472	all
Automobile mechanics - motor vehicle dealers	473,474	639
Automobile mechanics - gas stations	473,474	648
Automobile mechanics - auto repair services	473,474	757
Automobile mechanics - other industries	473,474	017-638,640-647,649-756,758-999
Other mechanics and repairmen	475,480,483,484,491-495	all
Heavy equipment mechanics, including diesel - manufacturing	481	107-399
Heavy equipment mechanics - other industries (exc. manufacturing)	481	017-106,400-999
Household appliance and accessory installers and mechanics	482	all
Radio and television mechanics	485	all
Railroad and car shop mechanics	486	all
Millwrights	502	all
Molders, metal	503,504,514	all
Painters - special trade contractors	510,511	069
Painters - except special trade contractors	510,511	017-068,070-999
Plasterers and paperhangers	512,520,521	all
Pattern and model makers, excluding paper	514	all
Plumbers - special trade contractors	522,523	069
Plumbers - except special trade contractors	522,523	017-068,070-999
Pressmen and plate printers	530,551	all
Roofers and slaters	534	all
Sheetmetal workers and tinsmiths	535,536	all
Stationary engineers	545	all
Structural metal craftsmen	550	all
Tailors	551	all
Telephone installers and repairmen	552	all
Telephone linemen and splicers	554	all
Upholsterers	561,562	all
Other craft workers - manufacturing industries	563, 401,404,405,426,434,435,444,445,501,505,506,515,516,525,533,540-543,546,560,571-575	107-399
Other craft workers - other industries	401,404,405,426,434,435,444,445,501,505,506,515,516,525,533,540-543,546,560,571-575	017-106,400-999

CAREER LINE CATEGORY	INCLUDED 1970 CENSUS OCCUPATIONS	INCLUDED 1970 CENSUS INDUSTRIES
OPERATIVES, EXCEPT TRANSPORT		
Assemblers - manufacturing, metals and nonelectric machinery	602	139-198
Assemblers - electrical machinery and equipment	602	199-209
Assemblers - transportation equipment	602	219-238
Assemblers - other industries	602	017-138,239-999
Bottling and canning operatives	604	all
Checkers and inspectors - electrical and transportation equipment	610	199-238
Checkers and inspectors - manufacturing, other durables	610	107-198,239-267
Checkers and inspectors - manufacturing, nondurables	610	268-398
Clothing ironers and pressers	611	all
Cutting operatives, n.e.c.	612	all
Dressmakers and seamstresses, except factory	613	all
Drillers, earth	614	all
Dry wall installers and lathers	615	all
Filers, polishers, sanders and buffers	621	all
Furnacemen, smeltermen, and pourers	622	all
Garage workers and gas station attendants	623	all
Graders and sorters	624,625	all
Laundry and dry cleaning operatives, n.e.c.	630	all
Meat cutters and butchers - manufacturing	633	all
Meat cutters and butchers - except manufacturing	631	all
Mine operatives, n.e.c.	640	all
Mixing operatives	641	all
Packers and wrappers, exc. meat and produce - nondurable goods	643	268-397
Packers and wrappers, exc. meat and produce - other industries	643	017-267,398-999
Painters, manufactured articles	644	all
Photographic process workers	645	all
Drill press operatives	650	all
Grinding machine operatives	651	all
Lathe and milling machine operatives	652	all
Precision machine operatives, n.e.c.	653	all
Punch and stamping press operatives	656	all
Sawyers	662	319
Sewers and stitchers - apparel and accessories	663	017-318,320-999
Sewers and stitchers - except apparel and accessories	663	all
Shoemaking machine operatives	664	all
Stationary firemen	666	all
Knitters, loopers and toppers	671	all
Spinners, twisters and winders	672	all
Weavers	673	all
Textile operatives other	670,674	all
Welders and flame-cutters - manufacturing	680	107-399
Welders and flame-cutters - except manufacturing industries	680	017-106,400-999
Winding operatives, n.e.c.	681	all
Other operatives - construction	601,603,605,620,626, 634-636,642,660,661, 665,690,692,694,695	067-077
Other operatives - lumber and wood products	601,603,605,620,626,	

...665,690,692,694,695,
601,603,605,620,626,
634-636,642,660,661,
665,690,692,694,695   107-118

Category	Codes	Page range
Other operatives - stone, clay and glass products	601,603,605,620,626, 634-636,642,660,661, 665,690,692,694,695	119-138
Other operatives - primary iron and steel industries	601,603,605,620,626, 634-636,642,660,661, 665,690,692,694,695	139-147
Other operatives - other metal industries	601,603,605,620,626, 634-636,642,660,661, 665,690,692,694,695	148-169
Other operatives - electrical machinery	601,603,605,620,626, 634-636,642,660,661, 665,690,692,694,695	199-209
Other operatives - nonelectrical machinery	601,603,605,620,626, 634-636,642,660,661, 665,690,692,694,695	177-198
Other operatives - transportation equipment	601,603,605,620,626, 634-636,642,660,661, 665,690,692,694,695	219-238
Other operatives - other durable goods	601,603,605,620,626, 634-636,642,660,661, 665,690,692,694,695	239-259
Other operatives - food industries	601,603,605,620,626, 634-636,642,660,661, 665,690,692,694,695	268-298
Other operatives - apparel	601,603,605,620,626, 634-636,642,660,661, 665,690,692,694,695	319-327
Other operatives - paper products	601,603,605,620,626, 634-636,642,660,661, 665,690,692,694,695	328-337
Other operatives - printing and publishing	601,603,605,620,626, 634-636,642,660,661, 665,690,692,694,695	338-339
Other operatives - chemicals	601,603,605,620,626, 634-636,642,660,661, 665,690,692,694,695	347-369
Other operatives - petroleum products	601,603,605,620,626, 634-636,642,660,661, 665,690,692,694,695	377-387
Other operatives - other nondurable goods	601,603,605,620,626, 634-636,642,660,661, 665,690,692,694,695	299,307-318,388-399
Other operatives - wholesale and retail trade	601,603,605,620,626, 634-636,642,660,661, 665,690,692,694,695	507-699
Other operatives - other industries	601,603,605,620,626, 634-636,642,660,661, 665,690,692,694,695	017-058,407-499,707-999

CAREER LINE CATEGORY	INCLUDED 1970 CENSUS OCCUPATIONS	INCLUDED 1970 CENSUS INDUSTRIES
TRANSPORT EQUIPMENT OPERATIVES		
Bus drivers, urban rail transit conductors and motormen	703,704	all
Deliverymen and routemen - wholesale and retail trade	705	507-699
Deliverymen and routemen - except wholesale and retail trade industries	705	017-506,700-999
Fork lift and tow motor operatives	706	all
Railroad brake and switchmen	712,713	all
Taxicab drivers and chauffeurs	714	all
Truck drivers - construction	715	067-078
Truck drivers - manufacturing industries	715	107-399
Truck drivers - other transportation, communications, & utilities	715	407-416, 418-499
Truck drivers - wholesale trade	715	507-599
Truck drivers - retail trade industries	715	607-699
Truck drivers - trucking services	715	417
Truck drivers - other industries	715	017-066,079-106,707-999
Transport equipment operatives	701,710,711	all
LABORERS, EXCEPT FARM		
Construction laborers - general bldg. & special trade contractors	750,751	067,069
Construction laborers - general contractors excluding building	750,751	068
Construction laborers - other industries	750,751	017-066,070-999
Freight and material handlers	753	all
Garbage collectors	754	all
Gardeners and groundskeepers, excluding farm	755	all
Longshoremen, stevedores and teamsters	760,763	all
Lumbermen, raftsmen, and woodchoppers	761	all
Stock handlers - grocery stores	762	628
Stock handlers - except grocery stores	762	017-627,629-999
Vehicle washers and equipment cleaners	764	all
Warehousemen, n.e.c.	770	all
Other laborers - manufacturing durables	740,752,780,785	107-259
Other laborers - manufacturing nondurables	740,752,780,785	268-399
Other laborers - transportation	740,752,780,785	407-429
Other laborers - other industries	740,752,780,785	017-106,447-999
FARMERS, FARM MANAGERS, FARM LABORERS, AND FARM FOREMAN		
Farmers (owners and tenants)	801	all
Farm managers and foremen	802,821	all
Farm laborers, wage workers	822	all
Self-employed farm service laborers and unpaid farm workers	823,824	all
SERVICE WORKERS, EXCEPT PRIVATE HOUSEHOLD		
Chambermaids and maids, except private household	901	all

Janitors – elementary and secondary schools	902	all
Janitors – manufacturing firms	903	857
Janitors – public administration	903	107-399
Janitors – other industries	903	907-937
	903	017-106,400-856,858-906, 938-999
Bartenders	910	all
Busboys	911	all
Cooks – eating and drinking places	912	669
Cooks – elementary and secondary schools	912	857
Cooks – other industries	912	017-668,670-856,858-999
Dishwashers	913	all
Food counter and fountain workers	914	all
Waiters – eating and drinking places	915	669
Waiters – other industries	915	017-668,670-999
Food service workers, n.e.c., excluding private household	916	all
Dental assistants	921	all
Nursing aides, orderlies, and attendants – except hospitals	925	017-837,839-999
Nursing aides, orderlies, and attendants – hospitals	925	838
Practical nurses	926	all
Other health service workers	922,923,924	all
Airline stewardesses	931	all
Attendants and ushers, recreation and amusement	932,953	all
Attendants, personal service other	933,934,945	all
Barbers	935	all
Child care workers, excluding private household	942	all
Hairdressers and cosmetologists	944	all
Housekeepers, excluding private household	950	all
Other personal service workers	940,941,943,952,954	all
Firemen, fire protection	961	all
Guards and watchmen	962	all
Policemen and detectives	964	all
Other protective service workers	960,963,965	all

PRIVATE HOUSEHOLD WORKERS

Child care workers, private household	980	all
Cooks, housekeepers, and laundresses – private household	981,982,983	all
Maids and servants, private household	984	all

Appendix B:
1966 Student
Questionnaire
(Form A)

WASHINGTON STATE UNIVERSITY
DEPARTMENT OF EDUCATION

Dear Student:

Washington State University is making a scientific study of the factors that influence the educational and occupational desires and plans of high school juniors and seniors in the State of Washington.

We are going to ask about 4,000 students in schools all over the state to fill out this questionnaire. The information you and other students provide will help teachers and school officials plan educational programs that meet the needs of students. This information will also provide answers to scientific questions.

Previous research has shown that students with similar scholastic ability may have very different educational plans. There may be several reasons for this. These include family background, the attitudes of friends, personal experiences in the classroom, other school related activities, and encouragement from teachers, counselors, or others. We hope to be able to determine the importance of each of these things on the basis of answers to the questions in this questionnaire.

Names and addresses are desired so that research workers can contact some students later to ask additional questions which have a bearing on educational and occupational plans. Special precautions have been set up to insure that your replies will be kept confidential and not revealed to anyone. After you write your name and address on the card which is attached to the front of the questionnaire, remove this card and send it to the front of the room. All name cards will be placed in an envelope which will be sealed immediately. It will not be opened until it is delivered to Washington State University.

WORK RAPIDLY. DO NOT MULL OVER ANY QUESTION. If you are not sure about the meaning of a question just answer it in keeping with your general impression of what the question means. If you are not sure what answer is best, give the one that is closest to your own feelings or opinion and move on. Your first impressions are generally the best. Do not change your answer unless you feel it is absolutely necessary. Work as rapidly as you can without feeling rushed.

You are not required to answer this questionnaire or any question in it if you do not wish to do so. Participation is entirely voluntary. However, we hope that you will decide to cooperate by answering the questions frankly and honestly.

Thank you very much.

135

December 1965
Form A

DEPARTMENT OF EDUCATION

WASHINGTON STATE UNIVERSITY

EDUCATIONAL AND OCCUPATIONAL PLANS OF HIGH SCHOOL STUDENTS

01

1. Sex
___ (1) Boy
___ (2) Girl

2. What grade are you in?
___ (1) 11th
___ (2) 12th

3. How old are you at your nearest birthday?
___ (1) 14 or younger
___ (2) 15
___ (3) 16
___ (4) 17
___ (5) 18
___ (6) 19 or older

4. Where do you live?
___ (1) City (2,500 or more)
___ (2) Town (under 2,500)
___ (3) On a farm
___ (4) Country, but not farm

5. What is your race? (optional)
___ (1) White
___ (2) Negro
___ (3) Oriental
___ (4) American Indian
___ (5) Other (what?)

6. How much thought have you given to your future educational needs and plans?
___ (1) None at all
___ (2) Very little
___ (3) Some
___ (4) A great deal

7. Mark the boxes at the left of the phrases that best describe your desires for future education. (Check all that apply.)
___ (1) Quit high school and not go to any kind of school again
___ (2) Graduate from high school
___ (3) Attend a business or commercial school (not college level)
___ (4) Attend a technical or vocational school (not college level)
___ (5) Attend a junior college - take a business or commercial course
___ (6) Attend a junior college - take a vocational or technical course
___ (7) Attend a junior college - take a regular college course
___ (8) Attend a college or university
___ (9) Graduate from a college or university
___ (10) After graduating from college spend one or more years doing advanced study in a specialized field
___ (11) Other (what?)

8. How certain are you that this is what you want to do about further education?
___ (1) Very sure
___ (2) Fairly sure
___ (3) Not at all sure

2

9. Mark the blanks at the left of the phrases which best describe that education you think you will **actually be able to get**. (Check all that apply.)
___ (1) Quit high school and not go to any kind of school again
___ (2) Graduate from high school
___ (3) Attend a business or commercial school (not college level)
___ (4) Attend a technical or vocational school (not college level)
___ (5) Attend a junior college - take a business or commercial course
___ (6) Attend a junior college - take a vocational or technical course
___ (7) Attend a junior college - take a regular college course
___ (8) Attend a college or university
___ (9) Graduate from a college or university
___ (10) After graduating from college spend one or more years doing advanced study in a specialized field
___ (11) Other (what?)

10. How sure are you that you will actually get the highest level of education you marked in question 9?
___ (1) Very sure
___ (2) Fairly sure
___ (3) Not at all sure

11. If you plan to get further education after high school, please name the school or schools you plan to attend. (Examples: Eastern Washington State College, Renton Vocational School, Spokane Beauty College.)

11a. What subject do you plan to major in?

12. Since completing the eighth grade, how many semesters will you have studied each of the following subjects by the end of high school? Circle the appropriate number.

(1) Agriculture   0 1 2 3 ++   (8) History   0 1 2 3 ++
(2) Art and music   0 1 2 3 ++   (9) Home economics   0 1 2 3 ++
(3) Biology   0 1 2 3 ++   (10) Mathematics   0 1 2 3 ++
(4) Business   0 1 2 3 ++   (11) Physical ed.   0 1 2 3 ++
(5) Chemistry   0 1 2 3 ++   (12) Physics   0 1 2 3 ++
(6) English   0 1 2 3 ++   (13) Shop   0 1 2 3 ++
(7) Foreign language   0 1 2 3 ++   (14) Social studies   0 1 2 3 ++

13. What school subjects do you like best? More than one can be marked.
___ (1) Agriculture   ___ (10) History
___ (2) Art and music   ___ (11) Home economics
___ (3) Algebra   ___ (12) Physical education
___ (4) Biology   ___ (13) Physics
___ (5) Business   ___ (14) Shop
___ (6) Chemistry   ___ (15) Social studies
___ (7) English   ___ (16) Trigonometry
___ (8) Foreign language   ___ (17) I don't like any of them
___ (9) Geometry   ___ (18) Other (what?)

14. What types of vocational training do you think should be available in your high school? Mark the types already available if you think they are important. More than one can be marked.

___ (1) Agriculture
___ (2) Home economics
___ (3) Business training
___ (4) Industrial arts
___ (5) Training in skilled trades - for example, electronics, carpentry and mechanics
___ (6) Training in trades for girls - for example, hair dressing and practical nursing
___ (7) A course in careers so that I would know what job to choose
___ (8) Vocational counseling to help me decide what job to choose
___ (9) None, school should concentrate on academic subjects
___ (10) Something else (what?)

15. How much of your school work are you interested in?

___ (1) All
___ (2) Most
___ (3) Some
___ (4) Little
___ (5) None

16. Circle a number to show how you feel about each of the statements below.

	(1) Agree	(2) Neither agree nor disagree	(3) Disagree	
(a)	1	2	3	I like school very much.
(b)	1	2	3	Most of my teachers are very helpful.
(c)	1	2	3	I often find myself watching the clock because my classes are so boring.
(d)	1	2	3	Lunch time is the most enjoyable time of the day.
(e)	1	2	3	School is difficult for me.
(f)	1	2	3	My teachers are the most helpful to the very good students.
(g)	1	2	3	The most important thing one gets out of high school is the diploma.
(h)	1	2	3	In my free time I would rather read than go to a movie.
(i)	1	2	3	In the evening I often find myself watching TV instead of doing my homework.
(j)	1	2	3	Education is important in preparing for a job.
(k)	1	2	3	High school seems to be little more than "serving time" until I can get out and go to work.
(l)	1	2	3	I appreciate the opportunity education gives me to learn more and broaden myself.

02

17. On your last report card did you get mostly: (Mark only one)

___ (1) A's
___ (2) A's and B's
___ (3) B's
___ (4) B's and C's
___ (5) C's
___ (6) C's and D's
___ (7) D's
___ (8) D's and F's

18. In which of the following organized activities do you participate? Circle a number to show how active you are in each.

	(1) Don't participate	(2) Not very active	(3) Quite active	(4) Very active	
(a)	1	2	3	4	Athletics
(b)	1	2	3	4	Music
(c)	1	2	3	4	Dramatics
(d)	1	2	3	4	Debate
(e)	1	2	3	4	School paper or annual
(f)	1	2	3	4	FFA or FHA
(g)	1	2	3	4	Hobby clubs
(h)	1	2	3	4	Pep club or pep rallies
(i)	1	2	3	4	Church youth groups
(j)	1	2	3	4	Hi-Y or Tri-Hi-Y
(k)	1	2	3	4	Others
(l)	1	2	3	4	_____
(m)	1	2	3	4	_____
(n)	1	2	3	4	_____
(o)	1	2	3	4	_____

19. How many high office positions (president, vice president, captain) have you held in the organized activities that you marked in the question above? _____

20. Are there any activities you would like to take part in that you aren't now participating in? Mark all that apply.

___ (1) Music
___ (2) Athletics
___ (3) Dramatics
___ (4) Debate
___ (5) School paper or annual
___ (6) Student government
___ (7) Church youth groups
___ (8) Hi-Y or Tri-Hi-Y
___ (9) FFA or FHA
___ (10) Hobby club
___ (11) Pep rallies or pep club
___ (12) None of these

21. On the following terms compare yourself to the rest of your classmates. Circle a number to show how you think your ability to do the things listed compares to the ability of your classmates.

	(1) Very much below average	(2) Somewhat below average	(3) About average	(4) Somewhat above average	(5) Very much above average	
(a)	1	2	3	4	5	Read and understand textbooks and other material assigned by teachers.
(b)	1	2	3	4	5	Memorize and remember facts and figures.
(c)	1	2	3	4	5	Write term papers, book reviews and short reports.

5

	(1) Very much below average	(2) Somewhat below average	(3) About average	(4) Somewhat above average	(5) Very much above average	
(d)	1	2	3	4	5	Study and prepare for tests.
(e)	1	2	3	4	5	Use encyclopedias, dictionaries, and other types of reference.
(f)	1	2	3	4	5	Understand and use new materials presented in class such as: a theory in science, formula in math, the cause of a historical event.
(g)	1	2	3	4	5	Take good notes from lectures or out of class reading.
(h)	1	2	3	4	5	Recite in class; give oral reports, participate in class discussion.
(i)	1	2	3	4	5	Get along with most teachers.

22. On the scale below please circle the number which best represents the way you feel about yourself.

EXAMPLES: I feel that I am slightly heavy, therefore, in the first sample (S-1) I circled the number "4" on the heavy side of the scale. In the next sample (S-2) I feel that I am very healthy; therefore, I circled the number "1" on the healthy side of the scale.

EXAMPLES:

	Very	Slightly	Neutral	Slightly	Very	
S-1	light	1	2	3	(4)	5	heavy
S-2	healthy	(1)	2	3	4	5	unhealthy

	Very	Slightly	Neutral	Slightly	Very	
intellectual	1	2	3	4	5	not intellectual
fast	1	2	3	4	5	slow
successful	1	2	3	4	5	unsuccessful
sharp	1	2	3	4	5	dull
alert	1	2	3	4	5	not alert

`03`

23. GIRLS ONLY.
Which of the following statements best describes what you think your interests and desires will be for most of your adult life? (Mark only one.)

_____ (1) Homemaking will be my major interest; I will not want to work at all after I am married.
_____ (2) Homemaking will be my major interest, but I will want to work occasionally or part time.
_____ (3) Homemaking will be my major interest, but I also want to work most of the time.
_____ (4) Work will be my major interest, but I will also want to have a family and be a homemaker.
_____ (5) Work will be my major interest. I will not want to spend much effort in homemaking.

6

24. Please circle a number to show whether or not each of the statements in this list agrees with your ideas of work.

	(1) Strongly agree	(2) Agree	(3) Neither agree nor disagree	(4) Disagree	(5) Strongly disagree	
(a)	1	2	3	4	5	Everyone who possibly can should work.
(b)	1	2	3	4	5	Even if I were financially secure and did not need a job I would probably work.
(c)	1	2	3	4	5	It is a person's duty to work.
(d)	1	2	3	4	5	If I did not work I would feel that I was not leading a "right life."
(e)	1	2	3	4	5	I find it hard to respect a man who doesn't work.
(f)	1	2	3	4	5	If I were financially well off, I think I could lead a perfectly happy and satisfying life without working.
(g)	1	2	3	4	5	A person who has never worked has missed a valuable experience.
(h)	1	2	3	4	5	If a person can live the way he wants to without working there is no reason for him to work.

GIRLS ONLY:

(i)	1	2	3	4	5	If I were married I would want my husband to do some kind of work even if he were financially secure and did not need a job.

25. Which of the following statements best describes the things you think you must do in order to prepare yourself for the kind of work you think you want to do?

_____ (1) I have never thought much about what I should do.
_____ (2) I must decide on a specific occupation and prepare myself for it.
_____ (3) I will develop abilities or skills useful in a number of different jobs and later make my choice.
_____ (4) I am not going to worry about preparing for a job until I see what type of job I can get.
_____ (5) The type of job I will get doesn't require any special preparation.

26. After finishing your education do you want to live in the community you are living in now?

_____ (1) Yes, definitely
_____ (2) Yes, I would prefer to
_____ (3) I don't care
_____ (4) No, I would rather leave
_____ (5) No, I definitely want to leave

27. Considering the kind of job and way of life you eventually wish to have, do you think it will be necessary for you to move from your present community?

_____ (1) No
_____ (2) I don't know
_____ (3) Yes

7

28. What kind of occupation would you most like to have as your career _if you could do whatever you chose?_ (Please be as specific as you can.)

_____

29. How sure are you that this is the occupation you really would want as your life's work?

____ (1) Very sure
____ (2) Fairly sure
____ (3) Not at all sure

30. For the occupation mentioned in question 28, the one you would most like as your life's work, do you think your abilities are:

____ (1) Very much above average
____ (2) Above average
____ (3) Just average
____ (4) Below average
____ (5) Very much below average
____ (6) I don't know yet because I have not yet made a choice

31. If an opportunity occurred to work in the occupation you listed in question 28, would you be willing to complete the training and education necessary to get the job?

____ (1) Yes
____ (2) No
____ (3) No occupation listed

32. What do you think are the possibilities that you might actually work at the occupation you listed in question 28?

____ (1) Very probable
____ (2) Quite probable
____ (3) Chances are 50-50
____ (4) Unlikely
____ (5) None at all

33. What would be your father's (or stepfather's) attitude be if you told him you were going to choose the occupation you listed in question 28 as your life's work?

____ (1) Very favorable
____ (2) Favorable
____ (3) Indifferent
____ (4) Unfavorable
____ (5) Very unfavorable
____ (6) I don't know
____ (7) Does not apply

34. What would your mother's (or stepmother's) attitude be if you told her you were going to choose the occupation you listed in question 28 as your life's work?

____ (1) Very favorable
____ (2) Favorable
____ (3) Indifferent
____ (4) Unfavorable
____ (5) Very unfavorable
____ (6) I don't know
____ (7) Does not apply

8

35. How much education do you think you would need to qualify for the occupation that you think you would really like to be in? (the one mentioned in question 28).

____ (1) Don't know
____ (2) I have enough now
____ (3) High school graduate
____ (4) Vocational or technical school
____ (5) Business or commercial school
____ (6) Some college, but not graduate from college
____ (7) Graduate from college
____ (8) Advanced study after graduation from college

36. Name some other occupations you would like almost as much as the occupation you listed in question 28.

a. _____

b. _____

c. _____

37. What occupation do you really expect to have as your life's work? (Please be as specific as you can.)

_____

38. How sure are you that you will actually have the occupation named in question 37 as your life's work?

____ (1) Very sure
____ (2) Fairly sure
____ (3) Not at all sure

38a. GIRLS WHO LISTED HOUSEWIFE OR HOMEMAKER IN QUESTION 37: Do you also expect to have some other job or occupation? If yes, what occupation do you have in mind?

_____

39. For the occupation mentioned in question 37, do you think your abilities are:

____ (1) Very much above average
____ (2) Somewhat above average
____ (3) Just average
____ (4) Somewhat below average
____ (5) Very much below average
____ (6) I don't know yet because I have not yet made a choice

40. How much education do you think you would need to qualify for work in the occupation that you say you expect to have? (the one mentioned in question 37).

____ (1) I don't know
____ (2) I have enough now
____ (3) Vocational or technical school
____ (4) Business or commercial school
____ (5) High school diploma
____ (6) Some college, but not graduate from college
____ (7) College degree
____ (8) Specialized study after graduation from college

This is not the end of the questionnaire. Please turn it around and answer the succeeding pages.

9

41. What would be your father's (or stepfather's) attitude if you told him you were going to choose the occupation you listed in question 37 as your life's work?

  (1) Very favorable
  (2) Favorable
  (3) Indifferent
  (4) Unfavorable
  (5) Very unfavorable
  (6) I don't know
  (7) Does not apply

42. What would be your mother's (or stepmother's) attitude if you told her you were going to choose the occupation you listed in question 37 as your life's work?

  (1) Very favorable
  (2) Favorable
  (3) Indifferent
  (4) Unfavorable
  (5) Very unfavorable
  (6) I don't know
  (7) Does not apply

43. What is the marital status of your mother and father?

  (1) Both alive, living together
  (2) Both alive, separated
  (3) Both alive, divorced
  (4) Father not living
  (5) Mother not living
  (6) Neither father nor mother living

44. Mark all of the following who live in your house at present.

  (1) Father
  (2) Mother
  (3) Stepfather
  (4) Stepmother
  (5) Brothers
  (6) Sisters
  (7) Grandmother
  (8) Grandfather
  (9) Husband
  (10) Wife
  (11) Other relatives
  (12) Persons who are not relatives

45. How many living brothers and sisters do you have?

_____

46. Are you:

  (1) The oldest child in your family
  (2) The youngest child
  (3) In between
  (4) The only child

47. What kind of work does your father (or stepfather) do for a living? What is his job called, what kind of business or industry does he work in, and what does he do? (For example: "Carpenter, works on a construction crew building new houses"; "Sales clerk, waits on customers in a department store"; "Owner and operator of a grocery store.")

48. With what kind of firm or outfit is your father associated in his work?

  (1) Own business
  (2) Own farm
  (3) Own professional office
  (4) Small private firm, organization or factory (50 employees or less)
  (5) Large private firm, organization or factory (over 50 employees)
  (6) Educational institution
  (7) Social agency
  (8) Other non-profit organization (what?) _____
  (9) Government bureau or agency
  (10) Other (what?)
  (11) Don't know

49. Does your mother work outside the home for pay?

  (1) Yes, full time
  (2) Yes, part time
  (3) No

50. In terms of income or wealth in my community, I think my family is

  (1) Considerably above average
  (2) Somewhat above average
  (3) Average
  (4) Somewhat below average
  (5) Considerably below average

04

51. Think for a minute about your family (father, mother, brothers and sisters). Some or maybe all of them have expressed certain attitudes concerning formal education (high school and college). When you look at the following statements, think of the members of your family and respond to the statements on the basis of your knowledge of the attitudes of those members. Mark only one answer for each statement.

	(1) All of them	(2) Most of them	(3) About half of them	(4) Only a few of them	(5) None of them
(a) They feel that formal education tends to take people away from their home community; and because of this it is undesirable.	1	2	3	4	5
(b) They are opposed to formal education beyond high school.	1	2	3	4	5
(c) They expect the younger members of the family to get all the education they can.	1	2	3	4	5
(d) They think formal education is very important.	1	2	3	4	5
(e) They believe that the most important thing in formal education is the diploma or degree.	1	2	3	4	5

52. What is the highest grade completed by your father?

____ (1) Grade school 1-7
____ (2) Grade school 8
____ (3) High school 9-11
____ (4) High school 12
____ (5) College 1-3
____ (6) College 4
____ (7) College 5 or more

53. What is the highest grade completed by your mother?

____ (1) Grade school 1-7
____ (2) Grade school 8
____ (3) High school 9-11
____ (4) High school 12
____ (5) College 1-3
____ (6) College 4
____ (7) College 5 or more

54. In which of the following would your parents be willing and able to help you financially? Mark all that apply.

____ (1) Farming
____ (2) College
____ (3) Vocational schooling
____ (4) Setting up a business of my own
____ (5) None of the above

55. Below is a list of statements dealing with your general feelings about yourself. Please circle a number to indicate your answer to each statement.

	(1) Strongly agree	(2) Agree	(3) Neither agree nor disagree	(4) Disagree	(5) Strongly disagree
(a) I feel that I am a person of worth at least on an equal plane with others.	1	2	3	4	5
(b) I feel that I have a number of good qualities.	1	2	3	4	5
(c) All in all, I am inclined to feel that I am a failure.	1	2	3	4	5
(d) I am able to do things as well as most other people.	1	2	3	4	5
(e) I feel I do not have much to be proud of.	1	2	3	4	5
(f) I take a positive attitude toward myself.	1	2	3	4	5
(g) On the whole, I am satisfied with myself.	1	2	3	4	5
(h) I wish I could have more respect for myself.	1	2	3	4	5
(i) I certainly feel useless at times.	1	2	3	4	5
(j) At times I think I am no good at all.	1	2	3	4	5

56. About how many close friends do you have?

57. When you do things with these friends, do you usually do them together as a group or with only one of them at a time?

____ (1) As a group, usually
____ (2) One at a time, usually
____ (3) Sometimes as a group, sometimes one at a time

58. Did any of your close friends drop out of school before graduating?

____ (1) Yes
____ (2) No

59. If yes, how many?

60. Think for a minute about your close friends. Circle a number in front of each of the statements listed below to show how well you think it describes the feelings of your friends about formal education (high school and college). How many of your close friends feel this way?

	(1) All of them	(2) Most of them	(3) About half of them	(4) Only a few of them	(5) None of them
(a) They feel that formal education tends to take people away from their home communities and because of this it is undesirable.	1	2	3	4	5
(b) They are opposed to formal education beyond high school.	1	2	3	4	5
(c) They feel that a good education helps a person to lead a better life.	1	2	3	4	5
(d) They think that formal education is very important.	1	2	3	4	5
(e) They believe that the most important thing in formal education is the diploma or degree.	1	2	3	4	5
(f) They expect the members of our group to get all of the education they can.	1	2	3	4	5

61. Think for a minute about your close friends. Think about the things they do in school. Mark the following statements according to how well you think they describe your group of friends. (Circle the appropriate number.)

	(1) All of them	(2) Most of them	(3) About half of them	(4) Only a few of them	(5) None of them
(a) They would probably quit school if they could find a way to quit without getting into an unpleasant situation.	1	2	3	4	5
(b) They sometimes get into trouble with teachers and school officials.	1	2	3	4	5
(c) For entertainment during out-of-school hours they generally run around with friends and do whatever seems interesting at the time, rather than go to school sponsored activities such as ball games, plays and dances.	1	2	3	4	5
(d) They enjoy high school.	1	2	3	4	5
(e) They participate in such activities as academic honor societies, science and language clubs, and other scholastic organizations.	1	2	3	4	5
(f) High grades (A's and B's) are important to them.	1	2	3	4	5

13

	(1) All of them	(2) Most of them	(3) About half of them	(4) Only a few of them	(5) None of them
(g) They are planning to go to college.	1	2	3	4	5
(h) They are planning to take vocational training.	1	2	3	4	5
(i) The boys are active in athletics.	1	2	3	4	5
(j) They are leaders in school activities.	1	2	3	4	5
(k) They are from farms.	1	2	3	4	5

62. Please circle a number to indicate the extent to which each of the statements below reflects the attitudes or feelings of the students you know at your school. (Think of all the students you know, not just your close friends.) How many of the students, in your opinion, have the feelings expressed in each of the statements?

	(1) All of them	(2) Most of them	(3) About half of them	(4) Only a few of them	(5) None of them
(a) The high school curriculum should be more directly related to specific jobs.	1	2	3	4	5
(b) Every student should try to go to college. If he can't make it there he can always get an ordinary job.	1	2	3	4	5
(c) There should be more emphasis on vocational and technical courses and less on college preparation.	1	2	3	4	5
(d) Courses like welding and wood working have no place in today's high school	1	2	3	4	5
(e) In modern society the skilled craftsman is as important as the scientist or the professional.	1	2	3	4	5
(f) Students enrolled in vocational or technical courses generally don't have the ability to master college preparatory courses.	1	2	3	4	5
(g) Shop courses are good preparation for the kind of work many students will be doing.	1	2	3	4	5
(h) Business courses like typing and shorthand are as important for girls as are college preparatory courses.	1	2	3	4	5
(i) High school should do more to provide students with skills useful in jobs and should not worry so much about college preparation.	1	2	3	4	5

14

63. Which person expects you to accomplish the most in the future?

(1) Father
(2) Mother
(3) Older brother or sister
(4) A friend in school
(5) A person about my own age (who is not in my school)
(6) A teacher, counselor or principal
(7) An adult other than those listed
(8) No other person

```
05
```

64. Please consider each occupation listed below and on the next page. Check a blank to show how well you think you would like that kind of work. Work quickly. Your first impression is the most valuable. (If you feel that you do not know enough about a particular occupation to make a realistic decision, place a check mark in the blank to the left of that occupation.)

(6)	OCCUPATION	(1) I would like this very much	(2) I would like this fairly well	(3) Indifferent	(4) I would dislike this a little	(5) I would dislike this very much
	Agricultural research scientist					
	Aide in child care center					
	Airline pilot					
	Airline stewardess					
	Automobile salesman					
	Automobile mechanic					
	Banker					
	Bank teller					
	Bookkeeper					
	Carpenter					
	Certified public accountant					
	Cook (restaurant)					
	College professor					
	Commercial artist					
	County agricultural agent					
	Computer programmer					
	Dietician					
	Dentist					
	Electrician					
	Elementary school teacher					
	Engineer					
	Factory manager					
	Farm operator					
	Foreman in factory					
	Home demonstration agent					
	Hair dresser or cosmetologist					
	Hotel-motel clerk					
	Janitor					
	Lawyer					
	Life insurance salesman					

OCCUPATION	(1) I would like this very much	(2) I would like this fairly well	(3) Indifferent	(4) I would dislike this a little	(5) I would dislike this very much
Machine operator in factory					
Maid - motel or hotel					
Manager of department store					
Manager of a loan company					
Mechanical draftsman					
Medical lab technologist					
Minister, priest or rabbi					
Nurse (R. N.)					
Nurse's aide					
Owner and operator of small business					
Physical therapist					
Physician					
Plumber					
Police officer					
Psychologist					
Radio announcer					
Recreational programs supervisor					
Reporter on daily newspaper					
Restaurant host or hostess					
Sales person of farm supplies					
Sales person in retail store					
Secretary					
Social worker					
Tailor or dressmaker					
Taxi driver					
Truck driver					
Veterinarian					
Waiter or waitress					
Warehouse worker					
Welder					
X-ray technician					

ANSWER THE REST OF THE QUESTIONNAIRE ONLY IF YOU HAVE LIVED ON A FARM

65. How many years have you lived on a farm?
(1) Less than one
(2) One to three
(3) Four to seven
(4) Eight to twelve
(5) Thirteen or more

66. If you did live on a farm, when was that?
(1) Sometime between birth and 12 years of age
(2) After 12 years of age
(3) Most of my life
(4) All of my life
(5) Other (what?) _____

67. How do you like farm life?
(1) Like it greatly
(2) Like it
(3) Neutral
(4) Dislike it
(5) Dislike it greatly

68. What is the most important factor in the choice of farming as an occupation? Mark the one factor you consider most important. (Mark only one.)
(1) Farming background
(2) Desire to farm
(3) Availability of an adequate farm
(4) Adequate financing

69. Is there a farm available if you want to go into farming?
(1) Yes
(2) No
(3) I don't know

70. If "yes," where is the farm located?
(1) Present home address
(2) Farm in present locality
(3) Farm in other section of Washington
(4) In a nearby state

71. Does most of your family income come from farm or non-farm employment?
(1) Mostly from farm
(2) Mostly from non-farm

Thank you for your cooperation.

Appendix C:
1966 Student Questionnaire
(Form B)

WASHINGTON STATE UNIVERSITY
DEPARTMENT OF EDUCATION

Dear Student:

Washington State University is making a scientific study of the factors that influence the educational and occupational desires and plans of high school juniors and seniors in the State of Washington.

We are going to ask about 4,000 students in schools all over the state to fill out this questionnaire. The information you and other students provide will help teachers and school officials plan educational programs that meet the needs of students. This information will also provide answers to scientific questions.

Previous research has shown that students with similar scholastic ability may have very different educational plans. There may be several reasons for this. These include family background, the attitudes of friends, personal experiences in the classroom, other school related activities, and encouragement from teachers, counselors, or others. We hope to be able to determine the importance of each of these things on the basis of answers to the questions in this questionnaire.

Names and addresses are desired so that research workers can contact some students later to ask additional questions which have a bearing on educational and occupational plans. Special precautions have been set up to insure that your replies will be kept confidential and not revealed to anyone. After you write your name and address on the card which is attached to the front of the questionnaire, remove this card and send it to the front of the room. All name cards will be placed in an envelope which will be sealed immediately. It will not be opened until it is delivered to Washington State University.

WORK RAPIDLY. DO NOT MULL OVER ANY QUESTION. If you are not sure about the meaning of a question just answer it in keeping with your general impression of what the question means. If you are not sure what answer is best, give the one that is closest to your own feelings or opinion and move on. Your first impressions are generally the best. Do not change your answer unless you feel it is absolutely necessary. Work as rapidly as you can without feeling rushed.

You are not required to answer this questionnaire or any question in it if you do not wish to do so. Participation is entirely voluntary. However, we hope that you will decide to cooperate by answering the questions frankly and honestly.

Thank you very much.

December 1965
Form B

2.

DEPARTMENT OF EDUCATION
WASHINGTON STATE UNIVERSITY

Educational and Occupational Plans
of High School Students

[01]

FIRST, WE WANT TO ASK SOME GENERAL QUESTIONS ABOUT YOU AND YOUR BACKGROUND.

1. Sex

___ (1) Boy
___ (2) Girl

2. What grade are you in?

___ (1) 11th
___ (2) 12th

3. Course of study:

___ (1) General
___ (2) Vocational
___ (3) Academic (including college preparatory)
___ (4) Commercial
___ (5) Other (please specify _____)

4. How old are you at your nearest birthday?

___ (1) 14 or younger
___ (2) 15
___ (3) 16
___ (4) 17
___ (5) 18
___ (6) 19 or older

5. Are you:

___ (1) The oldest child in your family
___ (2) The youngest child
___ (3) In between
___ (4) The only child

6. How many living brothers and sisters do you have?

7. Where do you live?

___ (1) City of 150,000 or larger
___ (2) City of 100,000 to 150,000
___ (3) City of 50,000 to 100,000
___ (4) City of 10,000 to 50,000
___ (5) City of 2,500 to 10,000
___ (6) Town under 2,500
___ (7) On a farm
___ (8) Country but not farm

8. What is your race? (Optional.)

___ (1) White
___ (2) Negro
___ (3) Oriental
___ (4) American Indian
___ (5) Other (what?)

9. What is the marital status of your mother and father?

___ (1) Both alive, living together
___ (2) Both alive, separated
___ (3) Both alive, divorced
___ (4) Father not living
___ (5) Mother not living
___ (6) Neither father nor mother living

Some of the questions that follow ask about your father and mother. If you live with your stepfather or stepmother, substitute "stepfather" for "father" or "stepmother" for "mother."

10. What kind of work does your father do for a living? What is his job called, what kind of business or industry does he work in, and what does he do? (For example: "Carpenter, works on a construction crew building new houses"; "Sales clerk, waits on customers in a department store"; "Owner and operator of a grocery store.")

11. With what kind of firm or outfit is your father associated in his work?

___ (1) Own business
___ (2) Own farm
___ (3) Own professional office
___ (4) Small private firm, organization, or factory (less than 50 employees)
___ (5) Large private firm, organization, or factory (50 employees or more)
___ (6) Educational institution
___ (7) Social Agency
___ (8) Other nonprofit organization (what?)
___ (9) Government bureau or agency
___ (10) Other (what?)

12. How much education did your parents get?

Father   Mother

___ ___ (1) Eighth grade or less
___ ___ (2) Some high school, but did not finish
___ ___ (3) High school graduate
___ ___ (4) Some college, but did not finish
___ ___ (5) College graduate
___ ___ (6) More than four years of college
___ ___ (7) Don't know

13. Did your father attend a vocational or technical school?

___ (1) Yes
___ (2) No
___ (3) I don't know

14. What are the occupations of the fathers of your three closest friends?

(1) _____

(2) _____

(3) _____

15. Approximately how many times did you change schools before you were 16 years of age (other than by graduation)?
   (1) Never
   (2) Once
   (3) Two to four times
   (4) Five to seven times
   (5) More than seven times

16. When you finish your education do you want to live in the community in which you are living now?
   (1) Yes
   (2) No
   (3) Not sure

17. Considering your future occupational plans, would you be able to do what you want to do in the community in which you are now living?
   (1) Yes
   (2) No
   (3) I don't know

18. If you were asked to use one of these names to describe your family's social group, which would you say your family belonged to?
   (1) Upper class
   (2) Upper-middle class
   (3) Middle class
   (4) Lower-middle class
   (5) Working class
   (6) Lower class

19. People in all communities make judgments and evaluations of each other regarding their respective rank in the community. Some people are considered low, others are placed more toward the middle, while others are judged to be toward the top. Place an X in the box to the right that best reflects what you think is your family's general standing in your community. ("1" represents very low standing and "10" represents very high standing.)

10	Above average
9	
8	
7	
6	
5	Average
4	
3	
2	
1	Below average

20. How confident are you that this is where other people in your community would rank your folks?
   (1) Very sure
   (2) Slightly sure
   (3) Not very sure
   (4) Not sure at all

21. Now place an X in the box at the right that best reflects the standing that you hope to achieve in the community in which you live when you become fully established in your own home or occupation. (Again, "1" represents very low standing and "10" represents very high standing.)

10	Above average
9	
8	
7	
6	
5	Average
4	
3	
2	
1	Below average

NOW WE WOULD LIKE TO KNOW SOMETHING ABOUT YOUR EDUCATIONAL PLANS AND DESIRES BEYOND HIGH SCHOOL, AS WELL AS YOUR ATTITUDES AND ACTIVITIES AS THESE RELATE TO HIGH SCHOOL.

22. Mark the boxes at the left of the phrases that best describe what you would like in the way of future education. (Mark all that apply.)
   (1) Quit high school and not go to any kind of school again
   (2) Graduate from high school
   (3) Attend a business or commercial school (not college level)
   (4) Attend a technical or vocational school (not college level)
   (5) Attend a junior college - take a business or commercial course
   (6) Attend a junior college - take a vocational or technical course
   (7) Attend a junior college - take a regular college course
   (8) Attend a college or university
   (9) Graduate from a college or university
   (10) After graduating from college, spend one or more years doing advanced study in a specialized field
   (11) Other (what?) _____

23. How certain are you that this is what you want to do about further education?
   (1) Very sure
   (2) Fairly sure
   (3) Not at all sure

24. Mark the blanks at the left of the phrases which describe the education you think you will actually be able to get. (Mark all that apply.)
   (1) Quit high school and not go to any kind of school again
   (2) Graduate from high school
   (3) Attend a business or commercial school (not college level)
   (4) Attend a technical or vocational school (not college level)
   (5) Attend a junior college - take a business or commercial course
   (6) Attend a junior college - take a vocational or technical course
   (7) Attend a junior college - take a regular college course
   (8) Attend a college or university
   (9) Graduate from a college or university
   (10) After graduating from college, spend one or more years doing advanced study in a specialized field
   (11) Other (what?) _____

5

25. How certain are you that you will actually get the highest level of education you checked in question 24?

(1) Not very certain
(2) Chances are 50-50
(3) Probably will
(4) Practically certain

26. ANSWER ONLY IF YOU ARE NOT PLANNING TO GO TO COLLEGE. Would you go to college if your parents could afford to send you?

(1) Yes
(2) No

27. ANSWER ONLY IF YOU WOULD LIKE TO TAKE VOCATIONAL, TECHNICAL, OR BUSINESS TRAINING, BUT DO NOT PLAN TO: Would you take vocational, technical, or business training if your parents could afford to pay for it?

(1) Yes
(2) No

28. On your last report card did you get mostly: (Check only one.)

(1) A's
(2) A's and B's
(3) B's
(4) B's and C's
(5) C's
(6) C's and D's
(7) D's
(8) D's and F's

29. How many high school activities are you active in and how many organizations do you belong to? (For example: Athletics, Music, Dramatics, Debate, School paper or annual, Student government, FFA or FHA, Hobby clubs, and any other clubs or organizations.)

30. Which of the following best describes your relationship with persons of the opposite sex? (Mark only one.)

(1) Married
(2) Formally engaged
(3) Not formally engaged, but have definite understanding to be married soon
(4) Going steady
(5) Date frequently
(6) Date occasionally
(7) Have some dates, but very few
(8) Do not date

31. GIRLS ONLY. BOYS GO DIRECTLY TO QUESTION 32.
If you are married or expect to get married soon, what occupation does (or will) your husband have?

6

02

HOW DO YOU THINK YOUR CLOSEST FRIEND WOULD RATE YOU IN THE FOLLOWING THINGS?

32. What kind of grades does your closest friend think you are capable of getting?

(1) Mostly A's
(2) Mostly B's
(3) Mostly C's
(4) Mostly D's
(5) Mostly F's

33. How would your closest friend rate you in school ability compared with those in your class at school?

(1) Among the best
(2) Above average
(3) Average
(4) Below average
(5) Among the poorest

34. In order to become a doctor, lawyer, or university professor, work beyond four years of college is necessary. How would your closest friend rank your capability for completing such advanced work?

(1) Very capable
(2) Somewhat capable
(3) Average capability
(4) Incapable
(5) Very incapable

35. Does your closest friend think you have the ability to complete college?

(1) Yes, definitely
(2) Yes, probably
(3) Not sure either way
(4) Probably not
(5) No

36. How do you think your closest friend would grade your work?

(1) Excellent
(2) Good
(3) Average
(4) Below average
(5) Much below average

37. Where do you think your closest friend would rank you in your class in high school?

(1) Among the best
(2) Above average
(3) Average
(4) Below average
(5) Among the poorest

38. How do you think your closest friend would rate you in school ability compared with your other close friends?

(1) The best
(2) Better than most
(3) About the same
(4) Not as good as most
(5) The poorest

39. Where do you think your closest friend would rank you in your class in college (if you actually go)?

(1) Among the best
(2) Above average
(3) Average
(4) Below average
(5) Among the poorest

NOW WE WOULD LIKE TO KNOW SOMETHING ABOUT YOUR JOB-RELATED DESIRES, PLANS AND ATTITUDES.

BOYS ONLY. GIRLS GO TO QUESTION 45.

40. Most students have daydreams about what they would like to be and do when they are adults. What kind of occupation would you most like to have as your career if you could do whatever you chose? (Please be specific)

41. How sure are you that this is the occupation you will actually have?

(1) Very sure
(2) Fairly sure
(3) Not at all sure

42. How sure are you that you know what kind of occupation you really want as a life-long career?

(1) Absolutely certain
(2) Quite certain
(3) Somewhat certain
(4) Very uncertain

43. Now, leaving your daydreams and wishes aside, what occupation do you really plan to have as your career?

(a) I have no definite plans

44. How often do you worry because you are not quite certain what you want in the way of an occupational career?

(1) Almost all the time
(2) Quite often
(3) Sometimes
(4) Seldom
(5) Never

GIRLS ONLY. BOYS GO TO QUESTION 52.

45. Which of the following statements best describes what you think your interests and desires will be for most of your adult life?

(1) Homemaking will be my major interest. I will not want to work at all after I am married.
(2) Homemaking will be my major interest, but I will want to work occasionally or work part time.
(3) Homemaking will be my major interest, but I will also want to work most of the time.
(4) Work will be my major interest but I will also want to have a family and be a homemaker.
(5) Work will be my major interest. I will not want to spend much effort in homemaking.
(6) Work will be my only interest. I will not want to spend much effort in homemaking.

GIRLS ONLY, continued. BOYS GO TO QUESTION 52.

46. If you checked 2, 3, 4, 5, or 6 in question 45, what occupation would you most want to have?

47. Do you actually expect to work after you finish your education?

(1) No
(2) Yes

48. If yes, what kind of job or occupation do you expect to have?

49. Do you agree or disagree with the following statements? Circle the appropriate number.

	(1) Strongly agree	(2) Agree	(3) Neither agree nor disagree	(4) Disagree	(5) Strongly disagree	
(a)	1	2	3	4	5	The abilities of women too often go unrecognized.
(b)	1	2	3	4	5	Women should be allowed to compete on equal terms with men in the occupational world.
(c)	1	2	3	4	5	The place for the adult female is in the home.
(d)	1	2	3	4	5	There would probably be fewer problems in the world if women had as much say-so in running things as men.
(c)	1	2	3	4	5	It is natural for women to have occupational positions which are inferior to those of men.

50. Do you feel that you personally will be prevented from realizing your educational or occupational ambitions because you are a female?

(1) Yes
(2) No

51. How do you personally feel about competing with males in the occupational world?

(1) Would like it very much
(2) Would like it somewhat
(3) Wouldn't make much difference
(4) Wouldn't usually like it
(5) Would never like it

52. Have you worked at all during the past year?

(1) Yes
(2) No

53. If you have worked, was the work that you did related to the kind of work you want as your career?

(1) Yes
(2) No

9

54. If yes, did this work change or influence your vocational preference?

___ (1) Yes
___ (2) No

BOYS ONLY. GIRLS GO TO QUESTION 57.

55. People have different opinions about the importance of a man's job. We would like to know high school students' opinions about this. Please indicate how you feel about the following statements by circling the appropriate number. Although it is possible that you may agree with a statement as it applies to most cases but can think of one or two exceptions, indicate how you feel about the statement as a general rule. Circle the appropriate number for each statement.

	(1) Strongly agree	(2) Agree	(3) Neither agree nor disagree	(4) Disagree	(5) Strongly disagree	
(a)	1	2	3	4	5	The most important thing in a man's life is his occupation.
(b)	1	2	3	4	5	Many times it is more important to have time for recreation than it is to work hard and achieve occupational advancement.
(c)	1	2	3	4	5	A man should always accept an occupational promotion even if this means moving to a strange community away from his close friends.
(d)	1	2	3	4	5	A man who already has a secure job with a modest income is foolish to go back to school even if additional education is necessary before he can expect to have a better job.
(e)	1	2	3	4	5	A man should be willing to give up time with his family and devote it to his job if this will help his occupational advancement.
(f)	1	2	3	4	5	A man should try hard to get farther ahead in the world than his parents.
(g)	1	2	3	4	5	The most important purpose of education is to prepare people for success.

56. When the time comes for you to take a job, would you take a job that required you to move far away from your community and parent?

___ (1) Definitely take the job
___ (2) Probably take the job
___ (3) Probably turn the job down
___ (4) Definitely turn the job down

10

57. BOYS:

Below are several pairs of occupations. The income for the two occupations in each pair is approximately equal. Please consider each pair of occupations and answer the following question: If you had to work in one or the other of these occupations as your life's work, which of the occupations in each pair would you choose? Please circle a number in each pair.

GIRLS:

Below are several pairs of occupations. The income for the two occupations in each pair is approximately equal. Please consider each pair of occupations and answer the following question: If your husband had to work in one or the other of these occupations as his life's work, which one of the occupations in each pair would you most like him to have? (Assume that he would be equally happy working at either job.) Please circle a number in each pair.

(a) 1. Railroad brakeman
     2. Draftsman

(b) 1. Clergyman (minister, priest, rabbi)
     2. Upholsterer

(c) 1. Plumber
     2. Photographer

(d) 1. Radio operator
     2. Locomotive fireman

(e) 1. Long shoreman or stevedore
     2. Bookkeeper

(f) 1. Foreman in a factory
     2. Editor or reporter

(g) 1. High school teacher
     2. Electrician

(h) 1. Tool and die maker
     2. Insurance agent

(i) 1. Cabinet maker
     2. Bank teller

(j) 1. College professor
     2. Locomotive engineer

(k) 1. Bus driver
     2. Manager of a service station

(l) 1. Medical or dental technician
     2. Baker

03

NOW WE WANT TO ASK YOU SOME QUESTIONS ABOUT YOURSELF AND YOUR OPINIONS.

Students have different opinions of their abilities. We would like to know how you evaluate your ability.

58. Where do you think you would rank in your class in high school?

___ (1) Among the best
___ (2) Above average
___ (3) Average
___ (4) Below average
___ (5) Among the poorest

59. Do you find yourself day-dreaming about the type of person you expect to be in the future?

___ (1) Very often
___ (2) Sometimes
___ (3) Rarely or never

60. Do you think you have the ability to complete college?

___ (1) Yes, definitely
___ (2) Yes, probably
___ (3) Not sure either way
___ (4) Probably not
___ (5) No

This is not the end of the questionnaire. Please turn it around and answer the succeeding pages.

11

61. How important to you personally is it to get ahead in life?

___ (1) Very important
___ (2) Fairly important
___ (3) Not very important
___ (4) Very unimportant

62. How do you rate yourself in school ability compared with those in your class at school?

___ (1) I am among the best
___ (2) I am above average
___ (3) I am average
___ (4) I am below average
___ (5) I am among the poorest

63. How much does it bother you to find that someone has a poor opinion of your intellectual abilities?

___ (1) Bothers me very much
___ (2) Bothers me somewhat
___ (3) Bothers me a little

64. Forget for a moment how others grade your work. In your own opinion how good do you think your work is?

___ (1) My work is excellent
___ (2) My work is good
___ (3) My work is average
___ (4) My work is below average
___ (5) My work is much below average

65. What kind of grades do you think you are capable of getting?

___ (1) Mostly A's
___ (2) Mostly B's
___ (3) Mostly C's
___ (4) Mostly D's
___ (5) Mostly F's

66. In order to become a doctor, lawyer, or university professor, work beyond four years of college is necessary. How capable do you think you are of completing such advanced work?

___ (1) Very capable
___ (2) Somewhat capable
___ (3) Not sure if you are capable
___ (4) Incapable
___ (5) Very incapable

67. Where do you think you would rank in your class in college (if you actually go)?

___ (1) Among the best
___ (2) Above average
___ (3) Average
___ (4) Below average
___ (5) Among the poorest

68. How do you rate yourself in school ability compared with your close friends?

___ (1) I am the best
___ (2) I am better than most
___ (3) I am about the same
___ (4) I am not as good as most
___ (5) I am the poorest

12

All high school students have ambitions and plans for life beyond high school. Your future occupational career and additional education are often included in these ambitions. There are people who say, however, that some students have more opportunities to realize their ambitions than others. How do you feel about the following statements?

69. Do you think you will be kept from achieving your educational or occupational desires because of your race?

___ (1) Yes
___ (2) No
___ (3) Uncertain

70. Do you think you will be kept from achieving your educational or occupational desires because of your family background?

___ (1) Yes
___ (2) No
___ (3) Uncertain

71. Do you think you will be kept from achieving your educational or occupational desires because of your parents' insufficient income?

___ (1) Yes
___ (2) No
___ (3) Uncertain

72. Do you think you will be kept from achieving your educational or occupational desires because of your religion?

___ (1) Yes
___ (2) No
___ (3) Uncertain

73. Studies show that adults in different occupations respond differently to most of the following statements and we would like to know if students with different educational and occupational plans also respond differently. Please indicate whether you agree or disagree with the following statements by circling the appropriate number. Although you may not completely agree or disagree with a statement, give the answer that comes closest to your own feelings.

	(1) Agree	(2) Disagree
(a) Most public officials are not really interested in the problems of the average man.	1	2
(b) Teenagers should not be permitted to drive.	1	2
(c) These days a person doesn't know whom he can count on.	1	2
(d) Anyone who has the ability should have the opportunity to get a college education.	1	2
(e) Nowadays a person has to live pretty much for today and let tomorrow take care of itself.	1	2
(f) Everyone can be trusted.	1	2
(g) In spite of what some people say, the lot of the average man is getting worse, not better.	1	2
(h) Individuals have more freedom under a democracy than under a dictatorship.	1	2
(i) Most people don't really care what happens to the next fellow.	1	2

13

74. Do you agree or disagree with the following statements? Please circle the appropriate number.

	(1) Strongly agree	(2) Agree	(3) Slightly agree	(4) Slightly disagree	(5) Disagree	(6) Strongly disagree	
(a)	1	2	3	4	5	6	I wish my father (or mother) had a better job.
(b)	1	2	3	4	5	6	I wish I lived in a nicer house.
(c)	1	2	3	4	5	6	The neighborhood I live in is not as nice as I would like.
(d)	1	2	3	4	5	6	My father's standing in the community is lower than the fathers' standing of my friends.
(e)	1	2	3	4	5	6	I wish I had nicer clothes.
(f)	1	2	3	4	5	6	The town I live in is a nice place to live.
(g)	1	2	3	4	5	6	I am sometimes embarrassed because I have to do without things that other kids have.
(h)	1	2	3	4	5	6	I am sometimes embarrassed because my folks do not have a car or because the car they have is not as nice as I would like.

75. How often do you have the feelings described below? Please circle the appropriate number.

	(1) Often	(2) Sometimes	(3) Never	
(a)	1	2	3	I feel bad because I don't have as much money to spend as most other kids do.
(b)	1	2	3	I have a hard time because it seems that my folks hardly ever have enough money.
(c)	1	2	3	I try to keep boys and girls away from my house because it isn't as nice as theirs.
(d)	1	2	3	I have to do without things that I like because my folks can't afford them.

WE NOW WANT TO ASK YOU SOME QUESTIONS ABOUT SITUATIONS THAT SOMETIMES OCCUR IN OCCUPA-
TIONS AND IN EDUCATIONAL INSTITUTIONS. Many people find themselves in these kinds of situations every
day, and many have a hard time choosing between the alternatives available. Although you may never find yourself in any of these exact situations, you will probably find yourself in similar situations several times during your
life. In any case, we would like to know what you think about the following problems.

76. Joe Smith is in charge of the desk at the school library. A certain book is in very heavy demand. Joe's close
friend, Jack Jones, is pressed for time and can only use the book at a certain hour. Jack suggests that Joe hide
the book for a while before his arrival so that he will be sure to get it. Jack needs it badly. What right does
Jack have to expect Joe to hide the book?

(1) He has a definite right as a friend to expect Joe to hide the book for him.
(2) He has some right as a friend to expect Joe to hide the book for him.
(3) He has no right as a friend to expect Joe to hide the book for him.

14

77. If you were Joe Smith, would you hide the book in view of your obligations to Jack as a friend and your
obligations to the library?

(1) Yes
(2) No

78. Doctor X is a doctor for an insurance company. He examines a close friend who is getting old and needs
more insurance. He finds that his friend is in pretty good shape, but is doubtful on one or two minor points
which are difficult to diagnose. What right does Doctor X's friend have to expect Doctor X to shade the
doubts in his favor?

(1) He would have a definite right as a friend to expect Doctor X to shade the doubts in his favor.
(2) He would have some right as a friend to expect Doctor X to shade the doubts in his favor.
(3) He would have no right as a friend to expect Doctor X to shade the doubts in his favor.

79. If you were Doctor X, do you think you would shade the doubts in favor of your friend?

(1) Yes
(2) No

80. John Brown is a New York drama critic. Henry Long, a close friend of his, has invested all his savings in a
new Broadway play. Brown really thinks the play is no good. What right does Long have to expect Brown to
go easy on the play in his review?

(1) He has a definite right as a friend to expect Brown to go easy on his play.
(2) He has some right as a friend to expect Brown to go easy on his play.
(3) He has no right as a friend to expect Brown to go easy on his play.

81. If you were in Brown's shoes, would you go easy on Long's play in your review in view of your obligations to
your readers and your obligations to Long, your friend?

(1) Yes
(2) No

82. Smith and Jones share a partnership in a department store. They wish to hire a young man to manage part
of the operation. They received two applications for the position. Applicant A had the best test scores and
his work experience was what Smith and Jones wanted. Smith wanted to hire Applicant A. Jones wanted to
hire Applicant B. Jones argued that because Applicant A came from another community, and because B and
his father were close friends of Smith and Jones, they were obligated to give the job to B. Whom do you
agree with?

(1) Smith
(2) Jones

83. Mr. Davis teaches high school mathematics. He has a pupil, Tom Black, who is failing Mr. Davis' course.
Because Mr. Davis and Tom's parents are close friends, Mr. Davis has gotten to know Tom quite well. He
knows that Tom is one of the brightest students in his class and that he is doing poor work because he must
work at night to help support his family. Since the school policy requires Davis to flunk a certain number of
students each term, he will have to flunk some other student who is really passing if he passes Tom. What
do you think Mr. Davis should do?

(1) Pass Tom and flunk the other student
(2) Flunk Tom and pass the other student

ONLY FOR THOSE WHO HAVE AT LEAST ONE BROTHER OR SISTER. OTHERS GO TO QUESTION 85.

84. Everything considered, one or more brothers or sisters has a happier life with your family than you have.

(1) Completely agree
(2) Agree
(3) Agree a little
(4) Disagree a little
(5) Disagree
(6) Completely disagree

16

85. Which parent do you think you resemble most in personality?

___ (1) Mother
___ (2) Father

NOW WE WANT TO ASK SOME QUESTIONS ABOUT YOUR PARENTS.

Some people believe that the way a teenager thinks his parents assess his ability will influence his educational and occupational ambitions and plans. Some people also believe that the relationship between parents and teenagers influences teenagers' ambitions and plans. We would like to check on these beliefs by having you answer the following questions.

FIRST SOME QUESTIONS ABOUT YOUR FATHER. IF YOU LIVE WITH YOUR STEPFATHER, ANSWER IN TERMS OF YOUR STEPFATHER.

86. Where do you think your father would rank you in your class in high school?

___ (1) Among the best
___ (2) Above average
___ (3) Average
___ (4) Below average
___ (5) Among the poorest

87. My father tries to understand my problems.

___ (1) Always
___ (2) Most of the time, but not always
___ (3) Sometimes
___ (4) Very rarely or never

88. What kind of grades does your father think you are capable of getting?

___ (1) Mostly A's
___ (2) Mostly B's
___ (3) Mostly C's
___ (4) Mostly D's
___ (5) Mostly F's

89. My father lets me know that he loves me.

___ (1) Frequently
___ (2) Sometimes, but not very often
___ (3) On rare occasions
___ (4) Never

90. How do you think your father would rate you in school ability compared with your close friend?

___ (1) The best
___ (2) Better than most
___ (3) About the same
___ (4) Not as good as most
___ (5) The poorest

91. How do you think your father would grade your work?

___ (1) Excellent
___ (2) Good
___ (3) Average
___ (4) Below average
___ (5) Much below average

92. How close would you say you were to your father?

___ (1) Extremely close
___ (2) Very close
___ (3) Considerably close
___ (4) Somewhat close
___ (5) A little close
___ (6) Not close at all

93. In order to become a doctor, lawyer, or university professor, work beyond four years of college is necessary. How would your father rank your capability for completing such advanced work?

___ (1) Very capable
___ (2) Somewhat capable
___ (3) He would not be sure if I am capable
___ (4) Incapable
___ (5) Very incapable

94. It helps me just to talk with my father when I am nervous or upset about something.

___ (1) Always
___ (2) Most of the time
___ (3) Sometimes
___ (4) Very rarely or never
___ (5) I never talk with my father

95. How would your father rate you in school ability compared with those in your class at school?

___ (1) Among the best
___ (2) Above average
___ (3) Average
___ (4) Below average
___ (5) Among the poorest

96. My father is an easy person to talk with.

___ (1) Always
___ (2) Most of the time, but not always
___ (3) Sometimes, but not very often
___ (4) Rarely or never

97. Does your father think you have the ability to complete college?

___ (1) Yes, definitely
___ (2) Yes, probably
___ (3) Not sure either way
___ (4) Probably not
___ (5) No

98. Where do you think your father would rank you in your class in college (if you actually go)?

___ (1) Among the best
___ (2) Above average
___ (3) Average
___ (4) Below average
___ (5) Among the poorest

99. My father feels warm and affectionate toward me.

___ (1) Rarely or never
___ (2) Sometimes, but not very often
___ (3) Most of the time, but not always
___ (4) Always

17

100. In comparison to your friends and their relationship with their fathers, how close do you think you are to your father?

   (1) Much less close than most of my friends
   (2) Somewhat less close than most of my friends
   (3) About the same as most of my friends
   (4) Somewhat closer than most of my friends
   (5) Much closer than most of my friends

NOW WE WANT TO ASK SOME QUESTIONS ABOUT YOUR MOTHER. IF YOU LIVE WITH YOUR STEPMOTHER, ANSWER IN TERMS OF YOUR STEPMOTHER.

101. My mother tries to understand my problems.

   (1) Always
   (2) Most of the time, but not always
   (3) Sometimes
   (4) Very rarely or never

102. My mother lets me know that she loves me.

   (1) Frequently
   (2) Sometimes, but not very often
   (3) On rare occasions

103. How close would you say you were to your mother?

   (1) Extremely close
   (2) Very close
   (3) Considerably close
   (4) Somewhat close
   (5) A little close
   (6) Not close at all

104. It helps me just to talk with my mother when I am nervous or upset about something.

   (1) Always
   (2) Most of the time
   (3) Sometimes
   (4) Very rarely or never
   (5) I never talk with my mother

105. My mother is an easy person to talk with.

   (1) Always
   (2) Most of the time
   (3) Sometimes, but not very often
   (4) Rarely or never

106. My mother feels warm and affectionate toward me.

   (1) Rarely or never
   (2) Sometimes, but not very often
   (3) Most of the time, but not always
   (4) Always

107. In comparison to your friends and their relationship with their mothers, how close do you think you are to your mother?

   (1) Much less close than most of my friends
   (2) Somewhat less close than most of my friends
   (3) About the same as most of my friends
   (4) Somewhat closer than most of my friends
   (5) Much closer than most of my friends

18

04

108. Do you agree or disagree with the following statements? Circle the appropriate number.

	(1) Strongly agree	(2) Agree	(3) Neither agree nor disagree	(4) Disagree	(5) Strongly disagree	
(a)	1	2	3	4	5	When I make plans, I am fairly sure that I can make them work.
(b)	1	2	3	4	5	It is not wise to plan too far ahead because most things turn out to be a matter of good or bad fortune anyhow.
(c)	1	2	3	4	5	People are lonely because they don't try to be friendly.
(d)	1	2	3	4	5	There's not much use in trying to please people; if they like you, they like you.
(e)	1	2	3	4	5	Many times I feel that I have little influence over the things that happen to me.
(f)	1	2	3	4	5	I do not believe that chance and luck are very important in life.
(g)	1	2	3	4	5	I have usually found that what is going to happen will happen, no matter what I do.
(h)	1	2	3	4	5	Many times I might just as well decide what to do by flipping a coin.
(i)	1	2	3	4	5	Becoming a success is a matter of hard work; luck has little or nothing to do with it.
(j)	1	2	3	4	5	Getting a good job depends mainly on being in the right place at the right time.
(k)	1	2	3	4	5	Most of the unhappy things in my life have been due to bad luck.
(l)	1	2	3	4	5	Most people don't realize how much their lives are the result of accidental happenings.

19

109. Do you agree or disagree with the following statements? Circle the appropriate number.

	(1) Strongly agree	(2) Agree	(3) Neither agree nor disagree	(4) Disagree	(5) Strongly disagree	
(a)	1	2	3	4	5	High school should be more concerned with developing social and personal skills; less concerned with developing vocational skills
(b)	1	2	3	4	5	There is too much emphasis on extra-curricular activities in high school, and not enough emphasis on developing job-related abilities.
(c)	1	2	3	4	5	In high school there should be more courses to prepare students for jobs in the outside world and fewer purely "academic" courses such as literature and history.
(d)	1	2	3	4	5	The primary function of a high school education should be to teach occupational skills.
(e)	1	2	3	4	5	High schools should be concerned more with occupational training than with preparation for college.
(f)	1	2	3	4	5	High schools should be more concerned with sponsoring activities that allow students to make friends with other students than with teaching vocational skills.

Appendix D:
1966 Student Interview
(Form A)

DEPARTMENT OF EDUCATION

WASHINGTON STATE UNIVERSITY

EDUCATIONAL AND OCCUPATIONAL PLANS OF
HIGH SCHOOL STUDENTS

JANUARY 1966
STUDENT INTERVIEW

I.D. NO. _____

INTERVIEWER'S NAME _____   DATE _____   TIME (MINUTES) _____

HELLO, GOOD MORNING, GOOD AFTERNOON, ETC. I am
from Washington State University. As you know, Washington State University is
conducting a study of the educational and occupational plans of young people.
You may recall filling out a questionnaire a few weeks ago. I'd like to ask you a
few additional questions. Your answers will be confidential. Do you mind being
interviewed?

IF CONSENTS: First let me get some general information about you.

1. How old will you be on your next birthday? _____

2. When is your next birthday?
    _____   _____   _____
      month   day   year

3. Are you a junior or a senior?
    _____ JUNIOR   _____ SENIOR

4. (INTERVIEWER: CHECK ONE)   _____ MALE   _____ FEMALE

5. Now, what would you like to do about your further education if you had a free
    choice? INTERVIEWER: PROBE TO THE FOLLOWING CATEGORIES. MARK HIGHEST
    LEVEL MENTIONED.

    DESIRES   EXPECTED
    (1) QUIT HIGH SCHOOL AND NOT GO TO ANY KIND OF SCHOOL AGAIN   (1) _____
    (2) GRADUATE FROM HIGH SCHOOL   (2) _____
    (3) ATTEND A BUSINESS OR COMMERCIAL SCHOOL (NOT COLLEGE LEVEL)   (3) _____
    (4) ATTEND A TECHNICAL OR VOCATIONAL SCHOOL (NOT COLLEGE LEVEL)   (4) _____
    (5) ATTEND A JUNIOR COLLEGE, TAKE A BUSINESS OR COMMERCIAL COURSE   (5) _____
    (6) ATTEND A JUNIOR COLLEGE, TAKE A VOCATIONAL OR TECHNICAL COURSE   (6) _____
    (7) ATTEND A JUNIOR COLLEGE, TAKE A REGULAR COLLEGE COURSE   (7) _____
    (8) ATTEND A COLLEGE OR UNIVERSITY   (8) _____
    (9) GRADUATE FROM A COLLEGE OR UNIVERSITY   (9) _____
    (10)AFTER GRADUATING FROM COLLEGE SPEND ONE OR MORE YEARS DOING
        ADVANCED STUDY IN A SPECIALIZED FIELD   (10) _____
    (11)OTHER (WHAT?) _____   (11) _____

6. How much education do you think you will actually be able to get?
    MARK "EXPECTED" BOXES.

                                                                          FORM A

7. Education is sometimes considered training for a job. Besides the
    education you have mentioned above, is there anything you plan to do to
    get the skills and knowledge you will need in the occupation you expect to
    be in?

    _____ YES

    _____ NO

    If yes, what is it? (INTERVIEWER: CONTINUE TO PROBE UNTIL NO OTHER
    THINGS ARE MENTIONED).

8. What kind of a job do you expect to get as your first full time job, that is
    is, what occupation do you expect to be in when you first go to work?

9. Is this the type of job you expect to have as your life's career?

    _____ YES

    _____ NO

    IF NO, ASK: What occupation do you expect to have as your life's
    career?

10. What are the chances that you will actually enter the job you mentioned as
    the one you expect to have as your career? INTERVIEWER: CODE TO THE
    FOLLOWING CATEGORIES.

    _____ (1) CERTAINLY WILL
    _____ (2) PROBABLY WILL
    _____ (3) CHANCES ARE 50-50
    _____ (4) PROBABLY WILL NOT
    _____ (5) NO JOB LISTED

2

3

11. Is there a particular person in this occupation whom you admire?

___ YES

___ NO

IF YES, ASK: Who is this person? (INTERVIEWER: IDENTIFY BY RELATIONSHIP TO STUDENT. e.g., FATHER, AUNT, FRIEND OF FAMILY, TEACHER, ETC.)

12. Has this person influenced you to choose this occupation?

___ YES

___ NO

IF YES, ASK: What did (he)(she) do or say that encouraged you?

13. Has anyone tried to influence your against this occupation?

___ YES

___ NO

IF YES, ASK: What did (he)(she) do or say?

4

14. As you may recall, several weeks ago you filled out a questionnaire. One of the questions in that questionnaire asked what occupation you expected to have as your life's work. Do you remember what occupation you named as the one you expected to have as your career?

___ YES

___ NO

IF YES, ASK: Was it the same occupation that you have just told me you expect to have as your life's work, or was it a different one?

___ SAME

___ DIFFERENT

IF DIFFERENT, ASK: What happened in the meantime that led you to change your mind?

People frequently find themselves in situations where they encounter the disapproval of some people.

15. Suppose that for reasons you considered important, you decided to drop out of high school. You know that your parents and your friends may disapprove of this. Whose disapproval would be hardest for you to take?

___ DISAPPROVAL OF PARENTS

___ DISAPPROVAL OF FRIENDS

16. Suppose you have been offered a job which you think you will like and you decide to accept it. You know that your parents and friends may not approve of the job you are going to accept. Whose disapproval would be hardest for you to take?

___ DISAPPROVAL OF PARENTS

___ DISAPPROVAL OF FRIENDS

17. Suppose that you have decided not to go to college. You know that your parents and your friends may disapprove of this decision. Whose disapproval would hurt you most?

_____ DISAPPROVAL OF PARENTS
_____ DISAPPROVAL OF FRIENDS

18. Suppose you have been offered a good job in a distant city and have decided to accept it. You know that your parents and your friends may disapprove of your moving so far away. Whose disapproval would hurt you most in this situation?

_____ DISAPPROVAL OF PARENTS
_____ DISAPPROVAL OF FRIENDS

19. Here is a card with several statements on it. Please read these statements and tell me the number of the one that best describes the attitude of your mother toward the question of whether you get any education after high school. (HAND RESPONDENT CARD I.)

_____ (1) NOT INTERESTED IN MY PLANS—DOESN'T CARE WHETHER I GET ANY MORE EDUCATION OR NOT.

_____ (2) INTERESTED IN MY PLANS BUT WANTS ME TO DO WHAT I WANT.

_____ (3) INTERESTED IN MY PLANS—HOPES THAT I GET A PARTICULAR KIND OF EDUCATION.

_____ (4) INTERESTED IN MY PLANS—INSISTS THAT I GET A PARTICULAR KIND OF EDUCATION.

_____ (5) I DON'T KNOW.

INTERVIEW: IF ANSWERS 3 OR 4, HAND RESPONDENT CARD II AND ASK: Which of these statements describes the education she wants you to get?

_____ (1) ATTEND A BUSINESS OR COMMERCIAL SCHOOL (NOT COLLEGE LEVEL)
_____ (2) ATTEND A TECHNICAL OR VOCATIONAL SCHOOL (NOT COLLEGE LEVEL)
_____ (3) ATTEND A JUNIOR COLLEGE, TAKE A BUSINESS OR COMMERCIAL COURSE
_____ (4) ATTEND A JUNIOR COLLEGE, TAKE A VOCATIONAL OR TECHNICAL COURSE
_____ (5) ATTEND A JUNIOR COLLEGE, TAKE A REGULAR COLLEGE COURSE
_____ (6) ATTEND A COLLEGE OR UNIVERSITY
_____ (7) GRADUATE FROM A COLLEGE OR UNIVERSITY
_____ (8) AFTER GRADUATING FROM COLLEGE SPEND ONE OR MORE YEARS DOING ADVANCED STUDY IN A SPECIALIZED FIELD
_____ (9) OTHER (WHAT?)

20. Now look at the statements again. Please tell me the number of the statement that best describes the attitude of your father toward the question of whether you get any education after high school.

_____ (1) NOT INTERESTED IN MY PLANS—DOESN'T CARE WHETHER I GET ANY MORE EDUCATION OR NOT.

_____ (2) INTERESTED IN MY PLANS BUT WANTS ME TO DO WHAT I WANT.

_____ (3) INTERESTED IN MY PLANS—HOPES THAT I GET A PARTICULAR KIND OF EDUCATION.

_____ (4) INTERESTED IN MY PLANS—INSISTS THAT I GET A PARTICULAR KIND OF EDUCATION.

_____ (5) I DON'T KNOW.

INTERVIEWER: IF ANSWERS 3 OR 4, SAY: Please look at card II again and tell me which statements describe the education you father wants you to get.

_____ (1) ATTEND A BUSINESS OR COMMERCIAL SCHOOL (NOT COLLEGE LEVEL)
_____ (2) ATTEND A TECHNICAL OR VOCATIONAL SCHOOL (NOT COLLEGE LEVEL)
_____ (3) ATTEND A JUNIOR COLLEGE, TAKE A BUSINESS OR COMMERCIAL COURSE
_____ (4) ATTEND A JUNIOR COLLEGE, TAKE A VOCATIONAL OR TECHNICAL COURSE
_____ (5) ATTEND A JUNIOR COLLEGE, TAKE A REGULAR COLLEGE COURSE
_____ (6) ATTEND A COLLEGE OR UNIVERSITY
_____ (7) GRADUATE FROM A COLLEGE OR UNIVERSITY
_____ (8) AFTER GRADUATING FROM COLLEGE SPEND ONE OR MORE YEARS DOING ADVANCED STUDY IN A SPECIALIZED FIELD
_____ (9) OTHER (WHAT?)

21. Here is another card. Please read the statements on this card and tell me the number of the one which best describes the way you think your mother feels about your occupational plans. (HAND RESPONDENT CARD III.)

_____ (1) NOT INTERESTED IN MY OCCUPATIONAL PLANS—DOESN'T CARE WHAT I DO.

_____ (2) INTERESTED IN MY OCCUPATIONAL PLANS—WANTS ME TO CHOOSE THE OCCUPATION I WANT.

_____ (3) INTERESTED IN MY PLANS—HOPES I CHOOSE A PARTICULAR KIND OF WORK.

_____ (4) INTERESTED IN MY PLANS—INSISTS THAT I CHOOSE A PARTICULAR KIND OF WORK.

_____ (5) I DON'T KNOW HER FEELINGS.

INTERVIEWER: IF RESPONDENT SELECTS RESPONSE 3 OR 4 ASK: What kind of work does she want you to choose?

22. Now read the statements again. Please tell me the number of the statement which best describes the way your father feels about your plans for your future occupation.

_____ (1) NOT INTERESTED IN MY OCCUPATIONAL PLANS--DOESN'T CARE WHAT I DO.

_____ (2) INTERESTED IN MY OCCUPATIONAL PLANS--BUT WANTS ME TO CHOOSE THE OCCUPATION I WANT.

_____ (3) INTERESTED IN MY PLANS--HOPES I CHOOSE A PARTICULAR KIND OF WORK.

_____ (4) INTERESTED IN MY PLANS--INSISTS THAT I CHOOSE A PARTICULAR KIND OF WORK.

_____ (5) I DON'T KNOW HIS FEELINGS.

INTERVIEWER: IF RESPONDENT SELECTS RESPONSE 3 OR 4 ASK: What kind of work does he want you to choose?

23. Some people say that the plans of young people are usually similar to those of their close friends. Others disagree. We would like to check this out on a scientific basis and it will help us to do this if you would be willing to tell us the names of the juniors and seniors in this school who are your best friends. Would you also tell us the occupations you think these students plan to enter.

NAMES   OCCUPATIONS

24. We would like to send letters to some parents of high school students to find out how they feel toward education and certain occupations. Would you have any objections if we sent a questionnaire to your parents?

IF NO OBJECTIONS ASK: What is you father's name and address?

Is your mother's address the same as your father's?

_____ YES

_____ NO

IF NO, ASK: What is her name and address?

Appendix E:
1966 Student Interview
(Form B)

2

DEPARTMENT OF EDUCATION

WASHINGTON STATE UNIVERSITY

EDUCATIONAL AND OCCUPATIONAL PLANS
OF HIGH SCHOOL STUDENTS

JANUARY 1966
STUDENT INTERVIEW

I.D. NO. _____ DATE _____ TIME (MINUTES) _____

INTERVIEWER'S NAME _____

HELLO. GOOD MORNING, GOOD AFTERNOON, ETC. I am
from Washington State University. As you know Washington State University is
conducting a study of the educational and occupational plans of young people.
You may recall filling out a questionnaire a few weeks ago. I'd like to ask you
a few additional questions. Your answers will be confidential. Do you mind
being interviewed?

IF CONSENTS: First let me get some general information about you.

1. How old will you be on your next birthday?

2. When is your next birthday?

3. Are you a junior or a senior? _____ JUNIOR _____ SENIOR

4. INTERVIEWER: CHECK ONE. _____ MALE _____ FEMALE

5. Now, what would you like to do about your future education if you had a
free choice? INTERVIEWER: PROBE AND CODE TO THE FOLLOWING CATEGORIES.
MARK THE HIGHEST LEVEL MENTIONED.

(1) QUIT HIGH SCHOOL AND NOT GO TO ANY KIND OF SCHOOL AGAIN.
(2) GRADUATE FROM HIGH SCHOOL.
(3) ATTEND A BUSINESS OR COMMERCIAL SCHOOL (NOT COLLEGE LEVEL)
(4) ATTEND A TECHNICAL OR VOCATIONAL SCHOOL (NOT COLLEGE LEVEL)
(5) ATTEND A JUNIOR COLLEGE, TAKE A BUSINESS OR COMMERCIAL COURSE
(6) ATTEND A JUNIOR COLLEGE, TAKE A VOCATIONAL OR TECHNICAL COURSE
(7) ATTEND A JUNIOR COLLEGE, TAKE A REGULAR COLLEGE COURSE
(8) ATTEND A COLLEGE OR UNIVERSITY
(9) GRADUATE FROM A COLLEGE OR UNIVERSITY
(10) AFTER GRADUATING FROM COLLEGE SPEND ONE OR MORE YEARS DOING ADVANCED
STUDY IN A SPECIALIZED FIELD.
(11) OTHER (WHAT?) _____

FORM B

Now we would like to know something about your job-related desires, plans and
attitudes.

BOYS ONLY:

6. Most students have daydreams about what they would like to be and do when
they are adults. What kind of occupation would you most like to have as
your career if you could do whatever you chose? (Please be specific.)

6a. Why does this occupation appeal to you?

7. Now, leaving your daydreams and wishes aside, what occupation do you really
plan to have as your career?

_____ (1) _____
_____ (2) I HAVE NO PLANS

GIRLS ONLY:

8. I now want to show you a card. HAND STUDENT CARD NO. I. On this card
there are six different things that you can do during your adult life--be a
homemaker and not work to having a career without ever marrying. Look at
each alternative carefully and tell me the number of the one alternative
that you think best describes what you think your interests and desires
will be for most of your adult life? INTERVIEWER: RECORD STUDENT'S
RESPONSE BELOW.

_____ (1) HOMEMAKING WILL BE MY MAJOR INTEREST. I WILL NOT WANT TO WORK AT
ALL AFTER I AM MARRIED.
_____ (2) HOMEMAKING WILL BE MY MAJOR INTEREST, BUT I WILL WANT TO WORK
OCCASIONALLY OR WORK PART TIME.
_____ (3) HOMEMAKING WILL BE MY MAJOR INTEREST BUT I WILL ALSO WANT TO WORK
MOST OF THE TIME.
_____ (4) WORK WILL BE MY MAJOR INTEREST BUT I WILL ALSO WANT TO HAVE A
FAMILY AND BE A HOMEMAKER.
_____ (5) WORK WILL BE MY MAJOR INTEREST. I WILL NOT WANT TO SPEND MUCH
EFFORT IN HOMEMAKING.
_____ (6) WORK WILL BE MY ONLY INTEREST. I DON'T WANT TO MARRY AND BE A
HOMEMAKER.

9. IF RESPONDENT ANSWERS QUESTION 8 WITH 2, 3, 4, 5 OR 6 ASK: What
occupation would you most want to have?

_____

4

We want to know now students think their mothers feel about their ability. HAND STUDENT CARD II. When I read you a question you look at the answers on this card and tell me the answer that you think is most like your mother's feelings.

Question 10. What kind of grades do you think your mother thinks you are capable of getting?

_____ (1) MOSTLY A'S
_____ (2) MOSTLY B'S
_____ (3) MOSTLY C'S
_____ (4) MOSTLY D'S
_____ (5) MOSTLY F'S

Question 11. How do you think your mother rates you in school ability compared with those in your class at school?

_____ (1) AMONG THE BEST
_____ (2) ABOVE AVERAGE
_____ (3) AVERAGE
_____ (4) BELOW AVERAGE
_____ (5) AMONG THE POOREST

Question 12. In order to become a doctor, lawyer, or university professor, work beyond four years of college is necessary. How do you think your mother would rank your capabilities for completing such advanced work?

_____ (1) VERY CAPABLE
_____ (2) SOMEWHAT CAPABLE
_____ (3) AVERAGE CAPABILITY
_____ (4) INCAPABLE
_____ (5) VERY INCAPABLE

Question 13. Do you think your mother thinks you have the ability to complete college?

_____ (1) YES, DEFINITELY
_____ (2) YES, PROBABLY
_____ (3) NOT SURE EITHER WAY
_____ (4) PROBABLY NOT
_____ (5) NO

Question 14. How do you think your mother would grade your work?

_____ (1) EXCELLENT
_____ (2) GOOD
_____ (3) AVERAGE
_____ (4) BELOW AVERAGE
_____ (5) MUCH BELOW AVERAGE

Question 15. Where do you think your mother would rank you in your class in high school?

_____ (1) AMONG THE BEST
_____ (2) ABOVE AVERAGE
_____ (3) AVERAGE
_____ (4) BELOW AVERAGE
_____ (5) AMONG THE POOREST

Question 16. How do you think your mother would rate you in school ability compared to your close friends?

_____ (1) THE BEST
_____ (2) ABOVE AVERAGE
_____ (3) AVERAGE
_____ (4) BELOW AVERAGE
_____ (5) THE POOREST

Question 17. Where do you think your mother would rank you in your class in college (if you actually go)?

_____ (1) AMONG THE BEST
_____ (2) ABOVE AVERAGE
_____ (3) AVERAGE
_____ (4) BELOW AVERAGE
_____ (5) AMONG THE POOREST

18. People in all communities make judgements of each other regarding their rank in the community. Some people are considered low, others are placed toward the middle, others are judged to be toward the top. Here is a card with ten boxes on it. HAND RESPONDENT CARD III. Number "1" represents very low standing, number "10" represents very high standing. Please tell me the number of the box that you think best reflects the standing of your family in the community.

10 _____ Above average
9 _____
8 _____
7 _____
6 _____
5 _____ Average
4 _____
3 _____
2 _____
1 _____ Below average

5

19. Now place an x in the box at the right that best reflects the standing that you hope to achieve in the community in which you live when you become fully established in your own home or occupation. (Again, "1" represents very low standing and "10" represents very high standing.)

10	Above average
9	
8	
7	
6	
5	Average
4	
3	
2	
1	Below average

20. I am going to read a list of items. Some parents have rules for their teenagers on these items. Others don't. Please tell me whether your parents have rules about these things.

Rules   No Rules

1. Time for being in at night on weekends
2. Amount of dating
3. Against going steady
4. Time spent watching TV
5. Time spent on homework
6. Against going around with certain boys
7. Against going around with certain girls
8. Eating dinner with the family

6

Now I would like for you to answer some questions about your feelings and attitudes. I am going to give you a booklet with a number of questions in it. The questions are not difficult; you should have no trouble answering them. INTERVIEWER: GIVE THE IPAT "SELF ANALYSIS FORM" TO THE RESPONDENT, READ THE INSTRUCTIONS WITH HIM, AND THEN APPEAR TO BE BUSY UNTIL THE RESPONDENT TELLS YOU HE HAS FINISHED.

As you know, students vary in their ability. Some are capable of doing excellent work in school, while others are only fair. We want to know what students think of their own ability. You may recall that several weeks ago we asked you some questions about this. We would like to ask you a few aditional questions today. Would you please read and answer the questions on this page while I arrange some of my papers. INTERVIEWER: SCORE THE IPAT WHILE RESPONDENT ANSWERS SELF-ASSESSMENT ITEMS.

PLEASE WRITE THE STUDENT'S NAME ON QUESTIONNAIRE SCHEDULE SUPPLEMENT.

8

21. Some people say that the plans of young people are usually similar to those of their close friends. Others disagree. We would like to check this out on a scientific basis and it will help us to do this if you would be willing to tell me the names of the juniors and seniors in this school who are your best friends. Would you please also tell me the occupations you think these students plan to enter.

NAME   OCCUPATION

_____ _____

_____ _____

_____ _____

22. We would like to send letters to some parents of high school students to find out how they feel toward education and certain occupations. Would you have any objections if we sent a questionnaire to your parents?

IF NO OBJECTIONS: What is your father's name and address?

_____ YES

_____ NO

    IF NO, what is her name and address?

Is your mother's address the same as your father's?

_____ YES

_____ NO

    IF NO, what is her name and address?

23. Where do you think you would rank in your class in high school?

_____ (1) Among the best
_____ (2) Above average
_____ (3) Average
_____ (4) Below average
_____ (5) Among the poorest

24. In order to become a doctor, lawyer, or university professor, work beyond four years of college is necessary. How capable do you think you are of completing such advanced work?

_____ (1) Very capable
_____ (2) Somewhat capable
_____ (3) Not sure if you are capable
_____ (4) Incapable
_____ (5) Very incapable

25. Do you think you have the ability to complete college?

_____ (1) Yes, definitely
_____ (2) Yes, probably
_____ (3) Not sure either way
_____ (4) Probably not
_____ (5) No

26. How do you rate yourself in school ability compared with those in your class at school?

_____ (1) I am among the best
_____ (2) I am above average
_____ (3) I am average
_____ (4) I am below average
_____ (5) I am among the poorest

27. Forget for a moment how others grade your work. In your own opinion how good do you think your work is?

_____ (1) My work is excellent
_____ (2) My work is good
_____ (3) My work is average
_____ (4) My work is below average
_____ (5) My work is much below average

28. What kind of grades do you think you are capable of getting?

_____ (1) Mostly A's
_____ (2) Mostly B's
_____ (3) Mostly C's
_____ (4) Mostly D's
_____ (5) Mostly F's

29. Where do you think you would rank in your class in college (if you actually go)?

_____ (1) Among the best
_____ (2) Above average
_____ (3) Average
_____ (4) Below average
_____ (5) Among the poorest

30. How do you rate yourself in school ability compared with your close friends?

_____ (1) I am among the best
_____ (2) I am above average
_____ (3) I am average
_____ (4) I am below average
_____ (5) I am the poorest

Appendix F:
1966 Counselors' and Administrators' Questionnaire (Form A)

NAME _____ I.D. NUMBER _____ FORM A

EDUCATIONAL AND OCCUPATIONAL ASPIRATIONS STUDY

Department of Education
Washington State University

Counselors and Administrators Questionnaire

A. Do you know this person well enough to give any opinions about (him)(her)?
_____(1) yes _____(2) no

B. What is your impression of the intellectual ability of this person?
_____(1) High _____(4) Below average
_____(2) Above average _____(5) Poor
_____(3) Average

C. In relation to (his)(her) ability (he)(she) is:
_____(1) An over achiever
_____(2) Average
_____(3) An under achiever

D. What level of education do you think this person would be able to obtain?
_____(1) Should probably drop out of high school
_____(2) High school only
_____(3) Junior College
_____(4) College
_____(5) Post graduate

E. Do you think this person should obtain some type of vocational or technical education?
_____(1) yes _____(2) no
_____(3) I don't know the student well enough to judge.

F. If yes, what type would you suggest?
_____(1) Stenographer or typist
_____(2) Clerical or business
_____(3) Mechanical
_____(4) Electrical
_____(5) Other trades for men (e.g., carpentry, plumbing.)
_____(6) Other trades for girls (e.g., hair dressing, practical nursing.)
_____(7) Other (what?) _____

G. Have you ever talked to this person about (his)(her) educational plans?
_____(1) yes _____(2) no

If yes, did you:

H. Encourage to go to college
_____(1) yes _____(2) no

I. Encourage to finish high school
_____(1) yes _____(2) no

J. Encourage to attend vocational-technical school
_____(1) yes _____(2) no

K. Have you ever talked to this person about (his)(her) occupational plans?
_____(1) yes _____(2) no

If yes, did you:

L. Explain job requirements or duties
_____(1) yes _____(2) no

M. Informed them of specific job opportunities
_____(1) yes _____(2) no

N. Recommended specific occupations to (him)(her)
_____(1) yes _____(2) no

O. Other
_____

P. What type of work would you say this person is best suited for?
_____(1) Professional
_____(2) Managerial or administrative
_____(3) Technical (lab technician, etc.)
_____(4) Manual-skilled (carpenter, electrician, etc.)
_____(5) Manual-unskilled
_____(6) Clerical
_____(7) Sales
_____(8) Farm operator
_____(9) Farm laboroer
_____(10) Other (specify) _____

Q. Any other comments pertaining to educational or occupational abilities or prospects of this student.

169

Appendix G:
1966 Counselors' and
Administrators'
Questionnaire
(Form B)

NAME _____

I.D. NUMBER _____

FORM B

EDUCATIONAL & OCCUPATIONAL ASPIRATIONS
STUDY

DEPARTMENT OF EDUCATION
WASHINGTON STATE UNIVERSITY

Counselors' and Administrators' Questionnaire

A. Do you know this person well enough to give any opinions about (him)(her)?

___ (1) yes   ___ (2) no

B. Do you know this student's I.Q. score?

___ (1) yes   ___ (2) no

    C. If yes, is it:

       ___ (1) 130+
       ___ (2) 120-129
       ___ (3) 110-119
       ___ (4) 100-109
       ___ (5) 90-99
       ___ (6) 80-89
       ___ (7) Below 80

D. Have you ever talked to this person about (his)(her) educational plans?

___ (1) yes   ___ (2) no

E. If yes, have you talked to him about vocational education?

___ (1) yes   ___ (2) no

F. Do you think this person should obtain some type of vocational or technical education?

___ (1) yes   ___ (2) no

G. If yes, what type would you suggest?

___ (1) Stenographer or typist
___ (2) Clerical or business
___ (3) Mechanical
___ (4) Electrical
___ (5) Other trades for men (e.g., carpentry, plumbing.)
___ (6) Other trades for women (e.g., hair dressing, practical nursing.)
___ (7) Other (what?)

H. What kind of grades do you think this student is capable of getting?

___ (1) Mostly A's
___ (2) Mostly B's
___ (3) Mostly C's
___ (4) Mostly D's
___ (5) Mostly F's

I. How would you rate this person in school ability compared with those in (his)(her) class at school?

___ (1) Among the best
___ (2) Above average
___ (3) Below average
___ (5) Among the poorest

J. In order to become a doctor, lawyer, or university professor, work beyond four years of college is necessary. How would you rate the capability of this student for completing such advanced work?

___ (1) Very capable
___ (2) Somewhat capable
___ (3) Average capability
___ (4) Incapable
___ (5) Very incapable

K. Do you think this student has the ability to complete college?

___ (1) Yes, definitely
___ (2) Yes, probably
___ (3) Not sure either way
___ (4) Probably not
___ (5) No

L. How would you grade this students's work?

___ (1) Excellent
___ (2) Good
___ (3) Average
___ (4) Below average
___ (5) Much below average

M. Where would you rank this student in (his)(her) class in high school?

___ (1) Among the best
___ (2) Above average
___ (3) Average
___ (4) Below average
___ (5) Among the poorest

N. How would you rate this student in school ability compared with (her)(her) friends?

___ (1) The best
___ (2) Better than most
___ (3) About the same
___ (4) Not as good as most
___ (5) The poorest

O. Where do you think this student would rank in (his)(her) class in college if (he)(she) actually goes?

___ (1) Among the best
___ (2) Above average
___ (3) Average
___ (4) Below average
___ (5) Among the poorest

Appendix H:
1966 Parent's
Questionnaire
(Form A)

WASHINGTON STATE UNIVERSITY
DEPARTMENT OF EDUCATION

Educational and Occupational Plans
of High School Students

Washington State University and the Washington State Office of Public Instruction are making a study of the factors which influence the educational and occupational plans of high school students. The results of this study will be used to plan educational programs that will help students reach their goals.

You can help in this work by taking a few minutes to answer the questions in this questionnaire. We will be grateful if you will do this.

The information you give will be used to check some ideas which people have about high school students and their parents. Some people say that nearly all parents want their children to go to college or take some other kind of schooling, but we are not sure this is the case. If the views of teenagers and their parents are not always the same, teachers and counselors can be more helpful to students if they know what the similarities and differences are. Facts about how much the desires of young people reflect the wishes of their parents will be helpful.

It will be greatly appreciated if you will take the time to fill out this questionnaire and return it in the enclosed postage-free envelope. Your replies will be handled in a confidential manner. We will use the information for statistical purposes only. We are not asking that names be placed on the questionnaires. This insures that the clerks who code the answers will not know whose questionnaires are being coded. The number which appears on the questionnaire will enable us to keep track of the returns as they come in, and thus avoid bothering you with a reminder if you have already returned your questionnaire.

Thank you for your cooperation.

Sincerely yours,

Roy T. Bowles
Staff Director

Design for a Study

Form A
February, 1966

DEPARTMENT OF EDUCATION
WASHINGTON STATE UNIVERSITY

Educational and Occupational Plans
of High School Students

Parent's Questionnaire

1. How many children in your family? (Include stepchildren and those no longer at home.) _____

2. How many of these were in high school any time during the 1965-66 school year? Boys _____ Girls _____

Now we would like to ask some questions concerning your feelings about the plans of your son or daughter who is a junior or senior in high school. IF YOU HAVE MORE THAN ONE CHILD IN THE ELEVENTH AND TWELFTH GRADES, Please answer these questions in terms of the oldest child who is in one of these grades. In each question, please circle the word "son" or "daughter" to indicate the sex of the child you are thinking of.

3. Mark the blank at the left of the phrase which best describes the highest level and type of education that you would like your son daughter (circle one) to achieve.

___ (1) Quit high school and not go to any kind of school again.
___ (2) Graduate from high school.
___ (3) Attend a business or commercial school (not college level).
___ (4) Attend a vocational or technical school (not college level).
___ (5) Attend a junior college, take a business or commercial course.
___ (6) Attend a junior college, take a vocational or technical course.
___ (7) Attend a junior college, take a regular college course.
___ (8) Attend a college of university.
___ (9) Graduate from a college or university.
___ (10) After graduating from college spend one or more years doing advanced study in a specialized field.
___ (11) Other (what?)

4. What course of study would you like your son daughter (circle one) to take? That is, what would you like him or her to major in?

5. What occupation or line of work would you most like your son daughter (circle one) to go into?

6. In which of the following would you be willing and able to help your son daughter (circle one) financially? Mark all that apply.
___ (1) Farming
___ (2) College
___ (3) Vocational schooling
___ (4) Business schooling
___ (5) Setting up a business of his or her own
___ (6) None of the above

7. Now we would like to know your general feelings about certain aspects of work and education. Please circle a number to show whether or not each of the statements in this list agrees with your ideas of work and education. (If retired, please give the responses which you would have given prior to retirement.)

	Strongly agree	Agree	Neither agree nor disagree	Disagree	Strongly disagree
(a) Everyone who possibly can should work.	1	2	3	4	5
(b) Even if I were financially secure and did not need a job I would probably work.	1	2	3	4	5
(c) It is a person's duty to work.	1	2	3	4	5
(d) If I did not work I would feel that I was not leading a "right life."	1	2	3	4	5

2

(e) I find it hard to respect a man who doesn't work.	1	2	3	4	5
(f) If I were financially well off, I think I could lead a perfectly happy and satisfying life without working.	1	2	3	4	5
(g) A person who has never worked has missed a valuable experience.	1	2	3	4	5
(h) If a person can live the way he wants to without working there is no reason for him to work.	1	2	3	4	5
WOMEN ONLY:					
(i) I would want my husband to do some kind of work even if he were financially secure and did not need a job.	1	2	3	4	5
(j) The high school curriculum should be more directly related to specific jobs.	1	2	3	4	5
(k) Every student should try to go to college; if he can't make it there he can always get an ordinary job.	1	2	3	4	5
(l) There should be more emphasis on vocational and technical courses and less on college preparation.	1	2	3	4	5
(m) Courses like welding and woodworking have no place in today's high school.	1	2	3	4	5
(n) In modern society the skilled craftsman is as important as the scientist or the professional.	1	2	3	4	5
(o) Students enrolled in vocational or technical courses generally don't have the ability to master college preparatory courses.	1	2	3	4	5
(p) Shop courses are preparation for the kind of work many students will be doing.	1	2	3	4	5
(q) Business courses like typing and shorthand are as important for girls as are college preparatory courses.	1	2	3	4	5
(r) High school should do more to provide students with skills useful in jobs and schould not worry so much about college preparation.	1	2	3	4	5
(s) I feel that formal education tends to take people away from their home communities and because of this it is undesirable.	1	2	3	4	5
(t) I am opposed to formal education beyond high school.	1	2	3	4	5
(u) I think that formal education is really very important.	1	2	3	4	5
(v) I believe that the most important thing in formal education is the diploma or degree.	1	2	3	4	5
(w) I expect my children to get all of the ecudation they can.	1	2	3	4	5

8. Please consider each occupation listed below and on the next page. Check a blank to show how you would feel if your son daughter (circle one) told you that he or she was going to choose this occupation as his or her life's work.

OCCUPATION	I would be very pleased	I would be pleased	I would be indifferent	I would be disappointed	I would be very displeased
Agricultural research scientist					
Aide in child care center					
Airline pilot					
Airline stewardess					
Automobile salesman					
Automobile mechanic					
Banker					
Bank teller					
Beautician					
Bookkeeper					
Carpenter					
Certified public accountant					
Cook (restaurant)					
College professor					
Commercial artist					
County agricultural agent					
Computer programmer					
Dentist					
Dietician					
Electrician					
Elementary school teacher					
Engineer					
Factory manager					
Farm operator					
Foreman in factory					
Home demonstration agent					
Hotel-motel clerk					
Janitor					
Lawyer					
Life insurance salesman					
Machine operator in factory					
Maid - motel or hotel					
Manager of department store					
Manager of a loan company					
Mechanical draftsman					
Medical lab technologist					
Minister, priest or rabbi					
Nurse (R.N.)					
Nurse's aide					
Owner and operator of small business					
Physical therapist					
Physician					
Plumber					
Police officer					
Psychologist					
Radio announcer					
Recreational programs supervisor					
Reporter on daily newspaper					

OCCUPATION	I would be very pleased	I would be pleased	I would be indifferent	I would be disappointed	I would be very displeased
Restaurant host or hostess					
Sales person of farm supplies					
Sales person in retail store					
Secretary					
Social worker					
Tailor or dressmaker					
Taxi driver					
Truck driver					
Veterinarian					
Waiter or waitress					
Warehouse worker					
Welder					
X-ray technician					

9. Where do you live?
___ (1) City of 150,000 or larger
___ (2) City of 100,000 to 150,000
___ (3) City of 50,000 to 100,000
___ (4) City of 10,000 to 50,000
___ (5) City of 2,500 to 10,000
___ (6) Town under 2,500
___ (7) On a farm
___ (8) Country but not farm

10. If you live on a farm, do you own or rent the farm?
___ (1) Own the farm
___ (2) Rent the farm

11. If you live in town, do you own or rent the house in which you are living?
___ (1) Own the house
___ (2) Rent the house

12. The 1965 income for my family from all sources was: (if you do not know exactly, make the best guess you can).
___ (1) Under $2,000
___ (2) $2,000 - 2,999
___ (3) $3,000 - 3,999
___ (4) $4,000 - 4,999
___ (5) $5,000 - 5,999
___ (6) $6,000 - 7,499
___ (7) $7,500 - 9,999
___ (8) $10,000 - 14,999
___ (9) $15,000 or over

13. In terms of income or wealth of families in my community, I think my family is:
___ (1) Considerably above average
___ (2) Somewhat above average
___ (3) Average
___ (4) Somewhat below average
___ (5) Considerably below average

14. What kind of work do you do for a living? What is your job called, what kind of business or industry do you work in, and what do you do? (For example: "Carpenter, work on construction crew building new house;" "Sales clerk, wait on customers in a department store;" "Owner and operator of a grocery store.") Mothers: Give husband's occupation.

15. What kind of firm or outfit are you (or is your husband) associated with in your work?
___ (1) Own business
___ (2) Own farm
___ (3) Own professional office
___ (4) Small private firm, organization or factory (50 employees or less)
___ (5) Large private firm, organization or factory (over 50 employees)
___ (6) Educational institution
___ (7) Social agency
___ (8) Other non-profit organization (what?) _____
___ (9) Government bureau or agency
___ (10) Other (what?) _____

This questionnaire was completed by a _____ man _____ woman.

Appendix I:
1966 Parent's
Questionnaire
(Form B)

WASHINGTON STATE UNIVERSITY
DEPARTMENT OF EDUCATION

Educational and Occupational Plans
of High School Students

Washington State University and the Washington State Office of Public Instruction are making a study of the factors which influence the educational and occupational plans of high school students. The results of this study will be used to plan educational programs that will help students reach their goals.

You can help in this work by taking a few minutes to answer the questions in this questionnaire. We will be grateful if you will do this.

The information you give will be used to check some ideas which people have about high school students and their parents. Some people say that nearly all parents want their children to go to college or take some other kind of schooling, but we are not sure this is the case. If the views of teenagers and their parents are not always the same, teachers and counselors can be more helpful to students if they know what the similarities and differences are. Facts about how much the desires of young people reflect the wishes of their parents will be helpful.

It will be greatly appreciated if you will take the time to fill out this questionnaire and return it in the enclosed postage-free envelope. Your replies will be handled in a confidential manner. We will use the information for statistical purposes only. We are not asking that names be placed on the questionnaires. This insures that the clerks who code the answers will not know whose questionnaires are being coded. The number which appears on the questionnaire will enable us to keep track of the returns as they come in, and thus avoid bothering you with a reminder if you have already returned your questionnaire.

Thank you for your cooperation.

Sincerely yours,

Roy T. Bowles

Roy T. Bowles
Staff Director

177

Form B
February, 1966

DEPARTMENT OF EDUCATION
WASHINGTON STATE UNIVERSITY
Educational and Occupational Plans
of High School Students

Parent's Questionnaire

1. How many children in your family? (Include stepchildren and those no longer at home.)

2. How many of these were in high school any time during the 1965-66 school year?

    Boys _____   Girls _____

Now we would like to ask some questions concerning your feelings about the plans of your son or daughter who is a junior or senior in high school. IF YOU HAVE MORE THAN ONE CHILD IN THE ELEVENTH AND TWELFTH GRADES, please answer these questions in terms of the oldest child who is in one of these grades. In each question, please circle the word 'son' or 'daughter' to indicate the sex of the child you are thinking of.

3. Mark the blank at the left of the phrase which best describes the highest level and type of education that you would like for your   son   daughter   (circle one) to achieve.

    ____ (1) Quit high school and not go to any kind of school again.
    ____ (2) Graduate from high school,
    ____ (3) Attend a business or commercial school (not college level)
    ____ (4) Attend a vocational or technical school (not college level)
    ____ (5) Attend a junior college, take a business or commercial course.
    ____ (6) Attend a junior college, take a vocational or technical course.
    ____ (7) Attend a junior college, take a regular college course.
    ____ (8) Attend a college or university,
    ____ (9) Graduate from a college or university,
    ____ (10) After graduating from college spend one or more years doing advanced study in a specialized field.
    ____ (11) Other (What?) _____

4. What course of study would you like your   son   daughter   (circle one) to take? That is, what would you like him or her to major in?

5. What occupation or line of work would you most like your   son   daughter   (circle one) to go into?

6. Below are several pairs of occupations. The income for the two occupations in each pair is approximately equal. Please consider each pair of occupations and answer the following question if you have a son in the eleventh or twelfth grade: If your son had to work in one or the other of these occupations as his life's work, which of the occupations in each pair would you prefer him to have?

    Or if you have a daughter in the eleventh or twelfth grade, answer in terms of the question: If your daughter's husband had to work in one or the other of these occupations in each pair which would you prefer him to have?

    Answer in terms of your oldest child who is in the eleventh or twelfth grade. This child is a   son   daughter   (circle one).

    A. Railroad brakeman   A. Longshoreman or stevedore
    B. Draftsman   B. Bookkeeper

    A. Clergyman (minister,   A. Cabinet maker
        priest, rabbi)   B. Bank teller
    B. Upholsterer

    A. Plumber   A. College professor
    B. Photographer   B. Locomotive engineer

    A. Radio operator   A. Bus driver
    B. Locomotive fireman   B. Manager of a service station

                                   A. High school teacher
                                   B. Electrician

                                   A. Tool and die maker
                                   B. Insurance agent

                                   A. Medical or dental technician
                                   B. Baker

2

7. In which of the following would you be willing and able to help your   son   daughter   (circle one) financially? Mark all that apply.

    ____ (1) Farming
    ____ (2) College
    ____ (3) Vocational schooling
    ____ (4) Business schooling
    ____ (5) Setting up a business of his or her own
    ____ (6) None of the above

    As everyone knows, not all children are alike in ability. We would like to know what you think of your son's (daughter's) ability. How would you rate your   son   daughter   (circle one) on the following? Please answer in terms of the oldest child who is in the eleventh or twelfth grade.

8. Where do you think your son (daughter) would rank in his (her) class in high school?

    ____ (1) Among the best
    ____ (2) Above average
    ____ (3) Average
    ____ (4) Below average
    ____ (5) Among the poorest

9. In order to become a doctor, lawyer, or university professor, work beyond four years of college is necessary. How capable do you think your son (daughter) is of completing such advanced work?

    ____ (1) Very capable
    ____ (2) Somewhat capable
    ____ (3) Not sure if he (she) is capable
    ____ (4) Incapable
    ____ (5) Very incapable

10. Do you think your son (daughter) has the ability to complete college?

    ____ (1) Yes, definitely
    ____ (2) Yes, probably
    ____ (3) Not sure either way
    ____ (4) Probably not
    ____ (5) No

11. How do you think your son (daughter) rates in school ability compared with those in his (her) class at school?

    ____ (1) Among the best
    ____ (2) Above average
    ____ (3) Average
    ____ (4) Below average
    ____ (5) Much below average

12. In your own opinion how good do you think your son's (daughter's) school work is?

    ____ (1) Excellent
    ____ (2) Good
    ____ (3) Average
    ____ (4) Below average
    ____ (5) Much below average

13. What kind of grades do you think your son (daughter) is capable of getting?

    ____ (1) Mostly A's
    ____ (2) Mostly B's
    ____ (3) Mostly C's
    ____ (4) Mostly D's
    ____ (5) Mostly F's

14. Where do you think your son (daughter) would rank in his (her) class in college (if he or she actually goes)?

___ (1) Among the best
___ (2) Above average
___ (3) Average
___ (4) Below average
___ (5) Among the poorest

15. How would you rate your son (daughter) in school ability compared with his (her) close friends?

___ (1) The best
___ (2) Above average
___ (3) About the same
___ (4) Below average
___ (5) The poorest

Parents usually have ambitions and plans for their children's educational and occupational careers. There are people who say, however, that some students have more opportunities to realize their ambitions than others. How do you feel about the following statements?

16. Do you think your son (daughter) will be kept from achieving his (her) educational or occupational desires because of race?

___ (1) Yes
___ (2) No
___ (3) Uncertain

17. Do you think your son (daughter) will be kept from achieving his (her) educational or occupational desires because of family background?

___ (1) Yes
___ (2) No
___ (3) Uncertain

18. Do you think your son (daughter) will be kept from achieving his (her) educational or occupational desires because of insufficient family income?

___ (1) Yes
___ (2) No
___ (3) Uncertain

19. Do you think your son (daughter) will be kept from achieving his (her) educational or occupational desires because of religious beliefs?

___ (1) Yes
___ (2) No
___ (3) Uncertain

20. Now we would like to know your general feelings about certain aspects of work and education. Please circle a number to show whether or not each of the statements in this list agrees with your ideas of work and education. (If retired, please give the responses which you would have given prior to retirement.)

	Strongly agree	Agree	Neither agree nor disagree	Disagree	Strongly disagree
(a) Everyone who possibly can should work.	1	2	3	4	5
(b) Even if I were financially secure and did not need a job I would probably work.	1	2	3	4	5
(c) It is a person's duty to work.	1	2	3	4	5
(d) If I did not work I would feel that I was not leading a "right life."	1	2	3	4	5
(e) I find it hard to respect a man who doesn't work.	1	2	3	4	5
(f) If I were financially well off, I think I could lead a perfectly happy and satisfying life without working.	1	2	3	4	5
(g) The most important thing in a man's life is his occupation.	1	2	3	4	5
(h) Many times it is more important to have time for recreation than it is to work hard and achieve occupational advancement.	1	2	3	4	5
(i) A man should always accept an occupational promotion even if this means moving to a strange community away from his close friends.	1	2	3	4	5
(j) A man who already has a secure job with a modest income is foolish to go back to school even if additional education is necessary before he can expect to have a better job.	1	2	3	4	5
(k) A man should be willing to give up time with his family and devote it to his job if this will help his occupational advancement.	1	2	3	4	5
(l) A man should try hard to get farther ahead in the world than his parents.	1	2	3	4	5
(m) The most important purpose of education is to prepare people for success.	1	2	3	4	5

21. Now we would like to know your attitudes on some other issues, statements listed below. Please circle a number to show how you feel about the following.

	Strongly agree	Agree	Neither agree nor disagree	Disagree	Strongly disagree
(a) It is not wise to plan too far ahead because most things turn out to be a matter of good or bad fortune anyhow.	1	2	3	4	5
(b) There's not much use in trying to please people. If they like you, they like you.	1	2	3	4	5
(c) The average citizen can have an influence on the way the government is run.	1	2	3	4	5
(d) This world is run by the few people in power, and there is not much the little guy can do about it.	1	2	3	4	5
(e) Many times I feel that I have little influence over the things that happen to me.	1	2	3	4	5
(f) I do not believe that chance and luck are very important in my life.	1	2	3	4	5
(g) Many times we might just as well decide what to do by flipping a coin.	1	2	3	4	5
(h) Becoming a success is a matter of hard work; luck has little or nothing to do with it.	1	2	3	4	5
(i) Getting a good job depends mainly on being in the right place at the right time.	1	2	3	4	5

5

22. **Please circle a number to show whether you agree or disagree with the following statements. Although you may not completely agree or disagree with a statement, give the answer that comes closest to your own feelings.**

	Agree	Disagree	
(a)	1	2	Most public officials are not really interested in the problems of the average man.
(b)	1	2	Honesty is always the best policy.
(c)	1	2	These days a person doesn't know whom he can count on.
(d)	1	2	Anyone who has the ability should have the opportunity to get a college education.
(e)	1	2	Nowadays a person has to live pretty much for today and let tomorrow take care of itself.
(f)	1	2	Everyone can be trusted.
(g)	1	2	In spite of what some people say, the lot of the average man is getting worse, not better.
(h)	1	2	Individuals have more freedom under a democracy than under a dictatorship.
(i)	1	2	Most people don't really care what happens to the next fellow.

Now we would like to ask some general questions about you and your family.

23. How much education did you get? (check one)

___ (1) Eighth grade or less
___ (2) Some high school, but did not finish
___ (3) High school graduate
___ (4) Some college, but did not finish
___ (5) College graduate
___ (6) More than college

FATHERS ONLY:

24. Have you ever attended a vocational or technical school?

___ (1) Yes
___ (2) No

If yes, what type of school was it?

_____

25. Where do you live?

___ (1) City of 150,000 or larger
___ (2) City of 100,000 to 150,000
___ (3) City of 50,000 to 100,000
___ (4) City of 10,000 to 50,000
___ (5) City of 2,500 to 10,000
___ (6) Town under 2,500
___ (7) On a farm
___ (8) Country but not farm

26. If you live on a farm, do you own or rent the farm?

___ (1) Own the farm
___ (2) Rent the farm

27. If you live in town, do you own or rent the house in which you are living?

___ (1) Own the house
___ (2) Rent the house

6

28. The 1965 income for my family from all sources was: (if you do not know exactly, make the best guess you can).

___ (1) Under $2,000
___ (2) $2,000 - 2,999
___ (3) $3,000 - 3,999
___ (4) $4,000 - 4,999
___ (5) $5,000 - 5,999
___ (6) $6,000 - 7,499
___ (7) $7,500 - 9,999
___ (8) $10,000 - 14,999
___ (9) $15,000 or over

29. In terms of income or wealth of families in my community, I think my family is:

___ (1) Considerably above average
___ (2) Somewhat above average
___ (3) Average
___ (4) Somewhat below average
___ (5) Considerably below average

30. What kind of work do you do for a living? What is your job called, what kind of business or industry do you work in, and what do you do? (For example: "Carpenter, work on construction crew building new houses"; "Sales clerk, wait on customers in a department store". Owner and operator of a grocery store.") Mothers: give husband's occupation.

_____

31. What kind of farm or outfit are you (or is your husband) associated with in your work?

___ (1) Own business
___ (2) Own farm
___ (3) Own professional office
___ (4) Small private firm, organization or factory (50 employees or less)
___ (5) Large private firm, organization or factory (over 50 employees)
___ (6) Educational institution
___ (7) Social agency
___ (8) Other non-profit organization (what)
___ (9) Government bureau or agency
___ (10) Other (what?)

32. About how many clubs and organizations in your community would you say you belonged to? (Include civic clubs, churches, lodges, fraternal orders, and other groups.)

_____

MOTHERS ONLY

33. Do you work outside the home for pay?

___ (1) Yes full-time
___ (2) Yes part-time
___ (3) No

If Yes, what kind of work do you do?

_____

Appendix J:
1979 Pre-Telephone-
Interview Cover Letter
and Information
Brochure

WASHINGTON STATE UNIVERSITY
PULLMAN, WASHINGTON 99164

CAREER DEVELOPMENT STUDY
SOCIAL RESEARCH CENTER

March 13, 1979

Penny Larsen
1114 Riverside Blvd
Tacoma, WA 98999

Dear Ms. Larsen:

You were part of a statewide study of high school students in
1966. At that time you were a senior at West Coast High School.
Together with 7,000 other Washington high school students, you
told us what you would like to do after leaving high school.

About 14 years have passed and we are now updating the information
that you and your classmates provided us in high school. As you
may know, over the past year we relocated your West Coast High
School classmates and the others who participated in the study.
We are now conducting short telephone interviews to talk to you
about the experiences you have had since leaving high school.

Within the next few weeks one of our interviewers will also telephone you. The call will be long distance. Please take a few
minutes to talk to the interviewer. If the interviewer should
call at a bad time, explain the situation and we will call back
when it is more convenient.

We have enclosed a short brochure to tell you more about the
Career Development Study. You began this study back in high
school. We will appreciate your participation in this
continuation.

Sincerely,

LUTHER B. OTTO, Ph.D.
Project Director

LBO/bim
Enclosures

181

Information Brochure

THE CAREER
DEVELOPMENT STUDY

*On these pages we'll try to answer
some questions about the study . . . .*

WHAT IS THE CAREER DEVELOPMENT STUDY?

In 1966 we conducted a statewide study of the educational and occupational plans of Washington high school students.

14 years have passed and we are now updating the information. We are studying whether these individuals have accomplished the goals they had while in high school.

WHY STUDY FORMER WASHINGTON HIGH SCHOOL STUDENTS?

Young men and women make decisions during high school that shape the rest of their lives

—whether to go to college
—what kind of job to get . . . and how to get it
—whether to get married.

While similar studies have been completed in the eastern states, little is known about the career problems and experiences of individuals who attended Washington and western high schools.

1966 and '67 were crucial years to leave high school

—educational systems were undergoing dramatic changes
—the war in Vietnam
—the economy was strong
—social and attitudinal changes were occurring.

We are studying how such changes affect individual lives.

WHO IS INCLUDED IN THE STUDY?

You

Most of your 1966 junior and senior classmates

About 7,000 former students from 28 high schools in the State of Washington.

WHY SHOULD I PARTICIPATE?

The main reason is to help us learn more about the problems young men and women face on leaving high school and how these problems are resolved. This will help parents who are preparing their sons and daughters for the future

—perhaps your own son or daughter.

DO I HAVE ANY CHOICE ABOUT THIS?

You certainly do. Participation in this study is strictly voluntary. We hope that you will continue to help us as you have in the past.

HOW WAS I CHOSEN TO PARTICIPATE IN THIS STUDY?

In 1966 twenty-eight high schools were scientifically selected to represent all public high schools in the State of Washington.

Your high school was selected.

In each school all junior and senior students agreed to answer a 16-page questionnaire. They provided their name and address so that researchers could contact them again in the future.

WHAT INFORMATION WAS OBTAINED IN 1966?

You were asked about your high school courses, your extracurricular activities, how well you were doing in school, and what things were difficult in completing your school work.

Questions were asked about your family and friends, what they wanted to do in the future, and your impressions about how they felt about you.

You told us about your plans for the future
—the education and jobs you would like to get
—the schools you wanted to attend
—your marriage plans.

HOW DID YOU FIND ME AFTER ALL THESE YEARS?

We started by mailing a letter to the address you provided us in 1966 asking your parents to provide us a current address for you.

We then mailed letters to addresses in ten-year class reunion booklets.

Finally, we telephoned former classmates, neighbors, and others in your community.

In this way we have located over 97% of the 7,000 individuals who helped us in 1966. There are only 233 people we have not been able to locate. We are still trying to contact them.

WHAT WILL BE MY PART IN THE CONTINUING STUDY?

Sometime during the next few weeks you will receive a long distance call from one of our interviewers.

For most people the interview will take about 15 to 20 minutes.

After the interview, we will send a small questionnaire to fill out at your leisure.

WHAT KINDS OF THINGS DO YOU WANT TO ASK ME?

The telephone interview will ask about the experiences you have had since leaving high school

—any education or training you have had

—the jobs you have held

—your family

—and any military experience.

The questionnaire will ask about your opinions

—your likes and dislikes

—leisure time activities and hobbies

—organizations you participate in

—and your plans for the future.

WHAT HAPPENS TO MY ANSWERS?

Your answers will be kept strictly confidential. They will be combined with the answers from other respondents. We will use this information to compare groups of people rather than individuals. For example, students from large cities will be compared with those from small towns. The results will be made public in the form of summaries and statistics.

WILL I EVER SEE THE RESULTS OF THIS SURVEY?

Yes, but it will be a year before the results are available. In the next few years you'll probably hear about the most important results from television or radio and read about them in the newspaper.

WILL MY ANSWERS BE KEPT CONFIDENTIAL?

Yes. All information will be kept strictly confidential.

WHO IS CONDUCTING THIS SURVEY?

In 1966 Washington State University conducted the first part of this study. The follow-up study is being conducted through a cooperative arrangement between the Social Research Center at Washington State University and the Center for the Study of Youth Development in Omaha, Nebraska. The interviewing will be done by a professional marketing firm, Audits & Surveys, in New York City.

WHAT IF I HAVE OTHER QUESTIONS ABOUT THIS STUDY?

If you have questions that this brochure did not answer, write to either:

Dr. Luther B. Otto
PO Box 34039
Omaha, NE 68134

OR

Dr. James F. Short, Jr., Director
Social Research Center
Washington State University
Pullman, WA 99164

**Appendix K:
1979 Telephone-
Interview Schedule**

CDS INTERVIEW SCHEDULE

Question 1-15
These are instructions to interviewers to enter respondent's characteristics for personalization of the computerized interview schedule.

Question 16
My name is (name), I am working with Washington State University. Perhaps you recall our letter. We would like to update the information you provided when you were a (class) at (name of high school). We would like to take a few minutes to talk to you about your experiences since leaving high school. May we proceed?

(1) Yes   LEADS TO QUESTION 17
(2) No - 'busy'   EXIT INTERVIEW
(3) No - 'refused'   EXIT INTERVIEW

Question 17
Just to make sure that our records are correct, what was your full name when you were a (class) at (high school name) high school back in 1966?

(1) SPECIFY   LEADS TO QUESTION 18

Question 18
INTERVIEWER: IS THERE A REASONABLE MATCH BETWEEN THE NAME GIVEN AND THE NAME (MAIDEN) ON THE FORM?

(1) Yes   LEADS TO QUESTION 20
(2) No   LEADS TO QUESTION 19

Question 19
Did you use the name (name on form) while at (name of high school) high school in 1966?

(1) Yes   LEADS TO QUESTION 20
(2) No   EXIT INTERVIEW
(3) Refused   EXIT INTERVIEW

Question 20
What is your date of birth?   (month - day - year)

(1) SPECIFY   LEADS TO QUESTION 21

Question 21
We would like to start by updating your educational accomplishments. In 1966 you were a (class). Since then, have you graduated from high school?

(1) Yes   LEADS TO QUESTION 26
(2) No   LEADS TO QUESTION 22
(3) Don't know/no response LEADS TO QUESTION 22

Question 22
What is the highest grade you have completed?

(1) Ninth   LEADS TO QUESTION 23
(2) Tenth   LEADS TO QUESTION 23
(3) Eleventh   LEADS TO QUESTION 23
(4) Twelfth   LEADS TO QUESTION 23
(5) Don't know/no response LEADS TO QUESTION 24

Question 23
In what month and year did you complete this grade?
INTERVIEWER: ENTER IN THE FORMAT MONTH-YEAR AND RECORD ON MARKER SHEET

(1) SPECIFY   LEADS TO QUESTION 24
(2) DON'T KNOW   BRANCHES TO 24

Question 24
Have you passed a high school equivalency test such as the G.E.D.?

(1) Yes   LEADS TO QUESTION 25
(2) No   LEADS TO QUESTION 30
(3) Don't know/no response LEADS TO QUESTION 30

Question 25
In what month and year did you pass this test?
INTERVIEWER: ENTER IN THE FORMAT MONTH-YEAR

(1) SPECIFY   LEADS TO QUESTION 30
(2) DON'T KNOW   BRANCHES TO 30

Question 26
In what month and year did you graduate from high school?
INTERVIEWER: ENTER IN THE FORMAT MONTH-YEAR AND RECORD ON MARKER SHEET

(1) SPECIFY   LEADS TO QUESTION 27
(2) DON'T KNOW   BRANCHES TO 27

Question 27
While in high school did you apply for admission to either a two or four year college or university?

(1) Yes   LEADS TO QUESTION 28
(2) No   LEADS TO QUESTION 30
(3) Don't know/no response LEADS TO QUESTION 30

Question 28
While in high school, or during the summer just after high school, did you apply for a scholarship, a financial grant, a student loan or some other form of financial aid to help pay for your first year of college?

(1) Yes   LEADS TO QUESTION 29
(2) No   LEADS TO QUESTION 30
(3) Don't know/no response LEADS TO QUESTION 30

Question 29
Did you receive any of the types of aid you applied for?

(1) Yes   LEADS TO QUESTION 30
(2) No   LEADS TO QUESTION 30
(3) Don't know/no response LEADS TO QUESTION 30

Question 30
Have you ever gone to college?

(1) Yes   LEADS TO QUESTION 31
(2) No   LEADS TO QUESTION 32
(3) Don't know/no response LEADS TO QUESTION 32

Question 31
What is the highest year in college that you have completed?

(1) Less than 1 year — LEADS TO QUESTION 32
(2) Freshman (1 year) — LEADS TO QUESTION 32
(3) Sophomore (2 years) — LEADS TO QUESTION 32
(4) Junior (3 years) — LEADS TO QUESTION 32
(5) Senior (4 years/B.S./B.A.) — LEADS TO QUESTION 32
(6) Post graduate, but not masters degree — LEADS TO QUESTION 32
(7) Masters degree — LEADS TO QUESTION 32
(8) Post masters, but not Ph.D., M.D., or D.D.S. — LEADS TO QUESTION 32
(9) Ph.D., M.D., D.D.S., or other professional degrees — LEADS TO QUESTION 32
(10) Don't know/no response — LEADS TO QUESTION 32

Question 32
Have you ever obtained a journeyman's card?

(1) Yes — LEADS TO QUESTION 33
(2) No — LEADS TO QUESTION 33
(3) Don't know/no response — LEADS TO QUESTION 33

Question 33
Not counting schools at which you took 2 or fewer courses, have you ever enrolled as a full- or part-time student in...
...a two-year junior or community college?

(1) Yes — LEADS TO QUESTION 34
(2) No — LEADS TO QUESTION 35
(3) Don't know/no response — LEADS TO QUESTION 35

Question 34
What junior or community colleges have you attended?
INTERVIEWER: ENTER COLLEGE(S) BY NAME, ONE TO A LINE
PROBE: ANY OTHER TWO-YEAR JUNIOR OR COMMUNITY COLLEGES?

(1) SPECIFY — LEADS TO QUESTION 35
THIS QUESTION IS A MULTIPLE ANSWER QUESTION
(2) DON'T KNOW — BRANCHES TO 35

Question 35
...a vocational, technical or trade school?

(1) Yes — LEADS TO QUESTION 36
(2) No — LEADS TO: IF Q 30 A 1 THEN Q 37 ELSE Q 39
(3) Don't know/no response — LEADS TO: IF Q 30 A 1 THEN Q 37 ELSE Q 39

Question 36
What vocational, technical or trade schools have you attended?
INTERVIEWER: ENTER SCHOOL(S) BY NAME, ONE TO A LINE
PROBE: ANY OTHER VOCATIONAL, TECHNICAL OR TRADE SCHOOLS?

(1) SPECIFY — LEADS TO: IF Q 30 A 1 THEN Q 37 ELSE Q 39
THIS QUESTION IS A MULTIPLE ANSWER QUESTION
(2) DON'T KNOW — BRANCHES TO: IF Q 30 A 1 THEN Q 37 ELSE Q 39

Question 37
...a four year college or university?

(1) Yes — LEADS TO QUESTION 38
(2) No — LEADS TO QUESTION 39
(3) Don't know/no response — LEADS TO QUESTION 39

Question 38
What four year colleges or universities have you attended as either an undergraduate or a graduate student?
INTERVIEWER: ENTER COLLEGE(S) BY NAME, ONE TO A LINE
PROBE: ANY OTHER FOUR YEAR COLLEGES OR UNIVERSITIES?

(1) SPECIFY — LEADS TO QUESTION 39
THIS QUESTION IS A MULTIPLE ANSWER QUESTION
(2) DON'T KNOW — BRANCHES TO 39

Question 39
...a business college or secretarial or nursing school?

(1) Yes — LEADS TO QUESTION 40
(2) No — LEADS TO: IF Q 30 A 1 THEN Q 41 ELSE Q 43
(3) Don't know/no response — LEADS TO: IF Q 30 A 1 THEN Q 41 ELSE Q 43

Question 40
What business, secretarial or nursing schools have you attended?
INTERVIEWER: ENTER SCHOOL(S) BY NAME, ONE TO A LINE
PROBE: ANY OTHER BUSINESS, SECRETARIAL OR NURSING SCHOOLS?

(1) SPECIFY — LEADS TO: IF Q 30 A 1 THEN Q 41 ELSE Q 43
THIS QUESTION IS A MULTIPLE ANSWER QUESTION
(2) DON'T KNOW — BRANCHES TO: IF Q 30 A 1 THEN Q 41 ELSE Q 43

Question 41
...or a professional school such as a medical, dental or law school; a seminary or any other similar school that requires previous college work for entrance?

(1) Yes — LEADS TO QUESTION 42
(2) No — LEADS TO QUESTION 43
(3) Don't know/no response — LEADS TO QUESTION 43

Question 42
What professional school(s) have you attended?
INTERVIEWER: PROBE: ANY OTHER PROFESSIONAL SCHOOLS?

(1) SPECIFY — LEADS TO QUESTION 43
THIS QUESTION IS A MULTIPLE ANSWER QUESTION
(2) DON'T KNOW — BRANCHES TO 43

Question 43

Are you currently enrolled in a school or college as a full- or part-time student?
INTERVIEWER: IF YES, PROBE: WHAT TYPE OF SCHOOL ARE YOU ENROLLED IN?

(1) Not currently enrolled
(2) Enrolled in: A 2 year junior or
      community college   LEADS TO QUESTION 44
(3) Enrolled in: A vocational/technical/
      trade school   LEADS TO QUESTION 44
(4) Enrolled in: A 4 year college or
      university   LEADS TO QUESTION 44
(5) Enrolled in: A business college or
      secretarial/nursing school   LEADS TO QUESTION 44
(6) Enrolled in: A professional school   LEADS TO QUESTION 44
(7) Don't know/no response   LEADS TO QUESTION 44

Question 44

Are there any other educational or training experiences you have had that we have not
talked about?
INTERVIEWER: DO NOT INCLUDE SPECIALIZED MILITARY TRAINING PROGRAMS OR INFORMAL ON-THE-JOB
             TRAINING.

(1) Yes   LEADS TO QUESTION 45
(2) No   LEADS TO QUESTION 46
(3) Don't know/no response   LEADS TO QUESTION 46

Question 45

What kind of education or training was that?
INTERVIEWER: PROBE: DID YOU HAVE ANY OTHER KIND OF EDUCATION OR TRAINING?

(1) A company training school or on-the-job
      training   LEADS TO QUESTION 285
(2) Correspondence courses   LEADS TO QUESTION 285
(3) Adult education courses   LEADS TO QUESTION 285
(4) Government training or job programs
      (C.E.T.A., Y.C.C., U.C.C., W.I.N.)   LEADS TO QUESTION 285
(5) Any training or educational program lasting
      less than 6 months   LEADS TO QUESTION 285
(6) Vocational/technical/trade training longer
      than 6 months   LEADS TO QUESTION 285
(7) Business/secretarial/nursing training
      longer than 6 months   LEADS TO QUESTION 285
(8) 2 year junior/community college longer
      than 6 months   LEADS TO QUESTION 285
(9) 4 year college/university longer than
      6 months   LEADS TO QUESTION 285
(10) Professional/post-college longer than
      6 months   LEADS TO QUESTION 285
(11) Don't know/no response   LEADS TO QUESTION 285
THIS QUESTION IS A MULTIPLE ANSWER QUESTION

Question 46

Now, thinking about your attendance at (school name): Could you give me the city and
state in which it is located?

                                                LEADS TO QUESTION 47
(1) SPECIFY
SPECIAL HANDLING #1
QUESTIONS 46 THROUGH 97 ARE DRIVEN BY THE SET OF ANSWERS TO QUESTIONS:
34 36 38 40 42
QUESTIONS WITHIN EACH ANSWER
THIS QUESTION IS A MULTIPLE ANSWER QUESTION
(2) DON'T KNOW   BRANCHES TO 47

Question 47

In what month and year did you start going to (school name)?
INTERVIEWER: ENTER IN THE FORMAT MONTH-YEAR AND RECORD ON MARKER SHEET

(1) SPECIFY   LEADS TO QUESTION 48
(2) DON'T KNOW   BRANCHES TO 48

Question 48

Not counting interruptions, in what month and year did you last attend (school name)?
INTERVIEWER: ENTER IN THE FORMAT MONTH-YEAR AND RECORD ON MARKER SHEET

(1) SPECIFY   LEADS TO QUESTION 49
(2) DON'T KNOW   BRANCHES TO 49

Question 49

Between the time you first enrolled and the time that you left (school name), did you ever
interrupt your schooling for a period of one month or more? Do not include regular school
breaks or summer vacations.

(1) Yes   LEADS TO QUESTION 50
(2) No   LEADS TO QUESTION 55
(3) Don't know/no response   LEADS TO QUESTION 55

Question 50

In what month and year did you first stop attending (school name)?
INTERVIEWER: ENTER IN THE FORMAT MONTH-YEAR AND RECORD ON MARKER SHEET

(1) SPECIFY   LEADS TO QUESTION 51
(2) DON'T KNOW   BRANCHES TO 51

Question 51

In what month and year did you return to (school name)?
INTERVIEWER: ENTER IN THE FORMAT MONTH-YEAR AND RECORD ON MARKER SHEET

(1) SPECIFY   LEADS TO QUESTION 52
(2) DON'T KNOW   BRANCHES TO 52

Question 52

And did you have any other major interruptions in your schooling at (school name)?

(1) Yes   LEADS TO QUESTION 53
(2) No   LEADS TO QUESTION 55
(3) Don't know/no response   LEADS TO QUESTION 55

Question 53
In what month and year did you next stop attending (school name)?
INTERVIEWER: ENTER IN THE FORMAT MONTH-YEAR AND RECORD ON MARKER SHEET

LEADS TO QUESTION 54
BRANCHES TO 54

(1) SPECIFY
(2) DON'T KNOW

Question 54
In what month and year did you return to (school name)?
INTERVIEWER: ENTER IN THE FORMAT MONTH-YEAR AND RECORD ON MARKER SHEET

LEADS TO QUESTION 52
BRANCHES TO 52

(1) SPECIFY
(2) DON'T KNOW

Question 55
Were you always enrolled as a full-time student?

(1) Yes   LEADS TO QUESTION 62
(2) No   LEADS TO QUESTION 56
(3) Don't know/no response   LEADS TO QUESTION 62

Question 56
Were you always enrolled as a part-time student?

(1) Yes   LEADS TO QUESTION 62
(2) No   LEADS TO QUESTION 57
(3) Don't know/no response   LEADS TO QUESTION 62

Question 57
When you started attending (school name), were you enrolled as a full- or part-time student?

(1) Full-time   LEADS TO QUESTION 58
(2) Part-time   LEADS TO QUESTION 60
(3) Don't know/no response   LEADS TO QUESTION 62

Question 58
In what month and year did you change to part-time enrollment?
INTERVIEWER: ENTER IN THE FORMAT MONTH-YEAR

LEADS TO QUESTION 59
BRANCHES TO 59

(1) SPECIFY
(2) DON'T KNOW

Question 59
Did you remain a part-time student for the rest of the time that you attended (school name)?

(1) Yes   LEADS TO QUESTION 62
(2) No   LEADS TO QUESTION 60
(3) Don't know/no response   LEADS TO QUESTION 62

Question 60
In what month and year did you change to full-time enrollment?
INTERVIEWER: ENTER IN THE FORMAT MONTH-YEAR

LEADS TO QUESTION 61
BRANCHES TO 61

(1) SPECIFY
(2) DON'T KNOW

Question 61
Did you remain a full-time student for the rest of the time that you attended (School name)?

(1) Yes   LEADS TO QUESTION 62
(2) No   LEADS TO QUESTION 58
(3) Don't know/no response   LEADS TO QUESTION 62

Question 62
While you were a student at (school name), did you ever hold a full-time job for more than one month during the school year? Do not include summer jobs or jobs held during school vacations or breaks. By "full-time" we mean working 25 hours or more in an average week and holding the job for more than one month.

(1) Yes   LEADS TO QUESTION 63
(2) No   LEADS TO QUESTION 63
(3) Don't know/no response   LEADS TO QUESTION 63

Question 63
What degrees, diplomas or certificates did you receive from (school name)?
INTERVIEWER: PROBE: ANY OTHERS? BEFORE GOING ON TO THE NEXT QUESTION, CHECK TO SEE IF 'OTHER CODE '6' WAS ENTERED. THE ANSWER TO THE NEXT QUESTION DEPENDS ON THAT ANSWER.

(1) A.A. associate degree   LEADS TO QUESTION 64
(2) B.S. or B.A. bachelor or arts/science   LEADS TO QUESTION 64
(3) M.S. or M.A. master of arts/science   LEADS TO QUESTION 64
(4) Ph.D./M.D./D.D.S./J.D./other professional degree   LEADS TO QUESTION 64
(5) Teaching certificate   LEADS TO QUESTION 64
(6) Other   LEADS TO QUESTION 64
(7) None   LEADS TO QUESTION 64
(8) Don't know/no response   LEADS TO QUESTION 64
THIS QUESTION IS A MULTIPLE ANSWER QUESTION

Question 64
INTERVIEWER: DID YOU ENTER AN 'OTHER' CODE '6' TO THE LAST QUESTION?

(1) Yes   LEADS TO QUESTION 65
(2) No   LEADS TO QUESTION 66

Question 65
INTERVIEWER: PROBE TO FIND OUT WHAT THE DEGREE CODED AS 'OTHER' WAS

(1) SPECIFY   LEADS TO QUESTION 66
THIS QUESTION IS A MULTIPLE ANSWER QUESTION   BRANCHES TO 66
(2) DON'T KNOW

Question 66
What was your major field of study or specialty at (school name)?

(1) SPECIFY   LEADS TO QUESTION 67
THIS QUESTION IS A MULTIPLE ANSWER QUESTION   BRANCHES TO 67
(2) DON'T KNOW

Question 67
On a scale of four to zero, about what was your cumulative grade point average for the years that you attended (school name)?
INTERVIEWER: IF RESPONDENT SAYS THEIR SCHOOL USED A DIFFERENT GRADING SYSTEM, THEN PROBE: IF FOUR POINT ZERO REPRESENTS STRAIGHT A'S, IF THREE POINT ZERO REPRESENTS AN AVERAGE OF B'S, IF A TWO POINT ZERO REPRESENTS MOSTLY C'S, AND A ONE POINT ZERO MEANS MOSTLY D'S, WHAT WOULD BE YOUR GRADE POINT AVERAGE?

(1) SPECIFY

At this point:
1) if the focal school was a two-year junior or community college, a vocational, technical, or trade school, or business, secretarial, or nursing school the interview proceeded to Question 94;
2) if the focal school was a four-year college or university the interview proceeded to Question 73; or
3) if the focal school was a professional school the interview proceeded to Questions 46-67 for the next school, or to Question 102 if questions had been asked for all schools elicited in Questions 34, 36, 38, 40, and 42.

Question 73
Did you attend (school name) as an undergraduate student, a graduate student or both?

(1) Under-graduate   LEADS TO QUESTION 74
(2) Graduate   LEADS TO QUESTION 102
(3) Both under-graduate and graduate   LEADS TO QUESTION 74
(4) Don't know/no response   LEADS TO QUESTION 102

Question 74
And did you receive a bachelor's degree from (school name)?

(1) Yes   LEADS TO QUESTION 75
(2) No   LEADS TO QUESTION 81
(3) Don't know/no response   LEADS TO QUESTION 81

Question 75
During their last year at college as an undergraduate, some people have definite plans for the future while others do not. Think back to about the time you received your bachelor's degree from (school name). About the time you received your degree, what were your plans for the year after you graduated from college? Did you plan on...
..getting a full-time job?

(1) Yes   LEADS TO QUESTION 78
(2) No   LEADS TO QUESTION 76
(3) Don't know/no response   LEADS TO QUESTION 76

Question 76
..getting a part-time job?

(1) Yes   LEADS TO QUESTION 77
(2) No   LEADS TO QUESTION 77
(3) Don't know/no response   LEADS TO QUESTION 77

9

Question 77
...entering the military?

(1) Yes   LEADS TO QUESTION 78
(2) No   LEADS TO QUESTION 78
(3) Don't know/no response   LEADS TO QUESTION 78

Question 78
...going to graduate or professional school?

(1) Yes   LEADS TO QUESTION 79
(2) No   LEADS TO QUESTION 79
(3) Don't know/no response   LEADS TO QUESTION 79

Question 79
...getting married?

(1) Yes   LEADS TO: IF Q 6 A 2 THEN Q 80 ELSE Q 87
(2) No   LEADS TO: IF Q 6 A 2 THEN Q 80 ELSE Q 87
(3) Don't know/no response   LEADS TO: IF Q 6 A 2 THEN Q 80 ELSE Q 87

Question 80
...keeping house?

(1) Yes   LEADS TO QUESTION 87
(2) No   LEADS TO QUESTION 87
(3) Don't know/no response   LEADS TO QUESTION 87

Question 81
During their last years at college as an undergraduate, some people have definite plans for the future while others do not, think back to about the time you left (school name), about the time you left college, what were your plans for the year after you left? Did you plan on...
...continuing in college?
INTERVIEWER: IF RESPONDENT IS CURRENTLY ENROLLED ASK ABOUT PLANS FOR NEXT YEAR

(1) Yes   LEADS TO QUESTION 82
(2) No   LEADS TO QUESTION 82
(3) Don't know/no response   LEADS TO QUESTION 82

Question 82
...getting a full-time job?

(1) Yes   LEADS TO QUESTION 85
(2) No   LEADS TO QUESTION 83
(3) Don't know/no response   LEADS TO QUESTION 83

Question 83
...getting a part-time job?

(1) Yes   LEADS TO QUESTION 84
(2) No   LEADS TO QUESTION 84
(3) Don't know/no response   LEADS TO QUESTION 84

10

12

Question 84
...entering the military?

(1) Yes	LEADS TO QUESTION 85
(2) No	LEADS TO QUESTION 85
(3) Don't know/no response	LEADS TO QUESTION 85

Question 85
...getting married?

(1) Yes	LEADS TO: IF Q 6 A 2 THEN Q 86 ELSE Q 87
(2) No	LEADS TO: IF Q 6 A 2 THEN Q 87 ELSE Q 87
(3) Don't know/no response	LEADS TO: IF Q 6 A 2 THEN Q 86 ELSE Q 87

Question 86
...keeping house?

(1) Yes	LEADS TO QUESTION 87
(2) No	LEADS TO QUESTION 87
(3) Don't know/no response	LEADS TO QUESTION 87

Question 87
While attending college as an undergraduate, how much did you participate in the following organized activities? Were you quite active, moderately active, not very active or not a participant in...
...intramural or coed sports?

(1) Quite active	LEADS TO QUESTION 88
(2) Moderately active	LEADS TO QUESTION 88
(3) Not very active	LEADS TO QUESTION 88
(4) Not a participant	LEADS TO QUESTION 88
(5) Don't know/no response	LEADS TO QUESTION 88

Question 88
...intercollegiate sports?

(1) Quite active	LEADS TO QUESTION 89
(2) Moderately active	LEADS TO QUESTION 89
(3) Not very active	LEADS TO QUESTION 89
(4) Not a participant	LEADS TO QUESTION 89
(5) Don't know/no response	LEADS TO QUESTION 89

Question 89
...band, chorus, orchestra, drama or other performing group or groups?

(1) Quite active	LEADS TO QUESTION 90
(2) Moderately active	LEADS TO QUESTION 90
(3) Not very active	LEADS TO QUESTION 90
(4) Not a participant	LEADS TO QUESTION 90
(5) Don't know/no response	LEADS TO QUESTION 90

Question 90
...church affiliated clubs, choruses or groups?

(1) Quite active	LEADS TO QUESTION 91
(2) Moderately active	LEADS TO QUESTION 91
(3) Not very active	LEADS TO QUESTION 91
(4) Not a participant	LEADS TO QUESTION 91
(5) Don't know/no response	LEADS TO QUESTION 91

Question 91
...student government or student newspapers or annuals?

(1) Quite active	LEADS TO QUESTION 92
(2) Moderately active	LEADS TO QUESTION 92
(3) Not very active	LEADS TO QUESTION 92
(4) Not a participant	LEADS TO QUESTION 92
(5) Don't know/no response	LEADS TO QUESTION 92

Question 92
...clubs sponsored or affiliated with your major area of study or your specialty?

(1) Quite active	LEADS TO QUESTION 102
(2) Moderately active	LEADS TO QUESTION 102
(3) Not very active	LEADS TO QUESTION 102
(4) Not a participant	LEADS TO QUESTION 102
(5) Don't know/no response	LEADS TO QUESTION 102

Question 94
While at (school name), did you participate in organizations such as the Future Business Leaders of America (FBLA), Distributive Education Clubs of America (DECA), Vocational Industrial Clubs of America (VICA) or other such student leadership organizations?

(1) Yes	LEADS TO QUESTION 95
(2) No	LEADS TO QUESTION 97
(3) Don't know/no response	LEADS TO QUESTION 97

Question 95
Which one did you participate in?

(1) FBLA (Future Business Leaders of America)	LEADS TO QUESTION 96
(2) DECA (Distributive Education Clubs of America)	LEADS TO QUESTION 96
(3) VICA (Vocational Industrial Clubs of America)	LEADS TO QUESTION 96
(4) Other	LEADS TO QUESTION 96
(5) Don't know/no response	LEADS TO QUESTION 96

THIS QUESTION IS A MULTIPLE ANSWER QUESTION

Question 96
How active a participant were you in this organization? Were you (read list)

(1) Very active	LEADS TO QUESTION 97
(2) Quite active	LEADS TO QUESTION 97
(3) Moderately active	LEADS TO QUESTION 97
(4) Not very active	LEADS TO QUESTION 97
(5) Not at all active	LEADS TO QUESTION 97
(6) Don't know/no response	LEADS TO QUESTION 97

14

Question 106
Why did you join the military?
INTERVIEWER: READ EACH OPTION AND ENTER ALL THAT APPLY.
      PROBE: DID YOU JOIN...

(1) To avoid the draft, that is, you thought
      you would be drafted anyway   LEADS TO QUESTION 107
(2) To get a job, to avoid unemployment   LEADS TO QUESTION 107
(3) For the education, training or benefits   LEADS TO QUESTION 107
(4) To get away from your home, city or family   LEADS TO QUESTION 107
(5) For the adventure, action or travel   LEADS TO QUESTION 107
(6) To serve your country   LEADS TO QUESTION 107
(7) Because you didn't know what else to do   LEADS TO QUESTION 107
(8) Other   LEADS TO QUESTION 107
(9) Don't know/no response   LEADS TO QUESTION 107
      THIS QUESTION IS A MULTIPLE ANSWER QUESTION

Question 107
INTERVIEWER: IF ONLY A SINGLE REASON WAS GIVEN TO THE LAST QUESTION, ENTER '11' AND DO
               NOT READ QUESTION, ELSE ASK: WHAT REASON WAS THE MOST IMPORTANT?

(1) None are important   LEADS TO QUESTION 108
(2) All are equally important   LEADS TO QUESTION 108
(3) To avoid the draft, that is, you thought
      you would be drafted anyway   LEADS TO QUESTION 108
(4) To get a job, to avoid unemployment   LEADS TO QUESTION 108
(5) For the education, training or benefits   LEADS TO QUESTION 108
(6) To get away from your city, home or family   LEADS TO QUESTION 108
(7) For the adventure, action or travel   LEADS TO QUESTION 108
(8) To serve your country   LEADS TO QUESTION 108
(9) Because you didn't know what else to do   LEADS TO QUESTION 108
(10) Other   LEADS TO QUESTION 108
(11) Only one reason given   LEADS TO QUESTION 108
(12) Don't know/no response   LEADS TO QUESTION 108

Question 108
In what month and year did you first begin in active duty?
INTERVIEWER: ENTER IN THE FORMAT MONTH-YEAR AND RECORD ON MARKER SHEET

(1) SPECIFY   LEADS TO QUESTION 109
(2) DON'T KNOW   BRANCHES TO 109

Question 109
Are you currently on active duty in the U.S. Armed Forces?

(1) Yes   LEADS TO QUESTION 112
(2) No   LEADS TO QUESTION 110
(3) Don't know/no response   LEADS TO QUESTION 110

Question 110
What was the month and year of your last separation from active service?
INTERVIEWER: ENTER IN THE FORMAT MONTH-YEAR AND RECORD ON MARKER SHEET

(1) SPECIFY   LEADS TO QUESTION 111
(2) DON'T KNOW   BRANCHES TO 111

13

Question 97
Is (school name) a private or a public school?

(1) Private   LEADS TO QUESTION 102
(2) Public   LEADS TO QUESTION 102
(3) Don't know/no response   LEADS TO QUESTION 102

Question 102
Now I want to shift to some questions about military service, if that applies to you.
Have you ever been on active duty in the U.S. Armed Forces?

(1) Yes   LEADS TO QUESTION 103
(2) No   LEADS TO QUESTION 103
(3) Don't know/no response   LEADS TO QUESTION 103

Question 103
Have you ever spent at least two months on active duty for training in the Reserves or the
National Guard?

(1) Yes   LEADS TO: If Q 102 A 1 THEN
                             Q 104 ELSE Q 128
(2) No   LEADS TO: IF Q 102 A 1 THEN
                             Q 104 ELSE Q 140
(3) Don't know/no response LEADS TO: IF Q 102 A 1
                             THEN Q 104 ELSE Q 140

Question 104
How did you first enter the Armed Forces? Were you drafted, did you enlist in the regular
services, the Reserves or the National Guard, or did you enter through college R.O.T.C.,
O.C.S. (Officer Candidate School), or a service academy?

(1) Drafted   LEADS TO QUESTION 108
(2) Enlisted   LEADS TO QUESTION 105
(3) Reserves or National Guard   LEADS TO QUESTION 128
(4) R.O.T.C., O.C.S. or service academy   LEADS TO QUESTION 105
(5) Other   LEADS TO QUESTION 105
(6) Don't know/no response   LEADS TO QUESTION 105

Question 105
At the time you entered the military, did you think of it more as...

(1) A new career   LEADS TO QUESTION 106
(2) An interruption of your previous civilian
      career   LEADS TO QUESTION 106
(3) Don't know/no response   LEADS TO QUESTION 106

Question 111
Between the time you first entered the military and when you were last separated, has there ever been a time when you were not in the military?

(1) Yes   LEADS TO QUESTION 113
(2) No   LEADS TO QUESTION 114
(3) Don't know/no response   LEADS TO QUESTION 114

Question 112
Between the time you first entered active military service and now was there ever a time when you were not in the military?

(1) Yes   LEADS TO QUESTION 113
(2) No   LEADS TO QUESTION 114
(3) Don't know/no response   LEADS TO QUESTION 114

Question 113
What was the date of your first separation from the military?
INTERVIEWER: ENTER IN THE FORMAT MONTH-YEAR

(1) SPECIFY
THIS QUESTION IS A MULTIPLE ANSWER QUESTION   LEADS TO QUESTION 290
(2) DON'T KNOW   BRANCHES TO 290

Question 114
Other than basic training, how many specialized military schools such as AIT (Advanced Individual Training) or NCO did you complete while in the Armed Forces? A specialized program is one that is not required of all members of that branch of the service.

(1) None   LEADS TO: IF Q 109 NOT A 1
                 THEN Q 117 ELSE Q 122
(2) One   LEADS TO: IF Q 109 NOT A 1
                 THEN Q 117 ELSE Q 122
(3) Two   LEADS TO: IF Q 109 NOT A 1
                 THEN Q 117 ELSE Q 122
(4) Three   LEADS TO: IF Q 109 NOT A 1
                 THEN Q 117 ELSE Q 122
(5) Four   LEADS TO: IF Q 109 NOT A 1
                 THEN Q 117 ELSE Q 122
(6) Five   LEADS TO: IF Q 109 NOT A 1
                 THEN Q 117 ELSE Q 122
(7) Six   LEADS TO: IF Q 109 NOT A 1
                 THEN Q 117 ELSE Q 122
(8) Seven or more   LEADS TO: IF Q 109 NOT A 1
                 THEN Q 117 ELSE Q 122
(9) Don't know/no response   LEADS TO: IF Q 109 NOT A 1
                 THEN Q 117 ELSE Q 122

Question 117
When you left, did you have a job or career waiting for you?

(1) Yes   LEADS TO QUESTION 118
(2) No   LEADS TO QUESTION 118
(3) Don't know/no response   LEADS TO QUESTION 118

Question 118
What was your pay grade when you were discharged?

(1) E1 . . . . (14)   01
(2) E2 . . . . (15)   02
(3) E3 . . . . (16)   03
(4) E4 . . . . (17)   04
(5) E5 . . . . (18)   05
(6) E6 . . . . (19)   06
(7) E7 . . . . (20)   07
(8) E8 . . . . (21)   08
(9) E9 . . . . (22)   09
(10) WO1 . . . . (23)   010
(11) WO2 . . . . (24)   Other pay grade
(12) WO3 . . . . (25)   Don't remember
(13) WO4 . . . . (26)   Don't know/no response

LEADS TO QUESTION 119

Question 119
Did you become interested in your civilian career because of your military training or work?

(1) Yes   LEADS TO QUESTION 120
(2) No   LEADS TO QUESTION 120
(3) Don't know/no response   LEADS TO QUESTION 120

Question 120
How much have you used your military training, skills or work experience in any of the jobs you have held since leaving the military? Would you say you have used them...

(1) All the time   LEADS TO QUESTION 121
(2) A lot   LEADS TO QUESTION 121
(3) Some   LEADS TO QUESTION 121
(4) Only a little   LEADS TO QUESTION 121
(5) Not at all   LEADS TO QUESTION 121
(6) Don't know/no response   LEADS TO QUESTION 121

Question 121
Since your separation from the military have you ever received any military pensions, disabilities or benefits, including use of the G.I. Bill?

(1) No, none   LEADS TO QUESTION 122
(2) G.I. Bill   LEADS TO QUESTION 122
(3) Disability - physical   LEADS TO QUESTION 122
(4) Disability - psychological   LEADS TO QUESTION 122
(5) Other   LEADS TO QUESTION 122
(6) Don't know/no response   LEADS TO QUESTION 122
THIS QUESTION IS A MULTIPLE ANSWER QUESTION

Question 122
Were you ever stationed in Southeast Asia during the Vietnam Conflict?
INTERVIEWER: NOTE: 'YES' ANSWERS ARE TO INCLUDE COUNTRIES SUCH AS VIETNAM, CAMBODIA, THAILAND, THE PHILLIPINES AND GUAM.

(1) Yes   LEADS TO QUESTION 123
(2) No   LEADS TO QUESTION 124
(3) Don't know/no response   LEADS TO QUESTION 124

Question 123
Was your duty in a combat or combat service-support unit?

(1) Yes   LEADS TO: IF Q 109 A   1 THEN Q 126 ELSE Q 124
(2) No   LEADS TO: IF Q 109 A   1 THEN Q 126 ELSE Q 124
(3) Don't know/no response   LEADS TO: IF Q 109 A   1 THEN Q 126 ELSE Q 124

Question 124
What branch of the service were you in?

(1) Navy or Naval Reserve   LEADS TO QUESTION 125
(2) Army or Army Reserve   LEADS TO QUESTION 125
(3) Air Force   LEADS TO QUESTION 125
(4) Marines   LEADS TO QUESTION 125
(5) Coast Guard   LEADS TO QUESTION 125
(6) National Guard   LEADS TO QUESTION 125
(7) Don't know/no response   LEADS TO QUESTION 125

Question 125
Think of the main kind of work you did while you were in the military. For what civilian job might that best prepare a person?
INTERVIEWER: FOR EXAMPLE: ELECTRICIAN, FILE CLERK, POLICEMAN, FOREMAN OR SUPERVISOR

(1) SPECIFY   LEADS TO: IF Q 103 A   1 THEN Q 128 ELSE Q 140
                   BRANCHES TO: IF Q 103 A   1 THEN Q 128 ELSE Q 140
(2) DON'T KNOW

Question 126
What branch of the service are you in?

(1) Navy or Naval Reserve   LEADS TO QUESTION 127
(2) Army or Army Reserve   LEADS TO QUESTION 127
(3) Air Force   LEADS TO QUESTION 127
(4) Marines   LEADS TO QUESTION 127
(5) Coast Guard   LEADS TO QUESTION 127
(6) National Guard   LEADS TO QUESTION 127
(7) Don't know/no response   LEADS TO QUESTION 127

Question 127
Think of the main kind of work you are doing in the military. For what civilian job might that best prepare a person?
INTERVIEWER: FOR EXAMPLE: ELECTRICIAN, FILE CLERK, POLICEMAN, FOREMAN OR SUPERVISOR

(1) SPECIFY   LEADS TO: IF Q 103 A   1 THEN Q 128 ELSE Q 140
                   BRANCHES TO: IF Q 103 A   1 THEN Q 128 ELSE Q 140
(2) DON'T KNOW

Question 128
Why did you join the Reserves or National Guard?
INTERVIEWER: READ EACH OPTION AND ENTER ALL THAT APPLY
PROBE: DID YOU JOIN...

(1) To avoid the draft, that is, you thought you would be drafted anyway   LEADS TO QUESTION 129
(2) For a part-time job for the extra money   LEADS TO QUESTION 129
(3) For the education, training or benefits   LEADS TO QUESTION 129
(4) For the adventure, action or travel   LEADS TO QUESTION 129
(5) To serve your country
(6) Because it was required as part of military duty   LEADS TO QUESTION 129
(7) Other reason   LEADS TO QUESTION 129
(8) Don't know/no response   LEADS TO QUESTION 129
THIS QUESTION IS A MULTIPLE ANSWER QUESTION

Question 129
INTERVIEWER: IF ONLY A SINGLE REASON WAS GIVEN TO THE LAST QUESTION, ENTER '111' AND DO NOT READ THE QUESTION, ELSE ASK: WHICH REASON WAS THE MOST IMPORTANT?

(1) None are important   LEADS TO QUESTION 130
(2) All are equally important   LEADS TO QUESTION 130
(3) To avoid the draft, that is, you thought you would be drafted anyway
(4) For a part-time job for the extra money   LEADS TO QUESTION 130
(5) For the education, training or benefits   LEADS TO QUESTION 130
(6) For the adventure, action or travel   LEADS TO QUESTION 130
(7) To serve your country   LEADS TO QUESTION 130
(8) Because it was required as part of military duty   LEADS TO QUESTION 130
(9) Other   LEADS TO QUESTION 130
(10) Don't know/no response   LEADS TO QUESTION 130
(11) Only one reason given   LEADS TO QUESTION 130

Question 130
In what month and year did you first enter the Reserves or National Guard?
INTERVIEWER: ENTER IN THE FORMAT MONTH-YEAR AND RECORD ON MARKER SHEET

(1) SPECIFY   LEADS TO QUESTION 131
(2) DON'T KNOW   BRANCHES TO 131

Question 131
Are you currently in the Reserves or National Guard?

(1) Yes   LEADS TO QUESTION 140
(2) No   LEADS TO QUESTION 132
(3) Don't know/no response   LEADS TO QUESTION 132

Question 132
What was the month and year of your last service in the Reserves or National Guard?
INTERVIEWER: ENTER IN THE FORMAT MONTH-YEAR AND RECORD ON MARKER SHEET

(1) SPECIFY   LEADS TO QUESTION 140
(2) DON'T KNOW   BRANCHES TO 140

Question 140
The next set of questions concerns your family life since you left high school.
Have you ever been married?
INTERVIEWER: ENTER CODE '3' ONLY IF RESPONDENT VOLUNTEERS THE INFORMATION

(1) Yes	LEADS TO QUESTION 142
(2) No	LEADS TO QUESTION 141
(3) No but currently living with member of the opposite sex	LEADS TO QUESTION 141
(4) Don't know/no response	LEADS TO QUESTION 141

Question 141
Do you plan to marry within the next year?

(1) Yes	LEADS TO QUESTION 230
(2) No	LEADS TO QUESTION 230
(3) Don't know/no response	LEADS TO QUESTION 230

Question 142
Are you currently married, separated, divorced or widowed?
INTERVIEWER: ENTER CODE '5' ONLY IF RESPONDENT VOLUNTEERS INFORMATION

(1) Currently married	LEADS TO QUESTION 143
(2) Currently separated	LEADS TO QUESTION 143
(3) Currently divorced	LEADS TO QUESTION 143
(4) Currently widowed	LEADS TO QUESTION 143
(5) Previously separated/widowed/divorced; currently cohabiting	LEADS TO QUESTION 143
(6) Don't know/no response	LEADS TO QUESTION 143

Question 143
How many times have you been married?
INTERVIEWER: INCLUDE CURRENT MARRIAGE IN COUNT

(1) Married once	LEADS TO QUESTION 144
(2) Married twice	LEADS TO QUESTION 144
(3) Married three times	LEADS TO QUESTION 144
(4) Married four times	LEADS TO QUESTION 144
(5) Married five times	LEADS TO QUESTION 144
(6) Married six or more times	LEADS TO QUESTION 144
(7) Don't know/no response	LEADS TO QUESTION 144

Question 144
INTERVIEWER: ENTER THE ANSWERS TO QUESTIONS 142 AND 143 (SHOWN BELOW) AS FOLLOWS:
A) IF MARRIED ONLY ONCE, ENTER CODE '1'
B) IF MARRIED MORE THAN ONCE AND CURRENTLY MARRIED, ENTER '2' AND '3'
C) IF MARRIED MORE THAN ONCE AND CURRENTLY WIDOWED, SEPARATED, DIVORCED OR
   COHABITING, ENTER '2' AND '4'

(1) Your first	LEADS TO QUESTION 147
(2) Your first	LEADS TO QUESTION 147
(3) Your current	LEADS TO QUESTION 147
(4) Your most recent	LEADS TO QUESTION 147
THIS QUESTION IS A MULTIPLE ANSWER QUESTION

QUESTIONS 147-209 ARE ASKED FOR FIRST, CURRENT, AND MOST RECENT MARRIAGES.

Question 147
What was the date of your (first, current, most recent) marriage?
INTERVIEWER: ENTER IN THE FORMAT MONTH-DAY-YEAR AND RECORD ON MARKER SHEET

(1) SPECIFY	LEADS TO QUESTION 148

Question 148
Approximately how many months did you date your (wife/husband) prior to your (first, current, most recent) marriage?

(1) SPECIFY	LEADS TO QUESTION 149
(2) DON'T KNOW	BRANCHES TO 149

Question 149
Approximately how many months were you engaged to your (wife/husband) before your (first, current, most recent) marriage?

(1) SPECIFY	LEADS TO QUESTION 150
(2) DON'T KNOW	BRANCHES TO 150

Question 150
Had your (first, current, most recent) (wife/husband) been married prior to your marriage?

(1) Yes	LEADS TO QUESTION 151
(2) No	LEADS TO QUESTION 151
(3) Don't know/no response	LEADS TO QUESTION 151

Question 151
What is your (first, current, most recent) (wife's/husband's) date of birth?
INTERVIEWER: ENTER IN FORMAT MONTH-DAY-YEAR

(1) SPECIFY	LEADS TO QUESTION 152
QUESTION 151 HAS ALPHANUMERIC ANSWERS	
(2) DON'T KNOW	BRANCHES TO 152

Question 152
(About your (first, current, most recent) marriage) Before you were married, what was the highest grade of regular school completed by your (first, current, most recent) (wife/husband)?

Grades 1 through 12

(1) First	(7) Seventh
(2) Second	(8) Eighth
(3) Third	(9) Ninth
(4) Fourth	(10) Tenth
(5) Fifth	(11) Eleventh
(6) Sixth	(12) Twelfth

College (academic years)

(13) Freshman (first year)	(17) Post-grad, but not master's degree
(14) Sophomore (second/associate's)	(18) Master's degree
(15) Junior (third year)	(19) Post master's but not M.D./PH.D.
(16) Senior (fourth/bachelor's)	(20) Doctorate (PH.D./M.D./J.D./D.D.S.)
INTERVIEWER: IF DON'T KNOW CODE '21'

(1) SPECIFY	LEADS TO QUESTION 153
(2) DON'T KNOW	BRANCHES TO 153

21

QUESTION 153
Aside from regular schooling, had your (first, current, most recent) (wife/husband) obtained any vocational or business school degree, certificate or diploma before your marriage?

(1) Yes   LEADS TO QUESTION 154
(2) No   LEADS TO QUESTION 154
(3) Don't know/no response   LEADS TO QUESTION 154

Question 154
During the first year of your (first, current, most recent) marriage did your (wife/husband) hold a full-time job? Do not include military service or summer school jobs.
INTERVIEWER: A "FULL-TIME" JOB MEANS WORKING 25 HOURS OR MORE IN AN AVERAGE WEEK FOR A PERIOD OF MORE THAN ONE MONTH

(1) Yes   LEADS TO QUESTION 157
(2) No   LEADS TO QUESTION 157
(3) Don't know/no response   LEADS TO QUESTION 157

Question 155
Was your (first, current, most recent) (wife/husband) unemployed or looking for work, unable to work or keeping house during the first year?

(1) No, none of the above   LEADS TO QUESTION 156
(2) Unemployed or looking for work   LEADS TO QUESTION 156
(3) Unable to work   LEADS TO QUESTION 156
(4) Keeping house   LEADS TO QUESTION 156
(5) Don't know/no response   LEADS TO QUESTION 156

Question 156
During the first year of your (first, current, most recent) marriage, was your (wife/husband) in the military or the reserves; or a full- or part-time student?

(1) Military   LEADS TO: IF Q 154 A 1 THEN Q 158 ELSE Q 166
(2) Reserves   LEADS TO: IF Q 154 A 1 THEN Q 158 ELSE Q 166
(3) Part-time student   LEADS TO: IF Q 154 A 1 THEN Q 158 ELSE Q 166
(4) Full-time student   LEADS TO: IF Q 154 A 1 THEN Q 158 ELSE Q 166
(5) Military and full- or part-time student   LEADS TO: IF Q 154 A 1 THEN Q 158 ELSE Q 166
(6) Reserves and full- or part-time student   LEADS TO: IF Q 154 A 1 THEN Q 158 ELSE Q 166
(7) None of the above   LEADS TO: IF Q 154 A 1 THEN Q 158 ELSE Q 166
(8) Don't know/no response   LEADS TO: IF Q 154 A 1 THEN Q 158 ELSE Q 166

Question 157
During the first year of your (first, current, most recent) marriage did your (wife/husband) hold a part-time job?

(1) Yes   LEADS TO QUESTION 156
(2) No   LEADS TO: IF Q 154 A 1 THEN Q 156 ELSE Q 155
(3) Don't know/no response   LEADS TO: IF Q 154 A 1 THEN Q 156 ELSE Q 155

22

Question 158
Again, referring to the first year of your (first, current, most recent) marriage, what kind of work was your (wife/husband) doing in (her/his) full-time job?
INTERVIEWER: FOR EXAMPLE: ELECTRICAL ENGINEER, SECRETARY, TRUCK DRIVER

(1) SPECIFY   LEADS TO QUESTION 159
THIS QUESTION IS A MULTIPLE ANSWER QUESTION
(2) DON'T KNOW   BRANCHES TO 159

Question 159
What were (her/his) most important activities or duties?
INTERVIEWER: FOR EXAMPLE: KEPT THE BOOKS, SOLD CARS, OPERATED PRINTING PRESS

(1) SPECIFY   LEADS TO QUESTION 160
THIS QUESTION IS A MULTIPLE ANSWER QUESTION
(2) DON'T KNOW   BRANCHES TO 160

Question 160
What kind of business or industry was this?
INTERVIEWER: FOR EXAMPLE: T.V. AND RADIO MFG., RETAIL SHOE STORE, STATE LABOR DEPT.

(1) SPECIFY   LEADS TO QUESTION 161
THIS QUESTION IS A MULTIPLE ANSWER QUESTION
(2) DON'T KNOW   BRANCHES TO 161

Question 161
Was this mainly manufacturing, wholesale trade, retail trade or something else?

(1) Manufacturing   LEADS TO QUESTION 162
(2) Wholesale   LEADS TO QUESTION 162
(3) Retail   LEADS TO QUESTION 162
(4) Something else   LEADS TO QUESTION 162
(5) Don't know/no response   LEADS TO QUESTION 162

Question 162
Was (she/he)...
INTERVIEWER: READ ALL CHOICES, CHECK ONLY ONE

(1) An employee of private company (business/individual) for wages/salary   LEADS TO QUESTION 164
(2) A government employee (federal, state, county or local)   LEADS TO QUESTION 164
(3) Self-employed in (her/his) own business, professional practice or farm   LEADS TO QUESTION 163
(4) Working without pay in a family business or farm   LEADS TO QUESTION 164
(5) Don't know/no response   LEADS TO QUESTION 164

Question 163
Was (her/his) business...

(1) Incorporated   LEADS TO QUESTION 164
(2) Not incorporated   LEADS TO QUESTION 164
(3) Don't know/no response   LEADS TO QUESTION 164

Question 164
Again, referring to your spouse's job during the first year of your (first, current, most recent) marriage, in an average week how many hours did (she/he) work at this job? Include overtime hours.

(1) SPECIFY   LEADS TO QUESTION 165
(2) DON'T KNOW   BRANCHES TO 165

Question 165
During that year, what was (her/his) salary?
INTERVIEWER: PROBE AND RECORD IF SALARY OR WAGE IS 'PER HOUR,' 'WEEK,' 'MONTH' OR 'PER YEAR.'

(1) SPECIFY   LEADS TO QUESTION 166
(2) DON'T KNOW   BRANCHES TO 166

Question 166
Now, several questions about your (first, current, most recent) (wife's/husband's) father. At the time your (first, current, most recent) (wife/husband) left high school, what kind of work was (her/his) father doing?
INTERVIEWER: FOR EXAMPLE: ELECTRICAL ENGINEER, STOCK CLERK, FARMER. IF NO BIOLOGICAL FATHER WAS PRESENT AT THE TIME, ASK ABOUT STEPFATHER. IF FATHER/STEPFATHER WAS DEAD AT THAT TIME, ENTER CODE '?'

(1) SPECIFY   LEADS TO QUESTION 167
THIS QUESTION IS A MULTIPLE ANSWER QUESTION
(2) DON'T KNOW   BRANCHES TO 173

Question 167
What were his most important activities?
INTERVIEWER: FOR EXAMPLE: KEPT ACCOUNT BOOKS, SOLD CARS, OPERATED A PRINTING PRESS, FINISHED CONCRETE

(1) SPECIFY   LEADS TO QUESTION 168
THIS QUESTION IS A MULTIPLE ANSWER QUESTION
(2) DON'T KNOW   BRANCHES TO 168

Question 168
What kind of business or industry was this?
INTERVIEWER: FOR EXAMPLE: T.V. AND RADIO MFG., RETAIL SHOE STORE, STATE LABOR DEPT.

(1) SPECIFY   LEADS TO QUESTION 169
THIS QUESTION IS A MULTIPLE ANSWER QUESTION
(2) DON'T KNOW   BRANCHES TO 169

Question 169
Was this mainly manufacturing, wholesale trade, retail trade or something else?

(1) Manufacturing   LEADS TO QUESTION 170
(2) Wholesale   LEADS TO QUESTION 170
(3) Retail   LEADS TO QUESTION 170
(4) Something else   LEADS TO QUESTION 170
(5) Don't know/no response   LEADS TO QUESTION 170

Question 170
Was he...
INTERVIEWER: READ ALL CHOICES, CHECK ONE

(1) An employee of a private company (business/individual) for wages/salary   LEADS TO QUESTION 172
(2) A government employee (federal, state, county or local)   LEADS TO QUESTION 172
(3) Self-employed in his own business (professional practice or farm)   LEADS TO QUESTION 171
(4) Working without pay in a family business or farm   LEADS TO QUESTION 172
(5) Don't know/no response   LEADS TO QUESTION 172

Question 171
Was his business...

(1) Incorporated   LEADS TO QUESTION 172
(2) Not incorporated   LEADS TO QUESTION 172
(3) Don't know/no response   LEADS TO QUESTION 172

Question 172
What was the highest grade of regular school completed by your (first, current, most recent) (wife's/husband's) father?

Grades 1 through 12
(1) First
(2) Second
(3) Third
(4) Fourth
(5) Fifth
(6) Sixth
(7) Seventh
(8) Eighth
(9) Ninth
(10) Tenth
(11) Eleventh
(12) Twelfth

College (academic years)
(13) Freshman (first year)
(14) Sophomore (second/associate's)
(15) Junior (third year)
(16) Senior (fourth/bachelor's)
(17) Post-grad, but not master's degree
(18) Master's degree
(19) Post master's but not M.D./PH.D.
(20) Doctorate (PH.D./M.D./J.D./D.D.S.)
INTERVIEWER: IF DON'T KNOW CODE '21'

(1) SPECIFY   LEADS TO QUESTION 173
(2) DON'T KNOW   BRANCHES TO 173

23

24

Question 173
What was the highest grade of regular school completed by your (wife's/husband's) mother?

Grades 1 through 12
(1) First
(2) Second
(3) Third
(4) Fourth
(5) Fifth
(6) Sixth
(7) Seventh
(8) Eighth
(9) Ninth
(10) Tenth
(11) Eleventh
(12) Twelfth

College (academic years)
(13) Freshman (first year)
(14) Sophomore (second/associate's)
(15) Junior (third year)
(16) Senior (fourth/bachelor's)
(17) Post-grad, but not master's degree
(18) Master's degree
(19) Post master's but not M.D./PH.D.
(20) Doctorate (PH.D./M.D./J.D./D.D.S.)
INTERVIEWER: IF DON'T KNOW CODE '21'

(1) SPECIFY
(2) DON'T KNOW

LEADS TO QUESTION 174
BRANCHES TO 174

Question 174
INTERVIEWER: PLEASE CODE (RESPONSE CODED PREVIOUSLY IN QUESTION 144)

(1) Your
(2) Your first
(3) Your current
(4) Your most recent

LEADS TO: IF Q 142 A   1 THEN
Q 177 ELSE Q 175
LEADS TO QUESTION 175
LEADS TO QUESTION 177
LEADS TO QUESTION 175

Question 175
At the end of your (first, current, most recent) marriage, what was the highest grade of regular school completed by your (wife/husband)?

Grades 1 through 12
(1) First
(2) Second
(3) Third
(4) Fourth
(5) Fifth
(6) Sixth
(7) Seventh
(8) Eighth
(9) Ninth
(10) Tenth
(11) Eleventh
(12) Twelfth

College (academic years)
(13) Freshman (first year)
(14) Sophomore (second/associate's)
(15) Junior (third year)
(16) Senior (fourth/bachelor's)
(17) Post-grad, but not master's degree
(18) Master's degree
(19) Post master's but not M.D./PH.D.
(20) Doctorate (PH.D./M.D./J.D./D.D.S.)
INTERVIEWER: IF DON'T KNOW CODE '21'

(1) SPECIFY
(2) DON'T KNOW

LEADS TO QUESTION 176
BRANCHES TO 176

25

Question 176
While you were married, had your (wife/husband) completed any vocational or business school degree, certificate or diploma other than what you have mentioned?

(1) Yes
(2) No
(3) Don't know/no response

LEADS TO: IF Q 174 A   2 THEN
Q 204 ELSE Q 191
LEADS TO: IF Q 174 A   2 THEN
Q 204 ELSE Q 191
LEADS TO: IF Q 174 A   2 THEN
Q 204 ELSE Q 191

Question 177
Currently, what is the highest grade of regular school completed by your (wife/husband)?

Grades 1 through 12
(1) First
(2) Second
(3) Third
(4) Fourth
(5) Fifth
(6) Sixth
(7) Seventh
(8) Eighth
(9) Ninth
(10) Tenth
(11) Eleventh
(12) Twelfth

College (academic years)
(13) Freshman (first year)
(14) Sophomore (second/associate's)
(15) Junior (third year)
(16) Senior (fourth/bachelor's)
(17) Post-grad, but not master's degree
(18) Master's degree
(19) Post master's but not M.D./PH.D.
(20) Doctorate (PH.D./M.D./J.D./D.D.S.)
INTERVIEWER: IF DON'T KNOW

LEADS TO QUESTION 178
BRANCHES TO 178

Question 178
Since you were married, has your (wife/husband) completed a vocational or business school degree, certificate or diploma?

(1) Yes
(2) No
(3) Don't know/no response

LEADS TO QUESTION 179
LEADS TO QUESTION 179
LEADS TO QUESTION 179

Question 179
At present, does your spouse have a full-time job? Do not include military service or summer school jobs.
INTERVIEWER: FULL-TIME MEANS WORKING MORE THAN 25 HOURS A WEEK ON THE AVERAGE AND HOLDING
THE JOB FOR MORE THAN ONE MONTH

(1) Yes
(2) No
(3) Don't know/no response

LEADS TO QUESTION 182
LEADS TO QUESTION 182
LEADS TO QUESTION 182

Question 180
Is (she/he) unemployed, unable to work or keeping house?

(1) No, none of the above
(2) Unemployed or looking for work
(3) Unable to work
(4) Keeping house
(5) Don't know/no response

LEADS TO QUESTION 181
LEADS TO QUESTION 181
LEADS TO QUESTION 181
LEADS TO QUESTION 181
LEADS TO QUESTION 181

26

Question 181
Is your (wife/husband) currently in the military or reserves; or a full- or part-time student?
INTERVIEWER: IF RESPONDENT SAYS 'YES' PROBE TO DETERMINE ACTIVITY

(1) Military — LEADS TO: IF Q 179 A 1 THEN Q 183 ELSE Q 191
(2) Reserves — LEADS TO: IF Q 179 A 1 THEN Q 183 ELSE Q 191
(3) Part-time student — LEADS TO: IF Q 179 A 1 THEN Q 183 ELSE Q 191
(4) Full-time student — LEADS TO: IF Q 179 A 1 THEN Q 183 ELSE Q 191
(5) Military and full- or part-time student — LEADS TO: IF Q 179 A 1 THEN Q 183 ELSE Q 191
(6) Reserves and full- or part-time student — LEADS TO: IF Q 179 A 1 THEN Q 183 ELSE Q 191
(7) None of the above — LEADS TO: IF Q 179 A 1 THEN Q 183 ELSE Q 191
(8) Don't know/no response — LEADS TO: IF Q 179 A 1 THEN Q 183 ELSE Q 191

Question 182
At present, does your spouse have a part-time job?
(1) Yes — LEADS TO QUESTION 181
(2) No — LEADS TO: IF Q 179 A 1 THEN Q 181 ELSE Q 180
(3) Don't know/no response — LEADS TO: IF Q 179 A 1 THEN Q 181 ELSE Q 180

Question 183
What kind of work is (she/he) doing?
INTERVIEWER: FOR EXAMPLE: ELECTRICAL ENGINEER, SECRETARY, TRUCK DRIVER
(1) SPECIFY — LEADS TO QUESTION 184
THIS QUESTION IS A MULTIPLE ANSWER QUESTION
(2) DON'T KNOW — BRANCHES TO 184

Question 184
What are (her/his) most important activities or duties?
INTERVIEWER: FOR EXAMPLE: KEPT THE BOOKS, SOLD CARS, OPERATED PRINTING PRESS
(1) SPECIFY — LEADS TO QUESTION 185
THIS QUESTION IS A MULTIPLE ANSWER QUESTION
(2) DON'T KNOW — BRANCHES TO 185

Question 185
What kind of business or industry is this?
INTERVIEWER: FOR EXAMPLE: T.V. AND RADIO MFG., RETAIL SHOE STORE, STATE LABOR DEPT.
(1) SPECIFY — LEADS TO QUESTION 186
THIS QUESTION IS A MULTIPLE ANSWER QUESTION
(2) DON'T KNOW — BRANCHES TO 186

Question 186
Is this mainly manufacturing, wholesale trade, retail trade or something else?

(1) Manufacturing — LEADS TO QUESTION 187
(2) Wholesale — LEADS TO QUESTION 187
(3) Retail — LEADS TO QUESTION 187
(4) Something else — LEADS TO QUESTION 187
(5) Don't know/no response — LEADS TO QUESTION 187

Question 187
Is (she/he)...
INTERVIEWER: READ ALL CHOICES, CHECK ONLY ONE

(1) An employee of private company (business/individual) for wages/salary — LEADS TO QUESTION 189
(2) A government employee (federal, state, county or local) — LEADS TO QUESTION 189
(3) Self-employed in (her/his) own business, professional practice or farm — LEADS TO QUESTION 188
(4) Working without pay in a family business or farm — LEADS TO QUESTION 189
(5) Don't know/no response — LEADS TO QUESTION 189

Question 188
Is (her/his) business...
(1) Incorporated — LEADS TO QUESTION 189
(2) Not incorporated — LEADS TO QUESTION 189
(3) Don't know/no response — LEADS TO QUESTION 189

Question 189
In an average week, how many hours does (she/he) work at this job, including over-time hours?
(1) SPECIFY — LEADS TO QUESTION 190
(2) DON'T KNOW — BRANCHES TO 190

Question 190
What is (her/his) current wage or salary?
INTERVIEWER: PROBE AND RECORD IF SALARY OR WAGE IS 'PER HOUR,' 'WEEK,' 'MONTH' OR 'YEAR'
(1) SPECIFY — LEADS TO QUESTION 191
(2) DON'T KNOW — BRANCHES TO 191

Question 191
Now, I'd like to ask you about your views and personal expectations about family size.
What do you think is the ideal number of children for a family?
(1) One — LEADS TO QUESTION 193
(2) Two — LEADS TO QUESTION 193
(3) Three — LEADS TO QUESTION 193
(4) Four — LEADS TO QUESTION 193
(5) Five — LEADS TO QUESTION 193
(6) Six — LEADS TO QUESTION 193
(7) Seven — LEADS TO QUESTION 193
(8) Eight — LEADS TO QUESTION 193
(9) Nine — LEADS TO QUESTION 193
(10) Ten — LEADS TO QUESTION 193
(11) Eleven or more — LEADS TO QUESTION 193
(12) None — LEADS TO QUESTION 193
(13) Don't know/no response — LEADS TO QUESTION 193

Question 193
How many children have you ever had, not counting still births, stepchildren or adoptions?
INTERVIEWER: INCLUDE DECEASED IN THE COUNT
(1) One   LEADS TO QUESTION 194
(2) Two   LEADS TO QUESTION 196
(3) Three   LEADS TO QUESTION 196
(4) Four   LEADS TO QUESTION 196
(5) Five   LEADS TO QUESTION 196
(6) Six   LEADS TO QUESTION 196
(7) Seven   LEADS TO QUESTION 196
(8) Eight   LEADS TO QUESTION 196
(9) Nine   LEADS TO QUESTION 196
(10) Ten   LEADS TO QUESTION 196
(11) Eleven or more LEADS TO QUESTION 196
(12) None   LEADS TO QUESTION 198
(13) Don't know/no response LEADS TO QUESTION 198

Question 194
What is your child's date of birth?
INTERVIEWER: ENTER IN FORMAT MONTH-DAY-YEAR AND RECORD ON MARKER SHEET
(1) SPECIFY   LEADS TO QUESTION 195
QUESTION 194 HAS ALPHANUMERIC ANSWERS
(2) DON'T KNOW   BRANCHES TO 195

Question 195
Does your child live with you at home?
(1) Yes   LEADS TO QUESTION 198
(2) No   LEADS TO QUESTION 198
(3) Don't know/no response LEADS TO QUESTION 198

Question 196
Starting with the oldest child, what is the date of birth for each child you have ever had?
INTERVIEWER: ENTER 1 LINE PER CHILD IN THE FORMAT MONTH-DAY-YEAR AND RECORD ON MARKER SHEET
(1) SPECIFY   LEADS TO QUESTION 197
THIS QUESTION IS A MULTIPLE ANSWER QUESTION
(2) DON'T KNOW   BRANCHES TO 197

Question 197
How many of these children currently live with you at home?
(1) One   LEADS TO QUESTION 198
(2) Two   LEADS TO QUESTION 198
(3) Three   LEADS TO QUESTION 198
(4) Four   LEADS TO QUESTION 198
(5) Five   LEADS TO QUESTION 198
(6) Six   LEADS TO QUESTION 198
(7) Seven   LEADS TO QUESTION 198
(8) Eight   LEADS TO QUESTION 198
(9) Nine   LEADS TO QUESTION 198
(10) Ten   LEADS TO QUESTION 198
(11) Eleven or more LEADS TO QUESTION 198
(12) None   LEADS TO QUESTION 198
(13) Don't know/no response LEADS TO QUESTION 198

Question 198
Not counting the ones you currently have, how many children do you expect to have in the future?
(1) One   LEADS TO QUESTION 199
(2) Two   LEADS TO QUESTION 199
(3) Three   LEADS TO QUESTION 199
(4) Four   LEADS TO QUESTION 199
(5) Five   LEADS TO QUESTION 199
(6) Six   LEADS TO QUESTION 199
(7) Seven   LEADS TO QUESTION 199
(8) Eight   LEADS TO QUESTION 199
(9) Nine   LEADS TO QUESTION 199
(10) Ten   LEADS TO QUESTION 199
(11) Eleven or more LEADS TO QUESTION 199
(12) None   LEADS TO QUESTION 199
(13) Don't know/no response LEADS TO QUESTION 199

Question 199
Have you ever adopted any children?
(1) Yes   LEADS TO QUESTION 200
(2) No   LEADS TO QUESTION 204
(3) Don't know/no response LEADS TO QUESTION 204

Question 200
How many children have you adopted?
INTERVIEWER: RECORD THIS NUMBER ON YOUR SCRATCH SHEET
(1) One   LEADS TO QUESTION 201
(2) Two   LEADS TO QUESTION 201
(3) Three   LEADS TO QUESTION 201
(4) Four   LEADS TO QUESTION 201
(5) Five   LEADS TO QUESTION 201
(6) Six   LEADS TO QUESTION 201
(7) Seven or more LEADS TO QUESTION 201
(8) Don't know/no response LEADS TO QUESTION 201

Question 201
How many of these children live with you at home?
INTERVIEWER: RECORD THIS NUMBER ON YOUR SCRATCH SHEET
(1) One   LEADS TO QUESTION 202
(2) Two   LEADS TO QUESTION 202
(3) Three   LEADS TO QUESTION 202
(4) Four   LEADS TO QUESTION 202
(5) Five   LEADS TO QUESTION 202
(6) Six   LEADS TO QUESTION 202
(7) Seven or more LEADS TO QUESTION 202
(8) None   LEADS TO QUESTION 202
(9) Don't know/no response LEADS TO QUESTION 202

Question 202
INTERVIEWER: DOES THE NUMBER OF CHILDREN ADOPTED EQUAL THE NUMBER OF CHILDREN CURRENTLY LIVING AT HOME?
(1) Yes   LEADS TO QUESTION 204
(2) No   LEADS TO QUESTION 203
QUESTION 202 CALLS FOR A RECALL OF ANSWERS TO THE FOLLOWING QUESTIONS: 200 THROUGH 201

Question 203
Now, think only of your adopted children who do not live at home with you. For how many of these children do you have financial responsibility (child support)?

(1) One — LEADS TO QUESTION 204
(2) Two — LEADS TO QUESTION 204
(3) Three — LEADS TO QUESTION 204
(4) Four — LEADS TO QUESTION 204
(5) Five — LEADS TO QUESTION 204
(6) Six — LEADS TO QUESTION 204
(7) Seven or more — LEADS TO QUESTION 204
(8) None — LEADS TO QUESTION 204
(9) Don't know/no response — LEADS TO QUESTION 204

Question 204
Did your (first, current, most recent) spouse have any children before your marriage to (her/him)?

(1) Yes — LEADS TO QUESTION 205
(2) No — LEADS TO QUESTION 210
(3) Don't know/no response — LEADS TO QUESTION 210

Question 205
How many?
INTERVIEWER: RECORD THIS NUMBER ON YOUR SCRATCH SHEET

(1) One — LEADS TO QUESTION 206
(2) Two — LEADS TO QUESTION 206
(3) Three — LEADS TO QUESTION 206
(4) Four — LEADS TO QUESTION 206
(5) Five — LEADS TO QUESTION 206
(6) Six — LEADS TO QUESTION 206
(7) Seven or more — LEADS TO QUESTION 206
(8) Don't know/no response — LEADS TO QUESTION 206

Question 206
How many of these children came to live with you when you were married?
INTERVIEWER: RECORD THIS NUMBER ON YOUR SCRATCH SHEET

(1) One — LEADS TO QUESTION 207
(2) Two — LEADS TO QUESTION 207
(3) Three — LEADS TO QUESTION 207
(4) Four — LEADS TO QUESTION 207
(5) Five — LEADS TO QUESTION 207
(6) Six — LEADS TO QUESTION 207
(7) Seven or more — LEADS TO QUESTION 207
(8) None — LEADS TO QUESTION 207
(9) Don't know/no response — LEADS TO QUESTION 207

Question 207
INTERVIEWER: DOES THE NUMBER OF CHILDREN SPOUSE HAD EQUAL THE NUMBER THAT CAME TO LIVE WHEN MARRIED?

(1) Yes — LEADS TO QUESTION 210
(2) No — LEADS TO QUESTION 209

QUESTION 207 CALLS FOR A RECALL OF ANSWERS TO THE FOLLOWING QUESTIONS: 205 THROUGH 206.

Question 209
For how many of these children not living at home (did/does) your (first, current, most recent) spouse have financial responsibility (child support)?

(1) One — LEADS TO QUESTION 210
(2) Two — LEADS TO QUESTION 210
(3) Three — LEADS TO QUESTION 210
(4) Four — LEADS TO QUESTION 210
(5) Five — LEADS TO QUESTION 210
(6) Six — LEADS TO QUESTION 210
(7) Seven or more — LEADS TO QUESTION 210
(8) None — LEADS TO QUESTION 210
(9) Don't know/no response — LEADS TO QUESTION 210

Question 210
Now let's see, you were married how many times?
INTERVIEWER: CODE IF YOU REMEMBER

(1) Married once — LEADS TO QUESTION 218
(2) Married twice — LEADS TO QUESTION 211
(3) Married three times — LEADS TO QUESTION 211
(4) Married four times — LEADS TO QUESTION 211
(5) Married five times — LEADS TO QUESTION 211
(6) Married six or more times — LEADS TO QUESTION 211
(7) Don't know/no response — LEADS TO QUESTION 250

Question 211
...and let's see, you are...

(1) Currently married — LEADS TO QUESTION 214
(2) Not currently married — LEADS TO QUESTION 212
(3) Don't know/no response — LEADS TO QUESTION 250

Question 212
Was your last marriage ended by death, divorce or separation?
INTERVIEWER: IF RESPONDENT SAYS 'SEPARATION/DESERTION' AND 'DIVORCE' THEN ENTER CODE '2'

(1) Death — LEADS TO QUESTION 213
(2) Divorce — LEADS TO QUESTION 213
(3) Separation/Desertion — LEADS TO QUESTION 213
(4) Don't know/no response — LEADS TO QUESTION 213

Question 213
And when did this occur?
INTERVIEWER: ENTER IN THE FORMAT MONTH-YEAR AND RECORD ON MARKER SHEET

(1) SPECIFY — LEADS TO QUESTION 214
(2) DON'T KNOW — BRANCHES TO 214

Question 214
Now, thinking about your first marriage...was this marriage ended by death, divorce or separation?
INTERVIEWER: IF RESPONDENT SAYS 'SEPARATION/DESERTION' AND 'DIVORCE' THEN ENTER CODE '2'

(1) Death — LEADS TO QUESTION 215
(2) Divorce — LEADS TO QUESTION 215
(3) Separation/Desertion — LEADS TO QUESTION 215
(4) Don't know/no response — LEADS TO QUESTION 215

Question 215
And when did this occur?
INTERVIEWER: ENTER IN THE FORMAT MONTH-YEAR AND RECORD ON MARKER SHEET

(1) SPECIFY   LEADS TO: IF Q 210 A   2 THEN
                       Q 224 ELSE Q 220
                       BRANCHES TO: IF Q 210 A   2
(2) DON'T KNOW   THEN Q 224 ELSE Q 220

Question 216
Was your marriage ended by death, divorce or separation?
INTERVIEWER: IF RESPONDENT SAYS 'SEPARATION/DESERTION' AND 'DIVORCE' THEN ENTER CODE '2'

(1) Death   LEADS TO QUESTION 217
(2) Divorce   LEADS TO QUESTION 217
(3) Separation/Desertion   LEADS TO QUESTION 217
(4) Don't know/no response   LEADS TO QUESTION 217

Question 217
And when did this occur?
INTERVIEWER: ENTER IN THE FORMAT MONTH-YEAR AND RECORD ON MARKER SHEET

(1) SPECIFY   LEADS TO: IF Q 216 A   2 THEN
                       Q 225 ELSE Q 230
                       BRANCHES TO: IF Q 216 A   2
(2) DON'T KNOW   THEN Q 225 ELSE Q 230

Question 218
...and let's see, you are...

(1) Currently married   LEADS TO QUESTION 230
(2) Not currently married   LEADS TO QUESTION 216
(3) Don't know/no response   LEADS TO QUESTION 230

Question 220
INTERVIEWER: IF 'MARRIED THREE TIMES' CODE A '1' AND '2'
             IF 'MARRIED FOUR TIMES' CODE A '1', '2' AND '3'
             IF 'MARRIED FIVE TIMES' CODE A '1', '2', '3' AND '4'
             IF 'MARRIED SIX OR MORE TIMES' CODE A '1', '2', '3' AND '4'

(1) Second   LEADS TO QUESTION 221
(2) Third   LEADS TO QUESTION 221
(3) Fourth   LEADS TO QUESTION 221
(4) Fifth   LEADS TO QUESTION 221
THIS QUESTION IS A MULTIPLE ANSWER QUESTION

Question 221
Now, thinking about your (first, current, most recent) marriage: What was the beginning date of your (first, current, most recent) marriage?
INTERVIEWER: ENTER IN THE FORMAT MONTH-YEAR AND RECORD ON MARKER SHEET

(1) SPECIFY   LEADS TO QUESTION 222
SPECIAL HANDLING 16
QUESTIONS 221 THROUGH 223 ARE DRIVEN BY THE SET OF ANSWERS TO QUESTION 220
(2) DON'T KNOW   BRANCHES TO 222

33

Question 222
And what was the ending date of your (first, current, most recent) marriage?
INTERVIEWER: ENTER IN THE FORMAT MONTH-YEAR AND RECORD ON MARKER SHEET

- (1) SPECIFY   LEADS TO QUESTION 223
(2) DON'T KNOW   BRANCHES TO 223

Question 223
And was your (first, current, most recent) marriage ended by death, divorce or separation?

(1) Death   LEADS TO QUESTION 224
(2) Divorce   LEADS TO QUESTION 224
(3) Separation/Desertion   LEADS TO QUESTION 224
(4) Don't know/no response   LEADS TO QUESTION 224

Question 224
INTERVIEWER: DID RESPONDENT SAY 'DIVORCED' TO ANY PRIOR MARRIAGE?

(1) Yes   LEADS TO QUESTION 225
(2) No   LEADS TO QUESTION 230
(3) Don't remember   LEADS TO QUESTION 230

Question 225
Are you currently making or receiving alimony payments?

(1) Yes   LEADS TO QUESTION 226
(2) No   LEADS TO QUESTION 230
(3) Don't know/no response   LEADS TO QUESTION 230

Question 226
Approximately how much per month do these payments amount to?

(1) SPECIFY   LEADS TO QUESTION 230
QUESTION 226 HAS ALPHANUMERIC ANSWERS
(2) DON'T KNOW   BRANCHES TO 230

Question 230
Now, we have a number of questions about jobs. We will be talking about both full-time and part-time jobs. By "full-time" we mean working 25 hours or more in an average week and holding the job for more than one month. By "part-time" we mean working 1 to 25 hours a week for pay.
Since leaving high school, have you ever held a full-time or part-time job for pay?

(1) Yes   LEADS TO QUESTION 231
(2) No   LEADS TO QUESTION 280
(3) Don't know/no response   LEADS TO QUESTION 280

Question 231
I will be mentioning some of the events and dates that you have already provided to help you remember...think about the first full-time job you remember after leaving high school. Do not include summer vacation jobs or part-time jobs. What kind of work were you doing on your first full-time job?
INTERVIEWER: FOR EXAMPLE: ELECTRICAL ENGINEERING, SECRETARY, TRUCK DRIVER

(1) SPECIFY   LEADS TO QUESTION 245
(2) DON'T KNOW   BRANCHES TO 245

34

Question 232
Have you had any other full-time jobs since leaving high school that we have not talked about? Do not include summer jobs during school vacations.

(1) Yes   LEADS TO QUESTION 244
(2) No   LEADS TO QUESTION 279
(3) Don't know/no response   LEADS TO QUESTION 279

Question 233
How long did you do this as your major activity? That is, in what month and year did you stop [***activity***]?

(1) SPECIFY   LEADS TO QUESTION 234
(2) DON'T KNOW   BRANCHES TO 234

Question 234
At any time during this period did you take a full-time job in the civilian labor force?

(1) Yes   LEADS TO QUESTION 244
(2) No   LEADS TO QUESTION 235
(3) Don't know/no response   LEADS TO QUESTION 235

Question 235
Let's see, that brings us to (****most recent date on marker sheet****). Did you then take another full-time or part-time job or did you do something else?
INTERVIEWER: NOTE: THIS IS A KEY QUESTION AND YOU MAY BE FLEXIBLE IN WORDING. REFER TO THE MARKER SHEET FOR DATES. READ EVENTS AND DATES TO THE RESPONDENT TO HELP THEM REMEMBER IF THEY ARE HAVING TROUBLE.
IF YOU ARE AT THE CURRENT DATE AND WISH TO EXIT THE JOB SECTION ENTER CODE '10'.

(1) Took a full-time job   LEADS TO QUESTION 244
(2) Entered the military   LEADS TO QUESTION 234
(3) Entered school   LEADS TO QUESTION 237
(4) Unemployed, looking for work   LEADS TO QUESTION 238
(5) Kept house, got married, raised a family   LEADS TO QUESTION 233
(6) Unable to work/disabled   LEADS TO QUESTION 240
(7) Part-time work (1-25 hours per week on
      the average)   LEADS TO QUESTION 233
(8) Other   LEADS TO QUESTION 233
(9) Don't know/no response   LEADS TO QUESTION 238
(10) ****** Exit job section ******   LEADS TO QUESTION 232

Question 237
At any time during this period when you were attending school, did you take a full-time job in the civilian labor force? Do not include summer vacation jobs or jobs held during school vacations or breaks.
INTERVIEWER: REFER TO MARKER SHEET

(1) Yes   LEADS TO QUESTION 244
(2) No - (period prior to present date)   LEADS TO QUESTION 235
(3) No - (period up to the present date)   LEADS TO QUESTION 232
(4) Don't know/no response   LEADS TO QUESTION 232

Question 238
How long did this period of looking for work or unemployment last?
INTERVIEWER: CODE DATE ENDED

(1) SPECIFY   LEADS TO QUESTION 239
(2) DON'T KNOW   BRANCHES TO 239

Question 239
During this time, what were the main things that you did to find work?
INTERVIEWER: ENTER ALL THAT APPLY; DO NOT READ LIST

(1) Public employment agency   LEADS TO QUESTION 235
(2) Private employment agency   LEADS TO QUESTION 235
(3) Contacted friends or relatives   LEADS TO QUESTION 235
(4) Placed or answered ads   LEADS TO QUESTION 235
(5) Civil service test or application with
      state, local or federal government   LEADS TO QUESTION 235
(6) Organization contact (urban league,
      welfare agency)   LEADS TO QUESTION 235
(7) School placement office   LEADS TO QUESTION 235
(8) Teachers or professors for job leads   LEADS TO QUESTION 235
(9) Labor union contact   LEADS TO QUESTION 235
(10) Contacted possible employer directly   LEADS TO QUESTION 235
(11) Nothing   LEADS TO QUESTION 235
(12) Other   LEADS TO QUESTION 235
(13) Don't know/no response   LEADS TO QUESTION 235
THIS QUESTION IS A MULTIPLE ANSWER QUESTION

Question 240
What was the main reason you were unable to work?

(1) Physical disability   LEADS TO QUESTION 241
(2) Psychological disability   LEADS TO QUESTION 241
(3) Family reasons   LEADS TO QUESTION 242
(4) Cannot find work   LEADS TO QUESTION 242
(5) Other   LEADS TO QUESTION 242
(6) Don't know/no response   LEADS TO QUESTION 242

Question 241
How long have you had this disability?

(1) SPECIFY   LEADS TO QUESTION 242
THIS QUESTION IS A MULTIPLE ANSWER QUESTION
(2) DON'T KNOW   BRANCHES TO 242

Question 242
When were you able to resume full-time employment or looking for work?
INTERVIEWER: ENTER IN THE FORMAT MONTH-YEAR AND RECORD ON MARKER SHEET

(1) SPECIFY   LEADS TO QUESTION 243
(2) DON'T KNOW   BRANCHES TO 242

Question 243
INTERVIEWER: DOES LAST DATE ENTERED EQUAL CURRENT DATE?

(1) Yes   LEADS TO QUESTION 232
(2) No   LEADS TO QUESTION 235

Question 244
What kind of work were you doing? FOR EXAMPLE: ELECTRICAL ENGINEERING, SECRETARY, TRUCK DRIVER

(1) SPECIFY   LEADS TO QUESTION 245
(2) DON'T KNOW   BRANCHES TO 245

37

Question 245
What were your most important activities or duties?
INTERVIEWER: FOR EXAMPLE: KEPT THE BOOKS, SOLD CARS, OPERATED PRINTING PRESS
THIS QUESTION IS A MULTIPLE ANSWER QUESTION   LEADS TO QUESTION 246
(1) SPECIFY
(2) DON'T KNOW   BRANCHES TO 246

Question 246
What kind of business or industry was this?
INTERVIEWER: FOR EXAMPLE: T.V. AND RADIO MFG., RETAIL SHOE STORE, STATE LABOR DEPT.
(1) SPECIFY   LEADS TO QUESTION 247
(2) DON'T KNOW   BRANCHES TO 247

Question 247
What was the name of the firm, company or employer you worked for?
(1) SPECIFY   LEADS TO QUESTION 248
(2) DON'T KNOW   BRANCHES TO 248

Question 248
Was this industry mainly manufacturing, wholesale trade, retail trade or something else?
(1) Manufacturing   LEADS TO QUESTION 249
(2) Wholesale   LEADS TO QUESTION 249
(3) Retail   LEADS TO QUESTION 249
(4) Something else   LEADS TO QUESTION 249
(5) Don't know/no response   LEADS TO QUESTION 249

Question 249
Were you an...
INTERVIEWER: READ ALL CHOICES, CHECK ONLY ONE
(1) An employee of private company
     (business/individual) for wages/salary   LEADS TO QUESTION 251
(2) A government employee (federal, state
     county or local)   LEADS TO QUESTION 251
(3) Self-employed in (her/his) own business,
     professional practice or farm   LEADS TO QUESTION 250
(4) Working without pay in a family business
     or farm   LEADS TO QUESTION 251
(5) Don't know/no response   LEADS TO QUESTION 251

Question 250
Was your business incorporated?
(1) Yes   LEADS TO QUESTION 251
(2) No   LEADS TO QUESTION 251
(3) Don't know/no response   LEADS TO QUESTION 251

Question 251
In what city and state was this?
(1) SPECIFY   LEADS TO QUESTION 252
THIS QUESTION IS A MULTIPLE ANSWER QUESTION
(2) DON'T KNOW   BRANCHES TO 252

38

Question 252
In an average week, how many hours did you actually work at this job, including over-time hours?
(1) SPECIFY   LEADS TO QUESTION 253
(2) DON'T KNOW   BRANCHES TO 253

Question 253
INTERVIEWER: DO YOU REMEMBER THE START DATE OF THIS JOB? IF SO, PROMPT RESPONDENT WITH "AND YOU STARTED THIS JOB IN ...., CORRECT?" AND ENTER THE DATE. ELSE, PROMPT "AND WHEN DID YOU BEGIN THIS JOB?"
(1) SPECIFY   LEADS TO QUESTION 254
(2) DON'T KNOW   BRANCHES TO 254

Question 254
While you were with this employer, did you have any promotions?
(1) Yes   LEADS TO QUESTION 255
(2) No   LEADS TO QUESTION 256
(3) Don't know/no response   LEADS TO QUESTION 256

Question 255
How many promotions were there?
(1) SPECIFY   LEADS TO QUESTION 256
(2) DON'T KNOW   BRANCHES TO 256

Question 256
Did you ever take a different job with this same employer?
(1) Yes   LEADS TO QUESTION 258
(2) No   LEADS TO QUESTION 257
(3) Don't know/no response   LEADS TO QUESTION 257

Question 257
When did you leave this job?
INTERVIEWER: ENTER IN THE FORMAT MONTH-YEAR AND RECORD ON MARKER SHEET
(1) SPECIFY   LEADS TO QUESTION 259
(2) DON'T KNOW   BRANCHES TO 259

Question 258
When did you leave this first job with this employer?
INTERVIEWER: ENTER IN THE FORMAT MONTH-YEAR AND RECORD ON MARKER SHEET
(1) SPECIFY   LEADS TO QUESTION 259
(2) DON'T KNOW   BRANCHES TO 259

Question 259
INTERVIEWER: IS THAT DATE LAST ENTERED ON THE MARKER SHEET THE CURRENT DATE?
(1) Yes   LEADS TO QUESTION 278
(2) No   LEADS TO QUESTION 260

Question 260
What was the main reason you left this job?

(1) Involuntary termination — LEADS TO: IF Q 6 A 2 THEN Q 261 ELSE Q 266

(2) Temporary laid off, seasonal job completed — LEADS TO: IF Q 6 A 2 THEN Q 261 ELSE Q 266

(3) Found better job or promotion — LEADS TO: IF Q 6 A 2 THEN Q 261 ELSE Q 266

(4) Any work-related reason (pay, co-workers, etc.) — LEADS TO QUESTION 263

(5) Get married, have children, raise a family — LEADS TO: IF Q 6 A 2 THEN Q 261 ELSE Q 266

(6) Spouse transferred or spouse took another job — LEADS TO: IF Q 6 A 2 THEN Q 261 ELSE Q 266

(7) No longer need the income — LEADS TO: IF Q 6 A 2 THEN Q 261 ELSE Q 266

(8) Returned to school — LEADS TO: IF Q 6 A 2 THEN Q 261 ELSE Q 266

(9) Entered the military — LEADS TO: IF Q 6 A 2 THEN Q 261 ELSE Q 266

(10) Your own illness or health reason — LEADS TO: IF Q 6 A 2 THEN Q 261 ELSE Q 266

(11) Other — LEADS TO: IF Q 6 A 2 THEN Q 261 ELSE Q 266

(12) Don't know/no response — LEADS TO: IF Q 6 A 2 THEN Q 261 ELSE Q 266

Question 261
At the end of this job, what was your wage or salary?
INTERVIEWER: PROBE AND RECORD IF SALARY IS 'PER HOUR,' 'WEEK,' 'MONTH' OR 'PER YEAR'

(1) SPECIFY — LEADS TO QUESTION 262
(2) DON'T KNOW — BRANCHES TO 262

Question 262
Did you view this job primarily as...
INTERVIEWER: READ ONLY THE FIRST 3 ITEMS ON THE LIST

(1) As a way to develop a career. — LEADS TO QUESTION 235
(2) As a way to get out of the house — LEADS TO QUESTION 235
(3) As a way to add to your own or your family income — LEADS TO QUESTION 235
(4) No, none of the above — LEADS TO QUESTION 235
(5) To develop a career and get out of the house — LEADS TO QUESTION 235
(6) To develop a career and add to income — LEADS TO QUESTION 235
(7) To get out of the house and add to income — LEADS TO QUESTION 235
(8) Don't know/no response — LEADS TO QUESTION 235

Question 263
INTERVIEWER: ENTER SPECIFIC REASON, PROBE AS NECESSARY

(1) SPECIFY — LEADS TO: IF Q 6 A 2 THEN Q 261 ELSE Q 266

THIS QUESTION IS A MULTIPLE ANSWER QUESTION
(2) DON'T KNOW — BRANCHES TO: IF Q 6 A 2 THEN Q 261 ELSE Q 266

Question 266
At the end of this job, what was your wage or salary?
INTERVIEWER: PROBE AND RECORD IF SALARY IS 'PER HOUR,' 'WEEK,' 'MONTH' OR 'PER YEAR'

(1) SPECIFY — LEADS TO QUESTION 235
(2) DON'T KNOW — BRANCHES TO 235

Question 278
What is your current wage or salary?
INTERVIEWER: PROBE AND RECORD IF SALARY IS 'PER HOUR,' 'WEEK,' 'MONTH' OR 'PER YEAR'

(1) SPECIFY — LEADS TO: IF Q 6 A 2 THEN Q 295 ELSE Q 232
BRANCHES TO: IF Q 6 A 2 THEN Q 295 ELSE Q 232
(2) DON'T KNOW

Question 279
INTERVIEWER: ARE THERE ANY MAJOR BLOCKS OF TIME (MORE THAN TWO YEARS) ON THE RESPONDENT'S MARKER SHEET DURING WHICH THEY MAY HAVE HELD A JOB? IF SO, PROBE: LET'S GO BACK FOR A MOMENT AND TALK ABOUT JOBS WE MAY HAVE MISSED, BACK IN [******* FROM MARKER SHEET *******] DID YOU HAVE A FULL-TIME JOB? IF THERE ARE NO MAJOR BLOCKS OF TIME OPEN, ENTER CODE '2'

(1) Yes — LEADS TO QUESTION 232
(2) No — LEADS TO QUESTION 280
(3) Don't know/no response — LEADS TO QUESTION 280

Question 280
That was the last question in the interview, as you may recall from our letter, we will be sending you a short questionnaire within the next week or so. If we mail it to:
(INTERVIEWER: READ ADDRESS OFF OF LABEL)
Is this address ok?

(1) Yes — LEADS TO QUESTION 282
(2) No (obtain address correction)

Question 282
I would like to urge you to complete the questionnaire at your earliest convenience as it is an important part of the study. Thank you very much for your time.
INTERVIEWER: TERMINATE INTERVIEW

Question 290
And when did you return to duty in the military?
INTERVIEWER: ENTER DATE IN THE FORMAT MONTH-YEAR

(1) SPECIFY — LEADS TO QUESTION 291
(2) DON'T KNOW — BRANCHES TO 291

Question 291
Did you have any other interruptions in your service in the military?

(1) Yes — LEADS TO QUESTION 292
(2) No — LEADS TO QUESTION 114
(3) Don't know/no response — LEADS TO QUESTION 114

Question 292
What was the date of this next separation from the military?
INTERVIEWER: ENTER IN THE FORMAT MONTH-YEAR

(1) SPECIFY — LEADS TO QUESTION 293
(2) DON'T KNOW — BRANCHES TO 293

40

41

Question 293
And when did you return to duty in the military?
INTERVIEWER: ENTER IN THE FORMAT MONTH-YEAR

(1) SPECIFY   LEADS TO QUESTION 114
(2) DON'T KNOW   BRANCHES TO 114

Question 295
Do you view your current job primarily as...
INTERVIEWER: READ ONLY THE FIRST 3 ITEMS ON THE LIST

(1) As a way to develop a career   LEADS TO QUESTION 252
(2) As a way to get out of the house   LEADS TO QUESTION 252
(3) As a way to add to your own or your
     family income   LEADS TO QUESTION 232
(4) No, none of the above,   LEADS TO QUESTION 232
(5) To develop a career and get out
     of the house   LEADS TO QUESTION 232
(6) To develop a career and add to income   LEADS TO QUESTION 232
(7) To get out of the house and add to income LEADS TO QUESTION 232
(8) Don't know/no response   LEADS TO QUESTION 232

Appendix L:
1979 Questionnaire
Cover Letter

WASHINGTON STATE UNIVERSITY
PULLMAN, WASHINGTON 99164

CAREER DEVELOPMENT STUDY
SOCIAL RESEARCH CENTER

June 6, 1979

George Parker
7777 Charles Ave
Spokane, WA 99999

Dear Mr. Parker:

Thank you for your help in this important research project.
Enclosed is the mail questionnaire mentioned in our telephone
interview. With it we are gathering information on how people
feel about their work, their accomplishments, and other aspects
of life.

This information is important. It will complete what you helped
us collect in the telephone interview. Your cooperation is
essential. We have attached a small honorarium to express our
appreciation for your continued help.

Let me emphasize again that the information you give us will be
strictly confidential. We have placed a number on the questionnaire
so that your name will not appear. This number will permit us to
know that you responded and to add this information to the information you provided while you were a junior at West Coast High
School. The information will be used only in statistical analysis
and will not be associated with your name in any way.

Please complete the questionnaire today and return it to us in the
envelope provided.

Sincerely,

LUTHER B. OTTO, Ph.D.
Project Director

LBO/mpr
Enclosures

THE CAREER DEVELOPMENT STUDY

Please answer all questions.

In some cases you may wish to qualify
your answers. If you do, please do so
in the margins. Your comments will be
taken into consideration.

Thank you for your cooperation.

1. First of all, when thinking about work, how important are the following things to you?

How important is . . . (check the appropriate box)

	VERY IMPORTANT	FAIRLY IMPORTANT	NOT PARTICULARLY IMPORTANT
A. the pay?	☐	☐	☐
B. the fringe benefits?	☐	☐	☐
C. how interesting the work is?	☐	☐	☐
D. the supervisor?	☐	☐	☐
E. your co-workers?	☐	☐	☐
F. how clean the work is?	☐	☐	☐
G. how tiring the work is?	☐	☐	☐
H. how highly people regard the job?	☐	☐	☐
I. job security?	☐	☐	☐
J. the amount of freedom you have?	☐	☐	☐
K. the chance to help people?	☐	☐	☐
L. not being under too much pressure?	☐	☐	☐
M. the chance to get ahead?	☐	☐	☐
N. the chance to use your abilities?	☐	☐	☐
O. the complexity of the work?	☐	☐	☐
P. living close to parents?	☐	☐	☐
Q. the number of hours worked?	☐	☐	☐
R. the amount of variety in the work?	☐	☐	☐
S. working during the daytime?	☐	☐	☐
T. the amount of repetition in the work?	☐	☐	☐
U. the region or climate?	☐	☐	☐
V. the distance from home to work?	☐	☐	☐

2. How much do you agree or disagree with the following statements? (Check the appropriate box)

	STRONGLY AGREE	AGREE	NEITHER AGREE NOR DISAGREE	DISAGREE	STRONGLY DISAGREE
A. People are lonely because they don't try to be friendly	☐	☐	☐	☐	☐
B. Men should share the work around the house with women such as doing dishes, cleaning, and so forth	☐	☐	☐	☐	☐
C. When I make plans, I am fairly sure that I can make them work	☐	☐	☐	☐	☐
D. Men and women should be paid the same money if they do the same work	☐	☐	☐	☐	☐
E. Becoming a success is a matter of hard work; luck has little or nothing to do with it	☐	☐	☐	☐	☐
F. I certainly feel useless at times	☐	☐	☐	☐	☐
G. The abilities of women too often go unrecognized	☐	☐	☐	☐	☐
H. I would be willing to move to another community to get a better job	☐	☐	☐	☐	☐
I. A preschool child is likely to suffer if the mother works	☐	☐	☐	☐	☐
J. It is more important for a wife to help her husband's career than to have a career herself	☐	☐	☐	☐	☐

3. Realistically, what kind of work do you expect to be doing 5 years from now?

TYPE OF WORK: _____ (for example: electrical engineer, stock clerk, farmer, elementary school teacher)

A. What kind of business or industry would that be in?

_____ (for example: TV and Radio manufacturing, retail shoe store, State Labor Department, farm)

B. Would that be working for yourself (self-employed) or for someone else?

_____ 1. SELF-EMPLOYED
_____ 2. SOMEONE ELSE

4

4. How much do you agree or disagree with the following statements? (Check the appropriate box)

	STRONGLY AGREE	AGREE	NEITHER AGREE NOR DISAGREE	DISAGREE	STRONGLY DISAGREE
A. Even if I were financially secure and did not need a job I would probably work	☐	☐	☐	☐	☐
B. I would be willing to move to another community so that my husband could get a better job	☐	☐	☐	☐	☐
C. A woman should have exactly the same job opportunities as a man	☐	☐	☐	☐	☐
D. A man should be willing to give up time with his family and devote it to his job if this will help his occupational advancement	☐	☐	☐	☐	☐
E. Women should be allowed to compete on equal terms with men in the occupational world	☐	☐	☐	☐	☐
F. There's not much use in trying to please people; if they like you, they like you	☐	☐	☐	☐	☐
G. Women should be considered as seriously as men for jobs as executives or politicians or even president	☐	☐	☐	☐	☐
H. My religious beliefs are very important to me	☐	☐	☐	☐	☐
I. A woman should be willing to give up time with her family and devote it to her job if this will help her occupational advancement	☐	☐	☐	☐	☐

5. Do you have any health problems or physical conditions that in any way limit the amount or kind of work you can do? (Check one)

_____ 1. NO

_____ 2. YES (If yes, please explain) _____

_____

_____

6. Have you ever held a full or part-time job in the last 5 years?

_____ 1. NO ⟶ (IF NO, GO TO QUESTION #22 ON PAGE #9)

_____ 2. YES

7. FOR THE NEXT SET OF QUESTIONS, THINK ABOUT YOUR PRESENT JOB. (IF YOU DO NOT PRESENTLY HOLD A JOB, THINK ABOUT YOUR MOST RECENT JOB). READ EACH OF THE STATEMENTS LISTED BELOW AND MARK 'YES' OR 'NO' WHETHER IT APPLIES TO YOU IN YOUR OWN WORK.

A. I have authority to hire or fire others .... _____ 1. NO _____ 2. YES

B. I can influence or set the rate of pay received by others .... _____ 1. NO _____ 2. YES

C. Someone else influences or sets my rate or amount of pay .... _____ 1. NO _____ 2. YES

D. I supervise the work of others. That is, what they produce or how much. _____ 1. NO _____ 2. YES

⟶ E. Do any of those persons supervise anyone else? .... _____ 1. NO _____ 2. YES

F. I decide both what others do and how they do it .... _____ 1. NO _____ 2. YES

G. I decide what others do, but they decide how to do it .... _____ 1. NO _____ 2. YES

H. Someone else supervises my work. That is, when I produce or how much. _____ 1. NO _____ 2. YES

⟶ I. Does that person have a supervisor on the job to whom he or she is directly responsible? .... _____ 1. NO _____ 2. YES

J. Someone else decides both what I do and how I do it .... _____ 1. NO _____ 2. YES

K. Someone else decides what I do, but I decide how to do it .... _____ 1. NO _____ 2. YES

L. My supervisor exercises little or no control over my work .... _____ 1. NO _____ 2. YES

(Go to next page)

3

5

8. Compared to other people in your occupation, would you say your own abilities for doing this job are: (Check one)

___ 1. VERY MUCH ABOVE AVERAGE
___ 2. ABOVE AVERAGE
___ 3. ABOUT AVERAGE
___ 4. BELOW AVERAGE
___ 5. VERY MUCH BELOW AVERAGE

9. When you are working at a challenging part of your job how confident are you that you can succeed? (Check one)

___ 1. VERY CONFIDENT
___ 2. CONFIDENT
___ 3. SOMEWHAT CONFIDENT
___ 4. NOT CONFIDENT
___ 5. NOT CONFIDENT AT ALL

10. When you are working at a challenging part of your job about how often do you succeed? Would you say all of the time (100%), none of the time (0%), or somewhere in between? (Check the correct percentage)

100% 90% 80% 70% 60% 50% 40% 30% 20% 10% 0%

11. When you succeed at a challenging part of your job, how often would you say it is because of: (Check one for each item)

	ALWAYS	FREQUENTLY	SOMETIMES	INFREQUENTLY	NEVER
A. Your high ability					
B. Good luck					
C. The task is easy					
D. You worked hard					

12. When you fail at a challenging part of your job, how often would you say it is because of: (Check one for each item)

	ALWAYS	FREQUENTLY	SOMETIMES	INFREQUENTLY	NEVER
A. Your low ability					
B. Bad luck					
C. The task is hard					
D. You didn't work hard enough					

6

13. Now lets think again about the items you ranked earlier. How satisfied are you with the following aspects of your present job (or most recent job)?

In your job, how satisfied are you with . . .
(Check the appropriate box for each)

	VERY SATISFIED	FAIRLY SATISFIED	SOMEWHAT DISSATISFIED	VERY DISSATISFIED	NOT RELEVANT
A. the pay?					
B. the fringe benefits?					
C. how interesting the work is?					
D. the supervisor?					
E. your co-workers?					
F. how clean the work is?					
G. how tiring the work is?					
H. how highly people regard the job?					
I. job security?					
J. the amount of freedom you have?					
K. the chance to help people?					
L. not being under too much pressure?					
M. the chance to get ahead?					
N. the chance to use your abilities?					
O. the complexity of the work?					
P. living close to parents?					
Q. the number of hours worked?					
R. the amount of variety in the work?					
S. working during the daytime?					
T. the amount of repetition in the work?					
U. the region or climate?					
V. the distance from home to work?					

8

14. **All things considered, how satisfied are you with your job as a whole—are you very satisfied, fairly satisfied, somewhat dissatisfied, or very dissatisfied?** (Check one)

——— 1. VERY SATISFIED
——— 2. FAIRLY SATISFIED
——— 3. SOMEWHAT DISSATISFIED
——— 4. VERY DISSATISFIED

15. **In an average day on your job, about how many hours do you spend on each of the following kinds of activities?** (Write in number)

A. Reading, writing and working with written materials ——— hours per day
B. Working with your hands, tools or equipment ——— hours per day
C. Dealing with people in your work (not including just passing the time of day) ——— hours per day

16. **In an average week, how many hours of overtime do you work?** (Write in number)

A. with pay: ——— hours per week
B. without pay: ——— hours per week

17. **In your current job do you feel you have ever been discriminated against because of your sex in:** (Check one for each item)

A. the kind of work you are assigned .... ——— 1. NO ——— 2. YES
B. the salary you receive .... ——— 1. NO ——— 2. YES
C. the opportunities you have for advancement or promotion .... ——— 1. NO ——— 2. YES
D. the fringe benefits available to you .... ——— 1. NO ——— 2. YES
E. the job security you have .... ——— 1. NO ——— 2. YES
F. the opportunities you have for training .... ——— 1. NO ——— 2. YES

17A. **Have you ever felt that sexual favors were being requested of you by a work supervisor in exchange for:** (Check one for each)

A. a pay raise? .... ——— 1. NO ——— 2. YES
B. a promotion .... ——— 1. NO ——— 2. YES
C. being hired for a job? .... ——— 1. NO ——— 2. YES
D. keeping your job? .... ——— 1. NO ——— 2. YES

17B. **Has such a request ever affected your decision to keep or leave a job?**

——— 1. NO ——— 2. YES

18. **About how many people work for your employer at all locations.** (Write in number)

ABOUT ——— PEOPLE

19. **About how many people work for your employer at the location that you work? We mean all types, areas, and departments at your particular location.** (Write in number)

ABOUT ——— PEOPLE

20. **About how many hours a week do you work at a part-time job in addition to your present full-time job?** (Specify number of hours)

——— 0 hours/week (do not have part- and/or a full-time job)
——— hours/week in part-time job

21. **Here is a list of things that might describe your present job (or most recent job if not currently employed)** (Check appropriate box for each)

	A LOT	SOME-WHAT	A LITTLE	NOT AT ALL
A. How much freedom does it allow you as to how you do your work?	☐	☐	☐	☐
B. How much does your job allow you to make a lot of decisions on your own?	☐	☐	☐	☐
C. Does your job allow you to do a variety of different things?	☐	☐	☐	☐
D. Does it require you to do things that are very repetitious (do things over and over)?	☐	☐	☐	☐

7

Design for a Study

25. Where were you born? _____ (city) _____ (state or country)

26. Where was your father born? _____ (city) _____ (state or country)

27. Where was your mother born? _____ (city) _____ (state or country)

28. What is the original nationality of your family on your FATHER's side? That is, what was it before coming to the United States? _____

(Example: Polish, German, Spanish, Russian)

THINK BACK TO YOUR JUNIOR YEAR IN HIGH SCHOOL. AT THAT TIME YOU WERE ABOUT 17.

29. During your junior year was your father and mother (or step parents) employed in a full or part-time job? (Fill in the blanks for your parents. Write 'none' if it doesn't apply).

FATHER | MOTHER

A. What type of work did he (she) do?
A. _____
(for example: electrical engineer, stock clerk, farmer, elementary school teacher)

B. What were his (her) most important activities or duties?
B. _____
(for example: kept account books, filed, sold cars, operated a printing press, finished concrete)

C. What kind of business would that be in?
C. _____
(for example: TV & Radio manufacturing, retail shoe store, State Labor Department, farm)

(Check one for father)
___ 1. SELF-EMPLOYED
___ 2. WORKING FOR SOMEONE ELSE
___ 3. A GOVERNMENT EMPLOYEE

(Check one for mother)
___ 1. SELF-EMPLOYED
___ 2. WORKING FOR SOMEONE ELSE
___ 3. A GOVERNMENT EMPLOYEE

D. Was he (she) self-employed or working for someone else:

E. Was this a full or part-time job?
___ 1. FULL-TIME
___ 2. PART-TIME

___ 1. FULL-TIME
___ 2. PART-TIME

---

22. Please indicate how much you agree or disagree with the following statements (Check the appropriate box)

	STRONGLY AGREE	AGREE	NEITHER AGREE NOR DISAGREE	DISAGREE	STRONGLY DISAGREE
A. On the whole, I am satisfied with myself	☐	☐	☐	☐	☐
B. Many times it is more important to have time for recreation than it is to work hard and achieve occupational advancement	☐	☐	☐	☐	☐
C. Women who do not want at least one child are being selfish	☐	☐	☐	☐	☐
D. Getting a good job depends mainly on being in the right place at the right time	☐	☐	☐	☐	☐
E. A woman can live a full and happy life without marrying	☐	☐	☐	☐	☐
F. The place for the adult female is in the home	☐	☐	☐	☐	☐
G. I do not believe that chance and luck are very important in life	☐	☐	☐	☐	☐
H. I wish I could have more respect for myself	☐	☐	☐	☐	☐
I. It is much better for everyone involved if the man is the achiever outside the home and the woman takes care of the home and family	☐	☐	☐	☐	☐

NOW WE WOULD LIKE TO ASK A FEW QUESTIONS ABOUT YOU AND YOUR PARENTS. THESE WILL ONLY BE USED FOR STATISTICAL PURPOSES.

23. About how old were your parents when they got married?
A. MY FATHER WAS ABOUT ___ YEARS OLD
B. MY MOTHER WAS ABOUT ___ YEARS OLD

24. About how many miles is it to your parents' closest current residence (or closest parent's residence if they are not presently living together)?
ABOUT ___ MILES

12

30. What was your and your parents' religious affiliation when you were a junior in high school? (Please write in the specific denomination. *For example, Episcopalian, Missouri Synod Lutheran, Southern Baptist, Jewish (Conservative), Roman Catholic.*)

FATHER'S (or stepfather's) AFFILIATION: _____

MOTHER'S (or stepmother's) AFFILIATION: _____

YOUR AFFILIATION WHILE A JUNIOR IN HIGH SCHOOL: _____

31. During your junior year, how often did you attend some religious service or church sponsored activity? (Check one)

_____ 1. ABOUT ONCE A WEEK OR MORE

_____ 2. ABOUT ONCE OR TWICE A MONTH

_____ 3. A FEW TIMES A YEAR

_____ 4. NEVER

32. How much do you agree or disagree with the following statements? (Check the appropriate box)

	STRONGLY AGREE	AGREE	NEITHER AGREE NOR DISAGREE	DISAGREE	STRONGLY DISAGREE
A. A working mother can establish just as warm and secure a relationship with her children as a mother who does not work	☐	☐	☐	☐	☐
B. There would probably be fewer problems in the world if women had as much say-so in running things as men	☐	☐	☐	☐	☐
C. I would not consider moving to another community unless I had a new job in hand	☐	☐	☐	☐	☐
D. Many times I feel that I have little influence over the things that happen to me	☐ ☐	☐ ☐	☐ ☐	☐ ☐	☐ ☐
E. Everyone who possibly can should work	☐	☐	☐	☐	☐
F. It is not wise to plan too far ahead because most things turn out to be a matter of good or bad fortune anyway	☐	☐	☐	☐	☐
G. Parents should encourage just as much independence in their daughters as in their sons	☐	☐	☐	☐	☐
H. A woman's job should be kept for her when she is having a baby	☐	☐	☐	☐	☐

33. How many of each of the following people live in the house or apartment in which you presently reside? (Write in the number of persons in each category: '0,' '1', '2', etc.)

RELATIVES

number

_____ 1. HUSBAND

_____ 2. CHILDREN (your own, or step-)

_____ 3. BROTHERS

_____ 4. SISTERS

_____ 5. FATHER (stepfather, father-in-law)

_____ 6. MOTHER (stepmother, mother-in-law)

_____ 7. GRANDPARENTS

_____ 8. OTHER RELATIVES

NON RELATIVES

number

_____ 9. ADULT MALES

_____ 10. ADULT FEMALES

_____ 11. CHILDREN

34. How many times have you been married? (Check one)

_____ 0 None ⟶ (IF NONE, GO TO QUESTION #40 ON PAGE #14)

_____ 1 Once

_____ 2 Two or more

35. What was your first husband's religious affiliation, if any? (Please specify denomination)

_____

36. About how far is it to your husband's parents' closest current residence (or closest parent's residence if they are not presently living together? (If not presently married, answer for your most recent husband.)

_____ MILES

37. What is your husband's present religious affiliation, if any? (Please specify denomination) (Or, most recent husband's denomination)

_____

11

14

40. With which religious denomination are you presently affiliated, if any?
(Please write in the specific denomination)

WE'RE INTERESTED IN THINGS PEOPLE DO IN THEIR SPARE TIME WHEN THEY AREN'T WORKING.
PLEASE ESTIMATE ABOUT HOW OFTEN YOU HAVE BEEN DOING THESE THINGS DURING THE
PAST YEAR.

41. How often do you engage in these activities? (Check the appropriate box)

	At Least Once a Week	Every 2 or 3 Weeks	12-15 Per Year	1-5 Per Year	"0" Per Year
A. Going to the movies	☐	☐	☐	☐	☐
B. Going to club meetings, activities (PTA, union, etc.)	☐	☐	☐	☐	☐
C. Going to church (or religious activities)	☐	☐	☐	☐	☐
D. Going to classes or lectures	☐	☐	☐	☐	☐
E. Going to watch sports events	☐	☐	☐	☐	☐
F. Fishing, camping, hunting, hiking,	☐	☐	☐	☐	☐
G. Boating, swimming, picnics, pleasure drives	☐	☐	☐	☐	☐
H. Playing active sports (bowling, softball, etc.)	☐	☐	☐	☐	☐
I. Visiting at husband's parents' home	☐	☐	☐	☐	☐
J. Going to nightclubs, bars, etc.	☐	☐	☐	☐	☐
K. Going to concerts, plays, etc.	☐	☐	☐	☐	☐
L. Going to fairs, museums, exhibits, etc.	☐	☐	☐	☐	☐
M. Playing cards, other indoor games	☐	☐	☐	☐	☐
N. Working on hobbies, painting or music	☐	☐	☐	☐	☐
O. Talking to your parents by phone	☐	☐	☐	☐	☐
P. Going out or visiting with friends	☐	☐	☐	☐	☐
Q. Going to civic or service group meetings	☐	☐	☐	☐	☐
R. Visiting at your parents' home	☐	☐	☐	☐	☐

13

38. Below are some things that married couples often do together. Which ones have you and your wife done together in the past few weeks? (If not presently married, answer for typical week in your last marriage)

	NO	YES
A. Had a good laugh together or shared a joke	☐	☐
B. Been affectionate toward each other	☐	☐
C. Spent an evening just chatting with each other	☐	☐
D. Did something the other particularly appreciated	☐	☐
E. Visited friends together	☐	☐
F. Entertained friends in your home	☐	☐
G. Taken a drive or walk for pleasure	☐	☐
H. Gone out together—movie, bowling, sporting or other entertainment	☐	☐
I. Had sex that was satisfying to both partners	☐	☐
J. Ate out in a restaurant together	☐	☐

39. Now here are some things about which husbands and wives sometimes agree and sometimes disagree: Which ones have caused differences of opinions or were problems in your marriage during the past few weeks? (Or, typical week in last marriage)

	NO	YES
A. Being tired	☐	☐
B. Irritating personal habits	☐	☐
C. Household expenses	☐	☐
D. Sex life	☐	☐
E. Being away from home	☐	☐
F. How to spend leisure	☐	☐
G. Time spent with friends	☐	☐
H. Your job	☐	☐
I. In-laws	☐	☐
J. Not showing love	☐	☐

42. One of the objectives of this study is to develop an understanding of the problems confronting young people as they leave high school. Would you take a minute and share with us what you feel are the major problems you have encountered in your life since leaving high school?

43. Given your experiences, what might be done in high school to help young people prepare for the future?

THANK YOU FOR YOUR HELP

PLEASE FILL OUT THE YELLOW INFORMATION SHEET AND INCLUDE IT

WITH THIS QUESTIONNAIRE IN THE RETURN ENVELOPE

**Appendix N:
1979 Transcript and
Tracking Form**

THREE FINAL THINGS . . . . . .

PAST -   - 1979 -   - FUTURE

FIRST: Some of the most important issues in education today center around the usefulness of high school courses and falling test scores. You provided us important information on these issues when you were in high school. Information is now needed about your high school coursework and test scores taken after the January 1966 survey was done. High schools will provide us this information if we receive a transcript request from you.

The transcript is the high school record that is normally sent to employers, schools and colleges when you apply for a job or college.

Please fill in the following for the **last high school** you attended.

PLEASE PRINT.

TO: _____

    (name of last high school attended)

_____ _____ _____
  (city)   (state)   (zip)

Please send a copy of my high school transcript and test scores to: Dr. Luther B. Otto
  Career Development Study
  Social Research Center
  Washington State University
  Pullman, Washington 99164

Date last attended high school: _____ 19 ____

Full name in 1966: _____

Birth date: _____ _____ 19 ____
       MONTH   DAY   YEAR

Signature: _____

Date: _____ 19 ____

SECOND: In another 10 or 15 years we may want to contact you again. Please give us the names and addresses of two people who would be able to help us locate you at that time (for example, brothers, sisters, friends, etc.).

1. NAME: _____

   ADDRESS: _____

   _____ _____ _____
     city   state   zip

   RELATIONSHIP: _____

2. NAME: _____

   ADDRESS: _____

   _____ _____ _____
     city   state   zip

   RELATIONSHIP: _____

IF MARRIED, Please PRINT your spouse's full name.

_____ _____ _____
 (first)   (middle)   (last)

THIS INFORMATION WILL BE KEPT IN STRICT CONFIDENCE AND WILL ONLY BE USED IN FUTURE FOLLOW-UPS OF THE CAREER DEVELOPMENT STUDY.

THIRD: HELP!

We have not been able to send information about this study to a few of your former classmates because we could not locate them. Every person in the study is important to us and cannot be replaced.

Please look over these names. Do you know where any of these people presently live or how we might get in touch with them or someone who knows where they are (for example brothers, sister, in-laws and the like)? Please note any information that may be helpful to us in locating them.

1966 JUNIORS

Copper Charles
Johnson Cynthia
Larsen Penny
Parker George

1966 SENIORS

Hansen Patty
Jones Timothy
Olson Helen
Smith John
Thomas William
Thompson Ruth

THANK YOU FOR YOUR HELP

PLEASE ENCLOSE THIS SHEET WITH THE QUESTIONNAIRE IN THE ENVELOPE WE HAVE PROVIDED FOR YOU

Indexes

Index of Authors

Abeles, Ronald, 100
Alexander, Karl, 52, 84, 86
Almquist, Elizabeth, 65
Althauser, Robert, 16, 17, 22
Alwin, Duane, 53, 89
Anderson, H. Dewey, 13
Angrist, Shirley, 65
Armstrong, J. Scott, 94
Avery, Robert, 25

Baltes, Paul, 101
Baron, James, 3, 7, 21-23, 99
Bartz, Karen Winch, 57, 58, 60
Bealer, Robert, 72
Becker, Gary, 50, 53
Bell, Daniel, 55
Bendix, Reinhard, 25
Berg, Ivar, 99
Bielby, William, 3, 7, 21-24, 34, 99
Bishop, Yvonne, 43
Blau, Peter, 1, 17, 52, 56
Blum, Zahava, 18, 74
Bowles, Samuel, 51, 52, 69, 71, 93
Braverman, Harry, 21, 32, 55
Brooks, Ralph, 72
Buehler, Charlotte, 13, 14
Bukholdt, 33

Cain, Glen, 7
Call, Vaughn, 28, 58, 60, 89
Carlson, Richard, 25
Carpenter, Edwin, 72
Carter, T. Michael, 59, 60
Charner, Ivan, 16
Christenson, James, 72
Chromy, James, 94
Clarridge, Brian, 72
Clausen, S., 19
Cogswell, Betty, 61
Coleman, James, 51, 52, 102
Collins, Randall, 34
Cook, Martha, 52
Cournoyer, Norman, 94

Cozan, Lee, 95
Crider, Donald, 72
Crites, John, 49
Cronbach, L., 102
Cutright, Phillips, 61

Dauffenbach, Robert, 25
Davidson, Percy, 13
Davis, Louis, 21
Deming, William Edwards, 33, 46
Denker, Elenor Rubin, 64
Dickinson, Peter, 32, 33
Dillman, Donald, 72, 74, 75
Doeringer, Peter, 7, 16, 22, 34, 53
Dohrenwend, Barbara Snell, 94
Duncan, Beverly, 52
Duncan, Otis Dudley, 1, 17, 52, 56, 87

Eck, Alan, 33
Eckhaus, Richard, 32, 35, 51, 53
Eckland, Bruce, 84, 86
Edwards, Richard, 32, 53
Elder, Glen, Jr., 59, 100, 101
Erdos, Paul, 94

Featherman, David, 17, 22, 25, 32, 34,
    51-54, 59-61, 84, 86, 87
Feinberg, Stephen, 46
Form, William, 13, 14
Freeman, Richard, 51
Frey, James, 72

Giddens, Anthony, 21
Ginsberg, Ralph, 31
Gintis, Herbert, 51, 52
Ginzberg, E., 65
Glaser, Barney, 57
Gleason, Edwin, 94
Goodman, Leo, 33
Gordon, David, 53
Grant, W. Vance, 60
Griffin, L., 84, 86, 99
Groeneveld, Lyle, 63, 101
Gross, Neal, 21

225

Index of Subjects

Accountants, 39, 42

Age: in data bases, 11; and developmental time, 4; and job mobility, 25

Age-graded career lines, 3, 9

Age-specific jobs, 9

Age-width of entry portals, 16, 36-37

Ambition and career lines, 54

Authority as job dimension, 24

Califano, Joseph, 103

Capital, 5

Capitalism, 7

Career: concepts and definitions of, 2, 3, 13-17; criticism of research on, 15; dimensions of, 21-25; framework for studying, 13-25; in human-capital theory, 6; as individual-level phenomenon, 16; as life-course phenomenon, 4. *See also* Career line(s); Gender and career; Job(s); Theories of work; Work

Career Development program of research: links structural and individual-level theories, 9, 20-21; overview of, 2, 103-105

Career Development Study, within Career Development program, 10; analysis priorities of, 20; focus on individual-level data, 10, 55, 67; job histories in, 47-48; and life-course perspective, 57; methodology of, 67-95; overview of, 98-99; and policy research, 102-103; sample in, 68-69, 82-93. *See also* Time 1 study (1966) procedures; Time 2 study (1979) procedures

Career-entry issues, 4

Career line(s), 13-25, 35-43, 47-66; access to, 9, 16-17, 20-21, 47-66; and community size, 55-56; construction of, 28-30; data base for, 9; definitions of, 3, 16, 25, 27, 28; empirical examples of, 35-43; empirical studies of, 13-14; estima-

tion and analysis of, 27-46; framework for studying, 13-25; and human-capital investment, 48-54; and interface with career, 3; and larger economy, 55; as link between individual and structural theories of work, 4, 99-100; and links to career data, 20-21; measurement of, 17-20; and monopoly, 7; priorities in research on, 20-21, 104; regional variation in, 34; strategies for analyzing, 18-20; as structural phenomenon, 16; typologies of, 20-21, 47-48; for women, 65. *See also* Career; Job(s); Job Dimensions; Job transitions; Work

Career-line set: as career tree, 19; construction of, 28-29; definition of, 16; diagrammed, 36, 40-42; example discussed, 37; transitions in, 39

Career tree, 17, 19

Census data: and career lines, 9, 57; linked to individual-level data, 47; measurement issue with, 33; as structural-level data base, 9-10

Census occupation-industry classifications, 28

Census Public Use Samples, 9-10

Community and access to career lines, 54-56

Complexity as job dimension, 23-24, 43-45

Conflict explanations of careers, 4, 6-8

Conservative explanations of careers, 4-6, 7-8, 49

Cross-sectional analysis. *See* Synthetic-cohort analysis

Data: in estimating career lines, 27; requirements for, 17-18, 67-68; summary of what collected (table), 72

Data bases, 9-11

About the Authors

Luther B. Otto is director of the Career Development Program and director of the Research Division at the Boys Town Center. He has served as acting director of the Social Research Center at Washington State University. His research interests have focused on social psychology, stratification and mobility, and the sociology of education. Dr. Otto has published widely and has presented numerous professional papers on his research on the achievement process. He is a reviewer and editorial consultant for several professional journals and publishers. He is a regular consultant to private and public agencies in the field of education and work.

Vaughn R.A. Call received the Ph.D. from Washington State University in 1977. Since then he has been a post-doctoral Fellow and research associate with the Career Development Program. Dr. Call's research interests, presentations, and published articles focus on age at marriage and other major family events as these influence and are affected by occupational, educational, and military life-course events.

Kenneth I. Spenner received the Ph.D. in sociology from the University of Wisconsin-Madison in 1977. Since then he has been a post-doctoral Fellow and research associate with the Career Development Program. His research and published articles have been on social psychology and social stratification. His current research work centers on occupational characteristics, classification systems, and work careers.